About Her Father's Business

A Journey of Ministry to Others

By

Kimberly Rae

authorHOUSE™

1663 LIBERTY DRIVE, SUITE 200
BLOOMINGTON, INDIANA 47403
(800) 839-8640
WWW.AUTHORHOUSE.COM

This book is a work of non-fiction. Names of people and places have been changed to protect their privacy.

© 2005 Kimberly Rae.
All Rights Reserved.

No part of this book may be reproduced, stored in a retrieval system, or transmitted by any means without the written permission of the author.

First published by AuthorHouse 02/22/05

ISBN: 1-4208-0416-2 (sc)

Library of Congress Control Number: 2004097510

Printed in the United States of America
Bloomington, Indiana

This book is printed on acid-free paper.

This book is **dedicated** to:

The Lord Jesus Christ who is my heavenly Bridegroom!

In honorable memory of my former, deceased husband, whose admirable legacy prompted me to make this "journey."

My present husband (he really *is* a gift); whose unfaltering encouragement, and faith in my abilities to write greatly helped in the "birth" of this book.

I would like to **acknowledge** and express my thanks to:

My husband, for his patience and in being a fair "sounding-board" of advice regarding the innumerable decisions and choices of my printing options; the helpfulness of his proof-reading endeavors; as well as, his willingness to sacrificially give me the time alone needed, often for days, so that I could prepare the final draft of this book for the publisher.

Linda-Sue, my long-time friend and Prayer Partner, for her loving *gift* of hard, long hours laboring to transcribe the original "report" from audio tapes into its first written draft. Hers was a kind and a massive undertaking! Also appreciated is Michelle S. who graciously and expertly did the book's final proof-reading in a timely manner.

Encouraging words and emotional support from many Christian friends, especially, Phyl R., Joanne E., Paul F., and Jill C.; along with the *"You go, girl!"* attitudes of my former and/or current elders and Pastors, most notably, Clay, Jeff and Mike.

...that they might be called trees of righteousness, the planting of the Lord, that He might be glorified.
(Isaiah 61:3b)

Lastly, there are countless "trees of righteous" which have effectively planted and watered much of the growth produced within my life, for the glory of the Lord. Past and current men and women of the faith whose teachings about the Lord God Almighty, whether through sermons from the pulpit, radio or tapes, Bible Study classes, written articles, books, devotionals, unsigned emails/slogans, or actual words of instruction directed at me, were used by the Master to shape my beliefs. This caused the vibrant Truths of Jesus to be absorbed into my very being.

Therefore, it is with sincere gratitude, that I acknowledge their profound contribution to my life and to this book. Also, it is with the utmost effort, that I shall attempt to give each person his/her adequate and accurate "credit due," but must beg their forgiveness if any errors are found within the following pages. You are encouraged to inform me of such; as it difficult indeed to now recall which lessons/sayings I learned from "man"....or from the Spirit of God Himself!

TABLE OF CONTENTS

Forward xi
Preface xxxv
Introduction xli
Chapter One - A Cowardly Heart 1
Chapter Two - Reach Out and Touch 7
Chapter Three - Never Give Up 15
Chapter Four - Kindness and Cruelty 23
Chapter Five - Courting with Honor 33
Chapter Six - Edify in Christ 39
Chapter Seven - Mistaken Lights 45
Chapter Eight - A Form Loved 53
Chapter Nine - Helpful Saints 61
Chapter Ten - Be Not Afraid 69
Chapter Eleven - Prayerfully Arrived 75
Chapter Twelve - Memorial Service 81
Chapter Thirteen - You Are Valued 87
Chapter Fourteen - Reminiscing and Praises 91
Chapter Fifteen - Down Memory Lane 97
Chapter Sixteen - Grief Expressed Becomes Less .. 101
Chapter Seventeen - Unfriendly Territory 113
Chapter Eighteen - Danger From Within 123
Chapter Nineteen - Covered in Prayer 131
Chapter Twenty-One - Distressed Daughter 139
Chapter Twenty-Two - And, yet…God! 145
Chapter Twenty-Three - Freedom and Forgiveness 167
Chapter Twenty-Four - A Loving Sister 175
Chapter Twenty-Five - Poor Life Choices 183
Chapter Twenty-Six - Of Worthy Stature 191
Chapter Twenty-Seven - Tidbits About Life 201
Chapter Twenty-Eight - Childlike Faith 207

Chapter Twenty-Nine - A Vow Challenged............213
Chapter Thirty - Rededicated Hearts 219
Chapter Thirty-One - Unavoidable Changes 227
Chapter Thirty-Two - Finishing the Journey...........235
Epilogue 243
Addendum...279
Appendix...285

** * * Scripture references and quotations are from the **King James Version** and their fuller content has been typed in the **Appendix** section of this book.*

Author's Note:

1.) While in the process of writing this book, in order to enhance clarification (especially within the main text), any italics within parenthesis are added statements, scriptures, or sources of information.

2.) As stated previously in the "disclaimer," most names and some dates or locations have been deleted or changed in order to protect the privacy of the people involved.

3.) To aide the book in remaining concise, yet flowing, occasional adjustments have been made. When two or more substantial topics were discussed within a given household, one of which was also "brought up" in another home or church letter, those of like subject matter were sometimes joined, as if only one family had asked the question. Yet, the words and statements remain as originally exact as was reasonably possible.

4.) Also, twice, on the way to visit a family, there occurred brief, yet potent encounters with travelers along the way. These people were NOT part of my planned visits, but their input and backgrounds were of enough value to the Gospel, that their contribution was "joined" within the tale of the next family on my journey.

FORWARD

The following items, presented chronologically, are included to help explain what occurred and led up to the event of my "journey." These shortened "excerpts" are from some of the actual letters, newspaper articles, my own personal writings or some comments to my church.

Annual Letter   (Jan. 2, 1996)

Hello

Kim and I send our warm greetings. We hope your holiday season was full of memories you will treasure for a long time.

As I write, we are in the biggest snowstorm we've had for many years. So far, we have about 27 inches and it's still coming down. Deep, powdery snow like this is very unusual here, and it sure is good to see for this ol' Colorado boy!

Even though nothing particularly outstanding happened to us during 1995 (unlike last year when Kim's health was in such jeopardy), it is a high honor to know our Creator and Redeemer, and being part of His plan is a wonderful thing.

Kim and I observed our 13th anniversary this past year and our tenth in North Carolina. I had a couple of milestones—it was 20 years ago when I left the Army to become a happy civilian, and 25 years ago when I first met Jesus.

Kim and I continue to do the music with the younger children of our church. While we sing, I play guitar and Kim does the hand motions. We love helping them learn scriptural principles through these fun songs.

Currently, Kim is taking several days to be alone, fasting and praying. She has a very strong concern for missionary and evangelistic efforts, and for people troubled by demonic oppression.

I am at the same printing company and bought a mountain bike last summer. Among other things this Christmas, Kim bought me a much-wanted pair of roller skates which I've already tried out in my neighbor's snow-cleared, asphalted driveway.

Y'all have a great '96!

(II Pet. 3:18) "Grow in the grace and knowledge of the Lord and Savior Jesus Christ."

---John & Kim Thomas

Marion Free Press *(Jan. 17, 1996)*

Blizzard of '96 - Good Samaritan Killed at Wreck

A local man died yesterday of injuries received after he stopped at the side of the road to help another motorist. John Thomas, almost 43, died when the pickup he had been driving was struck from the rear, pinning him between his truck and the car of a motorist who had run into a snowbank. Police gave this account of the 6:25 a.m. incident. Gerald Richards was traveling north when the right-hand lane ended, due to a buildup of plowed snow from the storms. Unable to move left because of traffic, he ran into a thick snowbank. Thomas stopped to help and he was between the front of his Dodge pickup and the rear of Richard's car when his truck was struck by a third vehicle, fatally injuring Thomas.

For Richards, the crash was something he will never forget and said, "The man was just trying to help. He went out of his way and look what happened. Thomas was one of the people driving in the open left lane. (Seeing I was in trouble), he went down to the next place he could to turn around and came back to help."

According to Richards, he and Thomas first tried to push the car out of the snow. Then Thomas got a shovel from his truck and tried that, but to no avail. At that point, Thomas decided to try pulling my car out with his truck. Thomas was preparing to hook on a tow when the crash occurred. Richards said, "I heard something and jumped back. Then I looked to see if Mr. Thomas got clear. He didn't."

The Daily News Tribune (Jan. 18, 1996)

Good Samaritan Dies

To those who knew him best, John Thomas was a man who devoted his life to helping people in trouble. This past Tuesday, his devotion to that very principle took his life from him. "We felt it was kind of appropriate, that he died helping someone," said

Thomas' co-pastor. "He was always doing things (for others) which brought no fanfare to himself."

As it was so frequent in his life, Thomas, who, according to his wife, Kim, usually carried a myriad of tools in his truck to help stranded motorists get back on the road, stopped to assist Richards. "Cars were whizzing past them," said Richards. He went to his truck to get a shovel. "He wouldn't let me do any of it, (to keep me out of harms way) he had to do all the hard work himself." Richards said, "He bent down to put the chain on my car and there was this God-awful boom. It was so fast. It hit him with such force."

Richards was unable to move Thomas, who had a faint pulse. "I kept telling him that help was on the way." I was praying that he wasn't going to die. But, a couple of minutes later, he closed his eyes. It's hard to believe that the man was doing a good deed and it ended up costing him his life."

Mrs. Thomas said her husband was a perfectionist, a man of integrity who inherently felt the need to help others. Not for money or glory, but because it was the right thing to do. He was so committed to his printing job, his wife said, that even the massive snowfall (and many still closed roads) didn't stop her Colorado-reared man from getting to work Monday. "They were behind on something," she said, "and John just used his cross-country skies to get there! The normally 20-minute drive took him two full hours."

John's co-pastor remarked, "He was known for his honesty and commitment to other people. That man was a true servant." Mrs. Thomas said she was relying on her faith in God to help her recover from the tragic and horrible loss of her husband, the same faith so ingrained in John. She said, "I'm glad he's not in pain and, someday, we will see each other again in heaven."

January 19, 1996

Dear Mrs. Kimberly Thomas,

It is with sorrow that I extend my condolences to you. The uncertainty of life is all the harder to understand when it ends under such circumstances.

I salute Mr. Thomas' compassion and his willingness to get involved. Many people would have passed by without stopping.

I wish I could have personally known him. People like him are indeed rare. The manner of his death touched the hearts of every officer in the Department.

Sincerely, Chief of Police

(**Note**: Shorter newspaper articles, similar to the ones above, also came out in the North Carolina circulation of the **Ashville Times-Dispatch** -1/20, as well as in the Colorado papers of the **Montezuma Sentinel** –1/22 and **The Weekly Star** -1/25.)

Kimberly's Journal

<u>Jan. 20, 1996</u> – Alas, today is my John's funeral. Help me, Jesus, to be brave for John's lost and hurting parents. And, praise You, for what was prepared for me to read during my quiet time, for this day's devotional.

("Morning By Morning" by C. H. Spureon) "Arise from the dead"... *(Eph. 5:14b)* "The hour is approaching when the message will come to us, as it comes to all, 'Arise, and go forth from your home, your city, your family and friends. Arise, take your last journey'. We know that there is a stormy river called 'Death.' God bids us cross it, promising to be with us. We will be departing from all we have known and loved here, but we will be going to our Father's house where Jesus is; to the 'royal city' *(Heb. 11:10)*. This will be our last move, to dwell forever with Him we love. Christian, be sure to look forward to heaven. It will help you to press on and forget the hard trials along the way. This world of woe is the stepping-stone to a world of bliss."

<u>Jan. 23, 1996</u> – Today is my 43rd birthday. Feeling much sadness that John is not here with me. His parents left very early this morning to fly home. Yet, as this day's devotional reminds me, Christ sympathizes and will help me to do more than survive, but also to grow!

("Morning By Morning" by C. H. Spureon) "The child of God can say, 'I have a Brother in heaven. I might be brokenhearted, but I have a Brother who loves and comforts His people.' In all of our sorrows,we

have His empathy. He, too, has known temptation, pain, disappointment, weakness, loneliness, poverty, and weariness. So, remember Christian, that however difficult or painful your road, it was marked by the footsteps of your Savior. Up ahead, royal feet have left a blood-red track to consecrate the thorny path, so that you can walk contented through every distressful situation in your life. Never forget that as you mature, you must experience continual change. Yet, be assured that, even though you are a pilgrim in this world, you can always feel right at home in *(the warmth of)* your God!"

* * **(That same evening)** *Got an unexpected call from the adoption agency. It was just the ugly and hurtful kind of "birthday surprise" Satan delights in giving! They did not know about John and had called to tell us that we could go meet our new son. Even though we had no preference as to gender, we did want a child under the age of two and would readily accept mild handicaps. So, they were proud to report that this baby boy was 18-months-old and completely healthy! They knew that John and I had spent thousands of dollars and gone through nearly insurmountable "red-tape" for almost five years, eagerly waiting to be told this "good news."*

Father God, I need Your forgiveness, for I am ashamed. It took every ounce of moral fiber to resist my intense desire to just go pick up the toddler, without telling the caseworker that John had died. How wonderful it would have been to cuddle my own child and love my sorrows away. But, such lack of integrity would have tainted Your name and John's memory;

plus being unfair to that sweet lad. Once the agency found out that I no longer had a "Daddy" here, they would have taken the child away. Then, both of us would've had to make another painful readjustment. Their intent was to grant the small boy a two-parent home...and I could no longer provide it.

Thank you, Jesus, for not allowing John's parents to be here during that phone call. None of his family or our friends needs anymore bad news right now. But, at least I have You to cry with and lean upon for comfort and recovery. Admittedly, if it were not that You have promised to never put on us "more than we can endure" (I Cor. 13:6-7), this new heartache would have been "the straw that broke the camel's back" in my resiliency. Master, please, heal this awful hurt!

January 26, 1996

(*Kimmy, this is the letter we sent to our other three kids. We wanted them to have all the details. Such a sad week and John is constantly in our thoughts. Take care! --Jake and Paula)

Dear Kids,
Just returned safely from North Carolina; John and Kim's neighbor friend, Geoffrey Daniels, along with his youngest son, drove us from and back to the airport. It feels strange and surreal being home in Colorado. But, we want to give you some insights into your brother, John. We can hardly rise above the

turmoil in our hearts, but we have to try because you should know what a wonderful person he really was.

<u>MOM:</u> Jan. 21, 1996 – Such an emotional time in NC for the funeral of my firstborn. So many feelings, but the strongest is the PRIDE we feel for him and I just wish I could have told him sooner. My regrets are that he couldn't stay longer and keep enjoying his life. He was so loved and had only 'blossomed' a few years ago, but WE hadn't been aware of it soon enough.

<u>DAD:</u> The funeral was two things; devastating and pleasantly overwhelming! It was packed with about 500 people, some who waited 1-1/2 hours just to come by and speak with us. I had no idea, but John had helped so many people and had so many interests. My, how he had expanded since he has been here in NC. I knew he sounded happier and now I know why. We both credit Kim for bringing John out of his shell so well and working with him and, mostly, just lovingly understanding him. We knew he was different than you other three kids, but we didn't know how to help, so we blundered along. I remember your Mom feeling helpless and not knowing what to do, so we just didn't DO anything; but that's never a solution to a problem. Don't you repeat our mistake with any of your own children!

<u>MOM:</u> For years, John had a low self-esteem, didn't like his looks and was so easily hurt by us, even by things WE thought didn't matter. He was a perfectionist and really tried hard, but often withdrew in failure. He didn't know how to verbally communicate well and that's what Kimmy helped him with. She also helped John to love himself. You see, he had a slight

disability, in that he could comprehend things visually much faster and better than verbally. My heart aches for this gentle, loving son I didn't know how to reach, so I just gave up even trying years ago.

<u>DAD:</u> As we listened to people "greeting" us after his funeral service yesterday, I was so amazed at the love and how many people would really miss John. They all had a story to tell or something good to say because he had given them so much of his time and energy. Everything he touched was done with love and care. I have sworn to change my life to be more like my oldest son. This is some of the good I feel is to come from his death. His example has taught me things that I needed to learn; to be more gentle, understanding, patient, loving and compassionate.

<u>MOM:</u> Jan. 22, 1996 – I don't know how Kim can take this and the hardest part will be when she lets down after we leave. Her whole life has changed, for she lived it mostly to please John, and also the God they both believed in. We talk about him a lot. "I love you, son, I wish I'd have told you more often."

<u>DAD:</u> His boss had all glowing things to say about John and showed us the whole plant and the area where he worked. John was in charge of the entire Graphics Arts Department and his boss said that John's work was the highest quality he had ever seen. The company truly expanded because of him, as many of the customers requested that only John work on their projects! He had received several bonuses and awards for "Employee of the Month and/or Quarter." In fact, Kim will go to his company's annual employee

luncheon Monday to receive John's most recent award which is the "Employee of the Year!"

<u>MOM:</u> Their home was cute: neither showy nor pretentious, but very clean and cozy. We could hardly walk around the yard without seeing John in everything, including his footprints frozen in the ground. And, in his small workshop was that wonderful spitting maul that he had custom-made. Due to his tall, strong arc, he kept breaking wooden handles, so John had a lead, 3' piece of heavy pipe welded onto the head, and it never broke again.

<u>DAD:</u> The sad time here has taught us that John was a dear soul, who had struggled many years to just be what WE, his family, considered "normal." He didn't know how to communicate well with others, despite the fact that he had a high level of intelligence. (There was another smart, yet slow-talking fellow, who was tall and gawky, thought he wasn't handsome, but was a man of integrity; his name was Lincoln.) Due to her experience in working with handicapped children, Kim discovered that, because of a mild Assimilation Delay (caused, we think, by his rough birth), John responded a bit slowly when just given verbal information, but his perceptions were much better when given visual clues. So, these past few years, she was helping him be able to change. He was so proud of his new abilities and wanted to show them to us, on their Colorado vacation this summer, so we could all know that he had finally 'blossomed'!

<u>MOM:</u> January 23, 1996 - Today is Kim's birthday and the one gift John never would have chosen for her is "Widowhood." This experience will affect my life

forever, as I now know devastation and deep loss and it will make me a kinder person. I won't be so easily judgmental and critical. "Oh, my gentle son John, we treated you, our unknown jewel, so poorly."

<u>DAD:</u> Choosing to not become Christians ourselves, we can take no credit for the fact that John had a strong faith and, unlike most people, he actually lived it everyday of his life. He was an honest, decent, hard-working, self-effacing soul with integrity. Even as parents, we had no idea how strong was his sense of responsibility and consideration for others. Each of us would do well to live by his fine example. ---

Love, Mom & Dad

February 11, 1996

To My " Church" Family,

I sense that many of you have been feeling awkward around me lately. I'd probably feel the same way, if I were in your place: not sure of how to deal with this new "widow." So, in trying to help ease some of your discomfort, here are a few things that would minister to my situation... I have no clue as to how others in mourning feel, so I can only give you insights from my own, current perspective. Perhaps some of these suggestions will be of help to you in the future, in dealing with others who are grieving a loss...

Although I don't seem to show lots of depression or frequent outbursts of stark, emotional pain, there are times when I get "weepy around the edges" from missing my "Honey-Bunch" and "Knight in Shining Armor!" There are occasions, like hearing the neighbors' truck pull into their driveway, which causes me to think, for a fleeting moment, that John has arrived home. Or, to go shopping and try to sadly alter every item to "just one person now, only just one." As well as entering a store and being unexpectedly hit, right in the raw emotions, with the force of all the visual reminders that Valentine's Day is near, knowing I no longer have my "Sweetheart" here with me. These are indeed the types of intense disappointments that pierce my heart deeply.

But, the reason I don't feel utterly devastated is that, for years now, my emotional and spiritual foundation depended mostly upon my life <u>in</u> Christ Jesus (Tim. 2:19a). It did not entirely depend on my life <u>with</u> my dear husband. Our shared Master is still right here with me. I've never felt abandoned or forsaken because my Father's love has never left me; nor ever will (I King 8:57).

Even so, being John's wife was a very blessed and pleasant experience. Also, I'm grateful to have had the privilege of helping John develop skills that enhanced and expanded friendships, which then led to his inner "call" of service to others. Who knows, in eternal value, perhaps that was the most important task which God wanted me to accomplish here on earth! Also, how nice it was to reap the added benefit of getting to watch John flourish and grow into the "man of God" his Master intended!

---In Jesus' Love, Kim

February 25, 1996

(*From the sister of the man John was helping when the accident occurred.)

Dearest Kimberly,

Just wanted to drop you a very special "thank you" for the wonderful taped message you sent to comfort our family. (*Which was the above longer version, spoken in front of Kim's church.) *I was so impressed! Today, while Mom, Gerald and his wife were here together, we intently listened to the tape, wiped away tears, nodding in agreement, and focusing on every word.*

I know you probably haven't given it much thought, but your straight forward approach to grief and handling life's problems could be a real comfort in so many peoples' lives. But, if that's to be, I know the Lord will lead you there and that you would be ready to answer the call. I hope your future will be filled with a purpose, one that helps to heal this change in your life.

I always heard to "rejoice at a funeral," but I never experienced it until John's. What a joy for us (who were still feeling that we were partly the cause of his death), to celebrate his life with his family and friends. Thank you so much for your kind thoughtfulness of inviting us and making us feel so welcomed. (I will never forget how you refused to allow my brother to blame himself.) You are a beautiful human being, <u>filled</u> with Jesus; it just bubbles over! He helps you to be and do remarkable things. The strength of the Lord's Spirit surrounds you. Continue your message of hope and faith; I heard it loud and clear! ---Love, Linda

The Daily News Tribune (February 29, 1996)

John Thomas Honored Posthumously

Today, Mr. Thomas was posthumously honored at his company's annual banquet with "The Employee of the Year" award. The recipient's wife, Kimberly, accepted the sterling silver engraved plate and bonus check with pride and gratitude. According to the CEO, no one was more deserving of the award this year than Thomas. "It epitomized what every employer loves to see in an employee: loyalty and dedication. Such attention to detail and self-sacrifice is unusual. But, that was John Thomas: a perfectionist, a leader and a knowledgeable and loyal employee."

Raleigh Leader (March 5, 1996)

Legislature Honors Thomas

A man, who was killed while helping another driver, was honored Monday by the North Carolina General Assembly passing a Resolution memorializing him as, "a Good Samaritan and a fine citizen." Thomas had already stopped to help three other motorists before then trying to lend a hand to Gerald Richards that fatal morning. John Thomas' actions, in stopping to help his fellow citizens in their time of need, was by all accounts typical of this generous, self-effacing and courageous man. Mr. Thomas' actions during the record storm are typical of the way we in this area think. Thomas' humanitarian actions are a true example of the values we strive to demonstrate. He gave the ultimate sacrifice, his life, to help another person. His unselfishness should be a testament and inspiration to us all. While it is unfortunate that John Thomas' life was cut short, it is with pride in the character that he represented that we honor him today as a true hero of our state.

Marion Free Press (March 6, 1996)

Council Honors Good Samaritan

Monday, City Council honored a man who died while trying to help others. Council presented a resolution to Mrs. Kimberly Thomas, widow of John Thomas, who died Jan. 16...

The City Attorney read the Resolution which characterized Thomas as, "A fine 20th Century Good Samaritan in the truest sense of the word. Whereas, this good citizen, friend, and neighbor has earned the respect and admiration of thousands who have never experienced the pleasure of knowing him and will be remembered as a hero who risked his life in service to humanity; now therefore, council officially recognizes the courage and compassion demonstrated by Mr. John Thomas in his life and in the sad circumstances of his death..."

Kimberly's Journal

<u>March 6, 1996:</u> - Sadly, today would have been John's 43rd birthday. Yet, as Beverly S., a dear sister-in-Christ reminded me, "John had the honor of dying the way he lived" and next he will be "worshipping in the very Presence of his risen Lord!" This past week, I made and sent copies of both surprise 'Resolutions' to his parents. It will make them so proud, as they will also be remembering his first "missed" birthday. But, as I remarked during the News broadcast, held after Monday night's Council meeting: "I don't believe that John's life was 'cut short'. No, as Peter Marshall once said, 'The measure of a (godly) man is not the duration, but the donation.' (How much of himself he gave in service to the King and to others while still on earth.) John simply gave more of himself <u>faster</u> than do most of us, so he got to go 'Home' sooner."

Such thoughts have done much to bring me a feeling of tranquil acceptance about the nearly fifteen years John and I got to spend loving each other. And, as these weeks of grace have passed, emotions have settled into a bearable pattern. Yet, thanks Lord, for today's devotional reading to lift my spirits and remind me that YOU understand!

("Days of Heaven on Earth", by A. B. Simpson)

"My grace is sufficient for thee."

(2 Cor. 12:9a)

"If none of God's saints were poor and tried, we would not know half so well the consolation of divine grace. We may see a pauper nearly starving on bread and water, but he still glories in Jesus. We may see a bereaved **widow** overwhelmed in affliction, yet still believing in Christ. What honor they reflect on the gospel! God's grace is illustrated and magnified in the poverty and trials of believers. Saints bear up under every discouragement, believing that all things work together for their best. They believe that out of apparent evils, a real blessing will ultimately spring. The master-works of God are those who stand in the midst of difficulties remaining steadfast and immoveable. Never dream of His failing you. The God, who has been sufficient until now, can be trusted until the end."

The Daily News Tribune (March 7, 1996)

Lawmakers Honor Good Samaritan

Tuesday, City Council honored a man who died while helping a motorist free his car from a snow bank last January. The North Carolina House of Delegates passed a joint Resolution (which was passed in the Senate the next day) *commemorating Thomas.*

A local delegate said, "Out here we all ban together to help our neighbors when they need a hand. Although they were strangers, he gave his energies selflessly to help his fellow citizens."

(*Similar article was put in the nearby city paper of **The Charlotte Observer**.)

NORTH CAROLINA – GENERAL ASSEMBLY

House Joint Resolution...
On the death of John L. Thomas

Agreed to by the: HOUSE of DELEGATES, March 7, 1996
Agreed to by the: SENATE, March 8, 1996

(Ending with...) *"Whereas, amidst the tragedy of John Thomas' untimely death, the example of his selfless and generous service to his neighbors and fellow citizens remains as a shining legacy; now therefore let it be*

RESOLVED by the House of Delegates, the Senate concurring, that the General Assembly mourns the loss of John L. Thomas... and that the clerk prepare a copy of this Resolution...as an expression of the great respect in which his memory is held by the members of this Assembly."

March 20, 1996

(An Ambassador card and poem, from our college professor.)

"It's hard to see tomorrow, when someone you love is gone; and it's harder still to realize, that your life will still go on..."
Kimberly,
I waited to write you until I was led to write with what I felt. My mind is awhirl with flashbacks of you

two in Colorado: our meetings at campus, your lovely smile, John's gentle presence, the dance sessions, your support of him even while dealing with the many burdens in your own life, his boyish grin when he had been quietly able to help someone, how the two of you <u>lived</u> what you stood for...I could go on and on. Since then, our contact has been by mail, but I can still clearly see you are "Ambassadors"...and I'm proud!

Now that John has been called home, the void must be immense. Yet, <u>you</u> have so much to continue giving...and receiving. In a world so crying out for love, what new pathways will God provide for you? "One with God is a majority!"

--Love, Gene and Lynn

Christian School Principal (April 7, 1996)

(Where Kim had worked/assisted, but recently gave 'notice' that she'd not be returning in the fall, as she had chosen to upgrade her Special Ed degree and work with infants/toddlers instead.)

Kim,
Thanks for sharing with me the letter concerning the donation of John's corneas so that two other folks have actually received sight, which they would not otherwise have had. May it be that God's rich blessings continue upon you and your life. Enjoyed the fine report and your praises of all the help*given by our church's "Work Crew" of men (a team that used to include John) at your home a couple of weeks ago. We

look forward to having a group of our student-workers visit with you this coming Friday to be of some yard help.   -John M.

*(They chopped down AND removed a few trees, put in our window a/c units, dismantled two crumbling, wooden sheds, and installed the upstairs shower for the "Elijah Room" quarters.)

April 15, 1996 - Elijah Room

Dear Friends and Neighbors,

As a married couple, John and I were often privileged to open our home to visiting pastors, evangelists, or fellow believers, especially those from other countries. We so enjoyed their fellowship and stories of God's prevailing ways, as we housed, fed and transported them around for a few days. But, soon after his death, a person made the comment, "Now that you are alone, visitors can't stay overnight here anymore. It just wouldn't be appropriate without John." Those words just did not settle well inside my spirit, so I asked the Lord to show me how to continue being able to invite His people to find rest within these walls. His answer became the upstairs quarters which are now called "The Elijah Room!"

Compressed all of my belongings to fit into just the downstairs rooms and have built a door at the bottom of the stairwell. This allows total privacy for me and for the smaller upstairs area, so as to meet the needs of any "guests" God sends. A shower has been installed in the half-bath up there, next to the extra bedroom. A small ice-box, microwave, dinette set and filled cabinets have become a tiny "kitchen nook," next to the small den. The new den used to be our "Prayer & Praise Room," but its long window has been made into door of entry from outside, and a walk-in closet was transformed to accommodate a cozy "Prayer Closet" to aid future visitors!

After an outside stairway is erected, the upstairs will soon be ready as a temporary, "no charge/ donations only" place of retreat for any Christians the Lord sends to this daughter to shelter. Like the widow who took care of the Prophet Elijah (I King 17:9-15), I fully trust that although my own funds are meager, God will provide for my basic needs, as I remain willing to provide for "His Guests."

--Love & Prayers, Kimberly

May 9, 1996

Dear Kimmy,
Each week your name is lifted before the throne of grace. We know that the pain does not easily wane. There may always be an empty spot as a result of John's passing. I've prayed a number of times that the words you share with others will bear spiritual fruit in their lives. As you continue to finish your commitment to the work (in Christ) *you've been given here, this verse applies: "I know the plans I have for you," declares the*

Lord, "plans to prosper you and not to harm you, plans to give you hope and a future." (Jeremiah 29:11)

Incidentally, your practical insights could well benefit others. Have you considered publishing ...to help them through (similar) *traumas?*

---In the Love of Jesus, Bill and Rosalind

Department of Veteran Affairs (June 9, 1996)

(Sent by the Director)

Dear Mrs. Thomas,

Internment of the remains of your husband, John L. Thomas, was accomplished today at the Denver National Cemetery. It will be approximately two months before his permanent headstone is received; at which time an official Memorial Service would be appropriate for his loved ones. Until then, a temporary marker is at the gravesite.

Church Announcements (July 28, 1996)

(Among other requests listed.)

Kim Thomas -- pray for her protection as she travels over 6,000 miles soon, mostly visiting John's friends and family members. She ought to have many opportunities to be an ambassador of Christ...

PREFACE

(* Following is the request of prayer-support for my journey from my "church family.")

August 4, 1996

John and I had planned to take our "driving-out-West" trip together this summer, as it would have been his first 3-week vacation since we had moved to North Carolina. His spirit felt pressed with much urgency to get back to see (and "reconnect with") his non-Christian parents, siblings, and older mid-West relatives; plus a few boyhood friends. As we depended on God's help, we were going to attempt, once again, to share our Jesus with them. John sensed that "time was running out" for some of them to grasp the privilege of Christ's salvation. Unknowingly, *we* thought it was *their* chances to accept the gospel that were waning, not actually John's own diminishing number of days, which were causing him to feel such an intense longing to see and speak with his family and cherished friends SOON!

So, in honor of the Master's Spirit that was prompting John "to go," and as a representative to them both, I am going on our planned 6,000+ mile trip alone (Except that Jesus will always be with me!). It will take 5 weeks to accomplish this task across 17 states, which is no small feat for a gal who is a self-avowed "home body" and hasn't a drop of gypsy blood in her!

On my way back to NC, I will stop to visit about ten households of my own relatives. But, out of 127 of John's kinfolk who are expecting me, I've only met eight of those people before! This kind of visiting is very much beyond my "comfort zone" or natural 'gifts.' Have always felt ill-at-ease among people that I don't already know, so I'm sure it is God who wants me to do this, as Kimmy would never have thought it a good idea on her own!

A couple of years ago, Jesus did allow John's prayers and information to be part of the help which caused his younger brother, who was formally entrenched in The Way International cult, to "come to the Lord." But, as far as John knew, most of his other family members were ardent intellectuals <u>without</u> Christ. Yet, 100% of the people on John's list, which he had hoped we could see together, are still allowing me to come visit them… even without him. I suspect that many are struggling with John's death and want some contact with his wife to help them feel less severed from him. Also, some may think that they are giving comfort to his grieving widow by inviting her to their homes for an afternoon or overnight to talk about him.

God's "timing" is for me to go see them all THIS summer, even though doing such will keep my own emotions rather raw. Yet, by next summer, when it would be much easier on me, I think several of them won't still have their doors or "ears" open to me or to God's Word!

Except for occasional letters or phone calls from a few of John's family, I will mostly be a complete "stranger" to them. And, as I pause in each sin-accustomed household, I may feel as insecure as someone who finds themselves enveloped within a foreign country. Possibly, I may also seem to *them* like an oddity or "alien" in their world. My words of hope and redemption and my preference to live a life truly pleasing to God may well be considered outlandish. But, I rest in the fact that God says His children will be known as a "peculiar people" *(I Peter 2:9)*. It's just that some of us are a tad MORE peculiar than others!

I do wish to be accepted and "at peace with all" *(Romans 12:18)* of John's family, as well as with my own non-Christian or Mormon clan. And, if anyone from Satan's camp rejects me because of my beliefs, it *will* hurt my feelings. But, I trust God to comfort and mend any such bruised emotions. Besides I would not want to so "compromise" my stand in Christ (in order to please others in their "worldly ways"), as to be mistaken as a fellow-citizen by the very kinds of people who consider my own dear Master an "outcast!" It is the Lord's acceptance/approval I want the most and I'd rather have His much sweeter company to share my lot with anyway. As it says, "He is a stranger with me." *(Ps. 39:12b)*

Accompanying me will be 15 years worth of special photos (from courting/engagement though marriage/funeral) for John's family and friends to look at and enjoy. But, the main reason for my going through the heart-wrenching task of collecting those pictures out of all of our albums, is that I'm certain they will be used as tools to better help me share John's life and <u>Who</u> he valued most in it! This gal expects that God will, probably, use her to assist many of John's family in bringing a "closure" to their grief, by showing them how fulfilled and happy were his last years. It has already ministered to his clan that I am respecting their own way of "mourning his loss," by taking this long drive to attend John's official Military Memorial Service on August 23, at the cemetery in Denver.

Suspect that it's also in my Father's plans to send me off with a HUGE bag of "spiritual seeds" to scatter among those lost souls which John so worried about and loved. I have no qualms about getting lost or remaining safe (even though my experience with maps is rather meager), because when our Master "sends," He also makes the way clear to "go." But, my prayer requests from you dears are:

1.) To be granted an extra measure, than is normal for me, of that "wisdom from above" to recognize any of those 'eternal opportunities' which may present themselves. To be extra sensitive to the Holy Spirit's guidance in knowing what to say, when and to whom! You know, "Have Kim get out of the way, so the Spirit can have *His* say"! (She needs to work on that.)

2.) To receive from you, my church family, a steadfast "prayer covering" to help protect me from attacks of Satan's forces. It is to be expected that he will send "trouble-makers" to try to hinder the going forth of God's Truth to those captive people. Pray for me while I'm under the roofs of so many who, unknown to them, are following the prince who is the enemy of my King!

3.) To keep my voice from becoming horse, or even being lost, due to so much extra talking. Thus being unable to give them the message of our Father's great love. Pray, too, that I somehow manage to get enough rest (or to be supernaturally fortified!), so as to not be unduly "at risk" while traveling all of those thousands of weary road miles alone.

Something which is appropriate to these requests was read during my quiet time, way back in May, which I think was from Oswald Chamber's book,

<u>Devotions for Morning and Evening</u>

"In the world ye shall have tribulation…" (John 16:33b)

Are you asking the reason for this, believer? Look… downward! Do you know what foes you have beneath your feet? Do you think that Satan will let you alone? No, he will always be at you, for he "goeth about like a roaring lion, seeking whom he may devour." (I Peter 5:8) Expect trouble…You are in an enemy's country, a stranger, a sojourner. The world is NOT your friend. Be assured that you will find enemies everywhere. But do not despair because God said, "I will be with thee in trouble; I will deliver thee and honor thee." (Psalm 91:15)

May the Spirit of Jesus help you to remember to send me "prayer hugs" from afar, while I'm on this "pilgrimage journey!"

   ---Thanks and Blessings to You,   Kimberly

INTRODUCTION

Dec. 15, 1996

Greetings and Salutations in the Lord!

In Psalm 74: 17, it says in part, "Thou hast made the summer and the winter." Sharing my life with John was my own dear season of "summer" and my soul's inner core has been a might uncomfortably "wintry" since his accident early last January, and as this first holiday season alone progresses. But, knowing that our King also rules the realms of 'frosty conditions,' helps remind me that good results will come from this time of being sadly afflicted *(Rom. 12:21)*.

In wondering why God allowed John to die, some people have thought it was the enemy trying to break up our united front and witness to Jesus as a couple and/or to damage my own walk and faith in the Lord. Others believed Satan knew John and I had planned to go see his kinfolk and friends this past summer, to try again to share Jesus with them, and a gleeful devil thought he'd win a big one against God this time by trying to spoil our plans. Yet, behold, how much *MORE* was the way opened to talk about spiritual and eternal matters because of John's death being on everyone's mind. Aha! Again, all the winning points go to God!

Others thought John was taken early to spare him some future evil or to begin training him now for a special part in the Lord's return later. But, none of the "whys" are really important to me. It is enough to know and believe that God is still in control, still loves both of us and, somehow, all of this will produce the best, ultimate results possible *(Phil. 1:12)*. A bounty of such lovely fruit already being produced is evidenced by His anointing hand upon the lives of the people with which He allowed me to be prepared to speak *(Col. 4:6)*. Bringing a touch of His love into their hearts in His Name, during this long trip. So, now friends, pay heed to the "tales of mighty valor" done by God's strong arm!

A few Christian friends have asked for a chance to hear about the details of my "journey," but most folks have been unable to gift me the time needed to share these memories with them in person. Therefore, since some of the things recalled are sweet and precious, yet others are a real inner torture to remember, this "report" appeared to be the best way to inform those folks who are interested about what happened, without forcing me to personally "dredge it all up again" over and over. When retelling the following events to one church couple, they asked for details about how each situation transpired and what God's Spirit gave me to say *(Matt. 10:19-20)*. So, I will try to accurately recount such details for you as well.

Therefore, including this introduction, what follows are the set of four audio tapes it took to record a verbal "report" *(transcribed now in this written form, nearly verbatim)* about events which occurred during my recent long, driving trip out West. Traveling lasted from **August 8th until Sept. 13th**. I have, purposely, left out and/or changed most peoples' names and even some places in order to protect their privacy regarding each circumstance and encounter. Yet, I have kept track of each person's identity in my written notes derived from my journal (upon which this "report" is based) as well as on the backs of related photos, so that I wouldn't forget their names.

It is always so precious to be able to recall the date of one's "rebirth," so these things are also being preserved for the benefit of "the new babes in Christ," born into the Kingdom during my travels. For their sakes, as you may notice, I rarely ever quote the book, chapter and verse to new or non-believers when telling them a gospel truth from the Bible (unless they ask for them). It's just not my style, due to negative memories of people sounding boastful and pride-filled when I was still so ignorant of God's Word. For me, such behavior was an early and huge "turn-off" regarding church people. Therefore, you are likely to hear what John used to teasingly refer to as "paraphrases by Kimmy!" He would say his wife never failed to give the "meat" of a text, but usually tried to sweeten it up a bit to make it more appealing to their taste and cut it into smaller portions to help it be easier for them to swallow. For me, it is so disagreeable to watch well-meaning Christians trying to force-feed and cram God's Word down non-believers' throats. Then be surprised or even hurt when their victims do not beam in gratitude and present them with a big "thank you" in return. Folks, that's just not reality! It is *not* human nature and it often causes damage and harm to that seeking person's viewpoint of Jesus and of His people. Sure, they need the nourishment of the true gospel, the inner nut, the kernel, the meat of God's grace and mercy, but why not coat the message with kindness and respectfulness by offering them the more pleasant taste of sweet, nut-covered, "Gospel M & Ms?" Often, they will ask for even more!

Lastly, many times on this trip, it was obvious that having me arrive as a visiting widow and knowing we'd talk about the often "taboo" subject of death, opened a multitude of spiritual doors. Because of that, praise God, almost no topic was "off-limits." Therefore, it was a very pleasant surprise to find that people just seemed less queasy asking questions about a variety of other serious matters, too!

CHAPTER ONE

A Cowardly Heart

From North Carolina, after a winding drive of long miles through many construction delays in West Virginia, I finally reached our friends, Charlie and Anita, in Ohio. It was already well after dark, so with hugs of warmth and a brief visit, we all soon went to bed. This gal was so pleased to begin her long drive by first stopping to visit with such a dear Christian family. She knew she'd be well blessed by their spiritual advice, covering and prayers at the beginning of this unsettling venture.

I spent most of the next day with Anita and her three children (ages 3-12), in times of light fun, as well as in moments of deep fellowship. We looked at the photos I'd brought and talked about how much we missed John. After awhile, we and her children enjoyed my supply of fun, word-picture flash cards which had, purposely, been brought along just for such times of pleasurable entertainment by any youngsters during my travels.

I didn't want my stay in different homes, to be a chore and really *boring* for the young people of the families visited. I can well remember how dull were such visits from adults who arrived to see *my* parents when I was younger! We kids had to tidy the house beforehand, according to Mom's strict standards, and stay out of the way while "their company" was around. Then, the following morning, we often had the unpleasant task of cleaning up any mess left by the partying adults the night before. Possibly, those earlier experiences are why I seem to have such a low "gifting" in hospitality and usually feel somewhat nervous, even now, when there are people coming over. So, while on this trip, I wanted to avoid creating similar feelings in those of more "tender years," which would be encountered along the way.

Soon after the husband, Charlie, got home, another out of state family of about six arrived to also spend the night with my friends. Everyone was getting along fine, but alas, during supper with the adults, I ran into the first of many challenges the Lord would have me experience on this trip. While we were eating, it soon became apparent that the other couple was intent on complaining about church people and varied disappointments within the family of God. I felt like a trapped audience and became very uncomfortable having to overhear gossip about things that were not my business and involving people I didn't even know. I rose from the table two or three times to get one item or another, in a purposeful attempt to be distracting, hoping that the annoying disturbances would help to change the folks' topic of discussion.

The tactic didn't work and I was getting very concerned, because the Master brought to my remembrance the gist of Leviticus 19:16a. It addressed the issue that negative tale-bearing, whether true or false, is strictly forbidden in God's Word! It can do injury to the teller, to each hearer, and to the person on whom the ill-report is being told. I knew God was nudging me to remind my friends, and their other guests, that the reputations of His people should always be carefully guarded and held in precious respect. Needful, yet "loving correction" *(Prov. 3:12)* should be administered directly; and <u>not</u> talked about behind their backs to others.

But, afraid of appearing ill-mannered and offending every adult present, I cowardly went to wash the supper dishes instead, so as to remove myself from hearing their conversation. Well, at least, that choice blessed the teenage daughter by offering to do her nightly chore. Once that task was finished and noting the focus of the grown-ups' visiting hadn't changed, I sat in with the large bunch of children. All the while, silently trying to muster up the courage to obey God and speak a word of admonition to their parents. Unsuccessful and feeling miserable, I shortly bid everyone a good-night and went off to bed.

Sleep? Forget it! Here I was afraid I would lose my nerve to witness to unbelievers further down the road on this trip, and now I couldn't even get beyond the "fear of man" *(Heb. 3:16)* to lovingly rebuke some kindly and true Christians. Satan's lackeys had a few hours of "hey day" making me wrestle with low self-esteem, causing my spirit to feel restless and agitated.

But then, by the Father's grace and mercy, the accuser threw at me the awful state of my "weakness" and that one word triggered the remembrance of II Corinthians 12:9a which says: "My strength is made perfect in your weakness." That scripture reminded me of the primary qualification for serving God...a healthy sense of our own weakness. God will allow no strength used in *His* battles, except for the strength which He Himself imparts. How wonderful is the blessing that God's Word will "not return void" *(Isa. 55:11)*, especially if you've made the effort to "hide it in your heart!" *(Ps. 119:11)* And, as you will soon see, during the next few weeks, God used and pulled out of me practically everything I had ever learned (about His ways and statutes); whether by intellect or through personal tough lessons, to "feed" someone at most every place I stopped. Oh, how I wished I had more to give them!

Believing that His victory was assured, I began to muster some courage again and knew that my own sense of being "cast down," was merely readying this vessel to be uplifted by His might! Soon falling deeply asleep, I knew that I'd be able to confess my own sin of disobedience and cowardliness the next morning either to Charlie or Anita, whichever one the Lord put in my path first. But, alas, I sensed that had I been prompt in obeying the Spirit's nudging, about the supper's conversation, the whole rest of the evening could have potentially gone far more sweetly and God-pleasing for everyone concerned. In a way I had let them all down by being too fearful about what they might think of me. After all, was not my own sin of not wanting to risk my pride getting hurt any less ugly than their gossiping? Absolutely not!

The next morning, with teary eyes, the Lord had me confess to the kind husband first and then to his dear wife who joined us. Charlie and Anita took the belated correction nobly and forgave me as well. After breakfast and photo-taking, I continued on with my

About Her Father's Business

journey. Praying for many miles though, that in doing what the Lord had commanded of me, I had not perhaps caused damage to the precious relationship John and I had shared with that Christian couple.

I should not have fretted though, as our God doesn't reward His children's obedience like that! After all, if I'd have asked for bread, He would not have given me a stone! *(Matt. 7:9, 11)* Weeks later, and a couple of days after I had returned home, Anita called. She wanted to know how I was faring after a satanic attack she'd heard about, half-way through the trip. And, also to thank me for giving that word of correction! She emphasized what a good lesson it turned out to be for even their children. The parents admitted what had transpired and told their youngsters that, sometimes, even grown-ups need to submit to the Lord's discipline. Praise His Name! This gal was one happy cookie!

CHAPTER TWO

Reach Out and Touch

The next stop, after traveling hours among rolling hills and farmlands, was Indiana. The husband, Stan, was a boyhood and neighborhood friend of John's and had a wife and three teenage children (ages 13-18). I had never met any of them before, yet Jesus granted all of us an instant rapport from the moment I stepped within their home at 4 p.m. But, with curiosity, I noticed that although everyone was friendly, only the husband shook my hand in greeting. Nor did I see anyone touching or sitting close to another person all evening. The husband didn't even kiss or hug his wife when she came home from work. I thought it odd, but hoped it only meant that they all were self-conscious in front of this stranger. Since I was only supposed to stay overnight, we three adults looked at photos (theirs and mine) all evening. Stan recalled old memories of our men's former school days, teen years and army service. Generally, we each talked like feather-brained magpies until after midnight.

The next morning I left early, but my car ran a bit rough upon starting. Driving about 25 minutes, I stopped at a one pump gas/cafe station in the very small town of Freedom. That's when my second challenge revealed itself. The car was all gassed up with miles ahead to go and guess what? It wouldn't start! It acted like it was totally empty and there wasn't even one mechanic residing in that little town to look at the problem *even* if it hadn't been a Saturday morning. So, I called the family I'd just left to see if they knew of a serviceman or auto-shop open nearby, to which I could have my car towed. Nope, it was to be temporarily "captive" in the town of Freedom.

Stan drove out to see if he could get my car started but was unable to, so we arranged to have it towed Monday, up to the next larger town about thirty miles away. Around that area, they were the only foreign car garage able to find the problem and order any needed part. So, with a "no nonsense" command to come back to their house, from that military ammunitions husband, I retraced my progress to "square one" of earlier that morning. Little did I know then, in the midst of feeling embarrassed for inconveniencing a family I'd just met, that God had "eternal plans" for these people. The delay was important as He wanted me to remain with them awhile longer. (Plus, the car trouble couldn't have happened at a safer place on my whole journey.) Also, unknown to me at the time, Stan's heart had been tugged the previous night, while he looked at John's photos and heard the tale of his daily faith. Now, God was about to move in that man's life…and in his family.

Stan was an unbeliever, but his wife had been brought up Christian. Yet, for years, the family had only attended her parent's church for events such as Easter, Christmas, funerals and weddings. I doubted, and soon found it to be true, that any of their children were saved. Twice on the drive home, Stan mentioned

About Her Father's Business

how glad he and his wife were to have me to themselves for more time. Both had expressed to the other that they'd felt an extra "presence of love" when John's wife had walked inside their home and had <u>so</u> wished her visit could have been longer. This yearning for me to stay amazed them both, as they had been nervous for days about this stranger coming to spend the night with them.

With that assurance of a welcome, I told Stan that my affectionate nature was too strong to feel comfortable for days among his clan if they didn't loosen up and think of me as "part of the family" and start touching each other again. He said, with all seriousness, that last night was perfectly "normal" for their household. His dad had always showed firm discipline, and with Stan remaining in the military, it certainly had not taught him to display his caring feelings for his wife and children over the years. So, with Stan's permission (and a silent prayer to the Lord to help me be tactful, yet brash enough – *Phil. 4:13*), he said I could show his family some of the benefits of being a healthy, affectionate unit.

The first opportunity to "step out in boldness" *(Eph. 6:19)* came as we entered the front door. The wife and kids were sitting on sofas and she "clucked" her sympathy over my car's dilemma, but only gave a glance of greeting to her husband and stayed seated. So, with a wide grin I walked over in front of her, reached down and took her by the arm, pulling her to her feet, and propelled the gal toward her husband. Laughingly, I said, "Noble woman of the household, arise and kiss thy good husband! For he has returned to the hearth, after successfully rescuing a "damsel in distress," and well deserves the reward of knowing you welcome him home!" (Oh dear, the shocked reaction from everyone in the room was priceless!) As that sweet-natured wife recovered, she turned towards her man. Stan was smiling down at her with a mischievous twinkle in his eye, as his wife stood close, looking up at him like a sheepish schoolgirl. By now, their teens were all smiling and "tee-heeing" behind their hands.

Well, the wife leaned up and gave her husband a quick peck on the cheek, but did that polite, almost motherly display of affection satisfy me? No way, Jose'! So, before the wife can back away, I tell her *that* kiss was "a good start… as an hor'dourve." And although I wasn't suggesting that she give her man a full course meal, right there in front of their children, didn't she think he, at least, merited a little more "meat and potatoes?" Here, let me explain …

"You see, dear, your very own 'Beloved' has just walked in the door! You are so pleased to see him that you, immediately "get off your duff" and with a smile of welcome and arms outstretched, do a comfy snuggle-bunny up to his side, under his strong "arm of protection." THEN, you give him a healthy 'smooch' on those pleasantly and conveniently located protrusions, under the nose and above the chin, which God gave each of us to use for more than just eating! You know, a 'peck' and a *real* kiss feel and sound a lot different. One is rather dry and sterile. Ah! But, the other is warm and pliable and needs to be resolutely planted on the lips." The young folks were now rolling with laughter, so I told them to help me with the "sound effects". "Come on, kids! Let's make some 'kissy-face' noises to help re-teach your parents something they seem to have forgotten back in their teen years." So, as the teens *loudly* and enthusiastically complied, their pink-faced yet, good-natured folks planted a resounding "smack" on each other! Then, with both of them grinning widely, Stan kept his arm draped over his wife's shoulders, as we all applauded and "whoop" our absolute approval!

Thus set the ever-comical tone of lessons teaching each member of that family the joys and benefits of learning to be comfortable in giving wholesome, affectionate touches. They had all been silently suffering with the need for physical human contact, but none of them had an inkling of how to change their situation or even that the others were feeling deprived as well. And, by the way, the *next* time her man came inside the door after work, his wife leapt into his arms in a draping and dramatic embrace. Joining in the mood of frolic, Stan then bent his gal slightly backwards to give her a really noisy kiss. Their behavior was accompanied by delighted squeals from their daughter and "way to go" wolf-whistles and shouts from their two sons!

The wife and the daughter thrived on the hugs immediately and were the first ones prone to give affection to the others. Stan was told that if he felt uncomfortable giving a frontal hug to his teenage daughter, (with her newly budding "front bumps"), then he could stand next to her and give his girl a squeeze across her shoulders, with a kiss on the top of her pretty head. After all, she wanted to be reassured that Daddy still thought of her as his "little princess!" Stan was further warned that if he didn't regularly put his affectionate 'arms of protection' around his daughter, then by sheer craving for that which she lacked at home, the gal was a prime candidate to seek such affection from another fella. And, it can almost be guaranteed that *he* would prey on her innocence and not be trustful to look out for her well being.

The daughter later thanked me for saying that, as one date had already been a bit more "friendly" than she liked; when all she wanted was to be held and cuddled. We talked in private awhile, as she hadn't known how to handle the situation and wanted instructions on how to not get stuck in another one like it.

The mother was told that, as she was talking to or listening to any of her teens, begin placing a gentle hand on the child's shoulder. Try to always pause and look at the person, and to stop averting her eyes or dividing her attention between them and her chores. She needed to confirm, with her actions, that *they* were more important than her tasks and merited her whole attention. No doubt, the teens would be more inclined to share their inner thoughts with her, if they felt she was genuinely interested.

The boys were informed that, even among "the guys," it was <u>not</u> "sissy" to show affection appropriately. If the occasion didn't seem to call for an actual "bear hug," they could deliver a manly, but not too rough, slap on the back. Even a "mock" punch to the other's shoulder, would demonstrate their caring, without getting too "mushy." I told the clan that, at first, my

About Her Father's Business

John had to be taught how to kiss, hold, and comfort me... until he became a real expert at it!

It was such a delightful blessing to be used by God during my elongated visit: To watch the beautiful development of lonely family members, who really did love each other, but hadn't known how to give expression to their caring, being transformed into doing silly, affectionate contests! The youngest boy joked that AT & T should be paying *me* for being such an example of their motto to "reach out and touch someone!"

How I wish each of you could see the vast difference in the stiff-posed, tight-grinned photo of that family, taken on the first evening I arrived, and the comparison of the picture taken on the morning I left them a few days later. In the latter one, no daylight can be seen between any of them; as they stand almost physically overlapping each other, with their hands put on a shoulder or back... and even the sister's head resting on her big brother's chest as he hugs her. And, the big smiles, oh dear sweet Jesus, how very beautiful are their expressions! Why, even the husband no longer resembled stern "Major Dad," but looked like a very friendly person who anyone would be glad to meet. Yet, by the time God let me move on, more than "human love" was found in their hearts.

CHAPTER THREE

Never Give Up

Stan was finally at ease enough, my first evening *back* with them, to venture a comment/question that was strongly on his mind. While everyone was still around the supper table, he recounted some of his more wild days and hateful, cruel mocking of anyone claiming to be a Christian. Stan admitted that he was resentful when John "got saved" at seventeen, as it had caused a rift in their close friendship. John began to get more stable, while most of the other guys in their late teens and early twenties were getting more out of control. Thus, soon he and John had little in common anymore.

At about 23-years-old, Stan had married his wife and had given up the drugs, booze and carousing. Yet, by then, all of his "decent" friends considered him a hopeless case and had long since deserted him. But, Stan remarked, "John never gave up on me." "He'd write to me once or twice a year and came over to visit whenever he was in town to see his folks. Although, I was usually stoned or drunk, John would stay and talk with me, making sure I knew that he really cared about my life and happiness. Often, though, in return for his loyal friendship, I'd treat him like "the scum of the earth." Not even writing him back for two or three years. Well, I've been wondering, does John's God sort of care about me the way he did? Or, is it too late for me to find out?"

So, for the first time in my life, I was given the privilege of helping one of God's lost children come unto Himself. Stan humbly prayed, after first allowing me to explain some things about the BIG step he was about to take. For example, scripture says that *(Col. 1:14)*, by faith, Stan had to receive and accept the gift of God's grace which gives all Believers eternal life with Him, through the sacrifice Jesus made on the cross which took away and pardoned all our sins. Christ needs to become real to Stan, not just the name of a historical figure, but consciously <u>alive</u> within his heart! He, then, belongs to Jesus as well as the Lord belongs to him... like actual family! The Master becomes his very own Savior and not even death can rob Stan of that love and mercy. Through the years, God will bless him with many precious things, but it is the gift of receiving Christ Himself, which Stan must always consider to be of the most value! Nothing else will aid him, or any of us, to keep life's joys and struggles in perspective.

By this time, Stan's wife was weeping for joy about her husband. Yet, she started to bemoan her own years of being a poor witness to those she has loved the most. In front of her kids, she confessed her wrongs and asked their forgiveness. She knew that, out of love and in submission to her own husband's wishes, she herself had wandered far from the Jesus of her youth. She had lost her zeal for God and how great was the value in His grace. She had often neglected prayer and, practically making her husband an idol, she had lost her "first love" of God *(Revelation 2:4)*. She had known that Christ would not honor a divided heart, so

About Her Father's Business

she wasn't even surprised when she sensed His Spirit withdrawing the very sunshine from her own soul.

But now, Stan's wife was not content with her state and wanted to rededicate her whole heart to Christ Jesus again! So, as her children stared in tearful silence their mother admitted to becoming a wayward child, humbling herself as I prayed for God's grace and strength to help her walk close to Him once more. Jesus would forgive her and lovingly lift her up, since it was His own heart's desire as well. He could, I knew, even "restore the years the locusts have eaten" and bring this welcomed daughter hope *(Joel 2:25a, 26)*. By then, we were all emotionally drained, yet called the wife's parents to tell them the good news and let them know to expect all of us at their church the next morning!

As decided beforehand, Stan and his wife "went forward at the invitation" (holding hands no less!) confessing their belief in Jesus Christ and their desire to be baptized. It was arranged to be done the very next Sunday. So many of their friends and family came up to congratulate them that the church service was almost an unheard of thirty minutes late that day!

The wife's elderly parents just kept weeping for joy and praising the Lord for answering their prayers. But, I overheard Stan tell them that it wasn't only *their* prayers which had helped cause this day of happiness. No, his old school buddy, John, had been praying faithfully for his lost childhood friend to "come to Christ" for over twenty-five years! And, Stan said, "That example has taught <u>me</u> the importance of never giving up on someone, no matter how hopeless the case may seem."

Back at their home after lunch, the kids hung around the table, instead of watching TV, to enjoy the surprising pleasure of getting reacquainted with their own folks. Before long, though, it became evident that the Lord's hand had not yet lifted His outpouring of blessing upon this family. Soon, both of the older teens expressed their desire to also become saved, then asked direct questions on how they were to personally begin serving Jesus!

To the oldest son, whose relationship with his beer-chugging girlfriend was now bothering his newly-birthed conscience, we talked about not being unequally yoked (II Cor. 6:4) and how God ordained that those of the light should be divided from those of the darkness. After all, when the Holy Spirit gives us spiritual light and opens our eyes to behold the glory of God, in Jesus Christ, we begin to look at sin in its true and ugly colors. We see our pathetic condition compared to the Almighty's pureness.

"But, remember," I told him "after you have explained your change and stand in Christ to your girlfriend, if she decides to still have nothing to do with God and His ways, then our Master says that the sons of Light are to have no fellowship ties with the deeds of darkness. Instead, pray that His Light will soon also shine in her heart. Watch out, too, for the pressures of peers, your so-called friends, who want to lead you away from Jesus with various temptations. Even things not as obvious, might be harmful to your

About Her Father's Business

new life in Christ, if you don't remember to ask His will on each matter."

For teens and young adults, peer pressure can be very strong. Being well acquainted with it in my own youth, it dared me into learning to scuba dive at 16, drive Malibu race track cars at 19, parachute at 22, and pilot a Cessna airplane at 26, yet each of those experiences almost cost my life... before I finally walked away from their lure. In themselves were they wrong? No, but for me, they were not ordained by God to get sidetracked with or involved in. And, Satan tried to use their excitement <u>and</u> danger to get rid of me *before* I'd yet had time to step over into the Kingdom of God. Beware, son, and guard against the enemy of your soul! *(Mark 8:36)*

The daughter, so full of appreciation for the newness of Life in her family, wondered how she could ever repay the Lord for His great gift. It was explained to her that we are all "debtors" and owe Jesus more than we could ever pay back *(Romans 8:1a, 12a)*. It has been said: Christians owe God's justice nothing only <u>because</u> Christ's mercy paid the debt when He became their receipt nailed to the cross, and said, "It is finished!" For that reason, we Believers owe even more...but to the debt of His love! The only way to begin to repay our Father is to simply give Him ourselves, and all that we have, to use for His glory.

Again, the girl fretted, because she felt that there was so little that she was able to give for the Master's use. She stated, "I only have my allowance and sometimes babysitting money. But, if I give every penny to some church or ministry or to poor folks, how can that tiny amount please God?" I asked her that if she knew our Jesus would be well pleased with the use and sacrifice of just one dime out of every dollar she earned, would her heart then be more at peace? Such began an explanation of the benefits and warnings of faithful tithing, like is stated in Haggai 1:9.

People are mistaken when they are miserly with their contributions to church ministry, needy people, and missionary outreaches, thinking the savings in their account is good economy. Little do they dream that such is actually taking away blessings of increased funds. Their excuse is often that they must better care for their own families, and they forget that to neglect the house of God is the surest way to bring poverty upon their own households. Scripture teaches that the Lord enriches the generous, but lets the stingy descend in poverty often…by the very means he had thought to increase his gain. Selfishness looks first to its own self, but godliness seeks first the Kingdom of God and His righteousness. It takes discipline and faith to always give to God first out of our earnings. Plus, to hold the remaining 90% with an open hand to offer Christ even more, when His Spirit prompts our heart to do so. After all, since our entire provisions are <u>gifts</u> from God, surely He is due the loyalty and thanks of such a tiny amount given back! Besides, Jesus knows, better than we do, where the greatest need is among His own children.

By now, it was time to begin supper, as the two older teens wanted to return to Sunday evening service and ask to also be baptized with their parents the next week. The youngest son wasn't ready yet to "jump on this

About Her Father's Business

band wagon" but admitted he sure liked the difference he was seeing in his family so far, and wondered how long all this niceness and "lovey-dovey" stuff would last. "Besides," he said with genuine concern, "what will my 'cool' school friends and teammates think of me?" I told him that is something to consider seriously because God does command His children to "Be ye separate (2 Cor 6:17)." A Christian is to live in the world, but not really be a part of its ways and actions: whatever he does should be for God's glory. Striving to be the best player on a team, a great pole-vaulter, or even some day making lots of money is not displeasing to the Lord *if* the motive to achieve those goals is to be a good witness for His name's sake or from a desire to have extra funds to be of regular help to God's own people. Also, "Be ye separate" from this "world's ways" regarding your everyday dealings. For instance, if a task or truth is right and honorable to do in God's sight then, even if you may lose something by doing it, it must still be done. Likewise, if an action or joke is wrong or doing someone else harm, a Christian must avoid that sin for the very love of His Master. We are not to let our eyes, which will one day see the King of Kings, be windows of lust, selfish gain, or unlovely pride. So, do think soberly about committing your heart and life to Jesus. He is well worth the cost, but only you can decide to receive Him into your own life.

* * * * * * * * * *

The next two days were likewise filled with fun, frolic and fortifying of these new "babes in Christ."

For me, it was an emotional strain to again have to leave all of them. I guess that, for a while, my closest link to John was his boyhood friend, Stan.

As of their last report, the daughter was saving her earnings (minus tithing) to go on a Teen Mania mission trip to Australia. The older son broke off with his former girlfriend and is doing better in his school grades and part-time job. The younger son is still teetering on the fencepost, but at school, he now defends his older siblings' choice to stand for Jesus and stifles any "razzing" he hears about them among his peers. (We all think he is very close to heaven's gate.) The family has remained faithful in their church attendance and growth in God's Word. Stan and his wife hope to visit me in North Carolina and use the "Elijah Room" for their second honeymoon retreat!

CHAPTER FOUR

Kindness and Cruelty

Late Tuesday afternoon, my car was repaired and ready to drive. A computer chip had suddenly gone out in the fuel injector system and it cost almost $550 to get a new one and have it replaced. As each day of delay passed, I had to readjust my traveling schedule and cancel getting to see some people. Since it was so very important to John for his own family to get a visit, I first notified my Mormon brother in Idaho, letting him know that I could not make it to their home after all. (It would not surprise me to someday learn that my King allowed the car repair delay in order to protect me <u>from</u> driving into that Mormon-dominated area.)

Then, I had to cancel getting to see our dear Christian friends in and near Glenwood Springs, Colorado. My schedule was now adjusted enough to continue visiting each of John's relatives and old friends, yet <u>still</u> be able to get to Denver in time for his official Memorial Service. Therefore, about 4 p.m. this gal started a 9-hour drive, which ended about midnight in Illinois, at John's Aunt Joyce's place (his mom's older sister).

* * * * * * * * *

With only a few hours of sleep that night, I got up to visit and share John's life with his aunt and uncle, who were both in their late seventies. Later that day for supper, we were to meet John's mother's brother, Tom, and wife, plus their newly married son and his bride. Nevertheless, for now, Jesus gave me the daylight hours to talk with John's sad and upset aunt.

After showing John's pictures, the newspaper articles and his city and state "Good Samaritan" Resolutions, his dear Aunt Joyce could not hold back her remorse any longer. She sobbed, "How can John ever forgive us? All of us treated him as if he was "dull-witted" throughout his life. We thought only stupid people needed the crutch of religion. Yet, how much better and honest and happy a person he turned out to be in comparison to most of us."

I told her that I was certain John had, indeed, forgiven all of them. However, that the only way <u>she</u> would ever feel sure about it herself was to meet and submit to the One from whom John had learned *how* to forgive. Aunt Joyce argued that she was too old and had done too many bad things to be so easily forgiven. Her words reminded me of Job 40:4 where it said "Behold I am vile." Understandably, she needed more encouragement and reassurance that she was not "too far gone" to still be saved and forgiven. Therefore, I told her that there is not a Christian who ever lived that did not feel ashamed in front of Christ and need to confess many, many wrongs. Nevertheless, Jesus beckons each one of us to "come unto Him" *(Matt. 11:28)*…just as we are. You cannot remove any of your sins from the past, but He is willing and able to erase all of them! With your contrite heart, confess and surrender to Him. You will find a complete pardon and be rewarded with a deep peace within. Therefore, with a silent nod of encouragement from stroke-impaired

About Her Father's Business

husband, John's elderly aunt repeated the sinner's prayer and became a new baby in God's family and a true "sister" to her own nephew, John!

Aunt Joyce spent the next 2-3 hours talking on the phone to family and friends about what had just happened to her. Physically and spiritually worn out, I went upstairs and took a nap. That evening, they took me out to meet John's other relatives for supper. Of course, by then, all of them had heard about Aunt Joyce's conversion and now got to see her radiant and glowing countenance.

Soon, Tom's son asked me a question that he and his bride wanted to know. They wanted the answer to, "How do we learn to love and trust each other like you and John did?" (Oh Lord, I thought, hold me down or this gal will be doing a "hallelujah-hop" right on the table because of these new "fish" You just plopped into her net!) Thus, right there in a busy restaurant, the older folks allowed me to minister advice and eternal direction to those two young people. Among other things, I told them that even "good people," who really love you, may let you down occasionally. Therefore, even as we are to forgive them, we are also to depend upon and trust in God, far more than any other person. Kindly, He often allows us to lean on and be a comfort to each other here. Yet, everyone who cares about you, no matter how much they would not mean to, has the potential to hurt your feelings or let you down in some way. We are, after all, still only imperfect humans trying to be Christ-like, but sometimes failing.

"Your best chance of harmony within your new marriage is for both of you to allow the Lord to guide all of your choices, decisions, and words. Develop a love and trust, mostly, in Jesus and never fully transfer all of your hopes, emotions, and mental stability onto just one person. Such a load is too heavy for them, as we all make mistakes, even if completely unintentionally. Besides, no matter how loving that person is, the bulk of your devotion and dependency belongs to God: He will *never* fail you! *(Heb. 13:5b)* With the help of Jesus, you and your spouse will be able to thrive and, as Gary Chapman says in his Five Love Languages video, to keep each others' 'love tank' full. Moreover, it is a very sweet blessing that God gives us the *gift* of other people in our lives with which to express and share our love." Obviously, the Holy Spirit had been at work in their hearts long before I got there, because each of those newlyweds very comfortably fell into God's embrace…as if it were the most natural thing for them to do… and, of course, it really was!

Early the next morning, I was packed and ready to depart. Yet, John's aunt kept weeping so much, not wanting me to leave, that her husband had trouble taking our 'farewell' picture. Oh, well; how delightful it must be to God to see prior "hearts of stone" turned into soft, loving flesh. Was I ever so thankful that the Master fortified my spirit with such a whole-hearted acceptance and committed change in Aunt Joyce and her other relatives. Because, unknown to me, I would soon be facing an unpleasant revenge from Satan, for my participation in the "freeing" of some those Illinois "captives" *(Isa. 61:1)*. No doubt about it, his composure was *dis*turbed!

About Her Father's Business

* * * * * * * * * *

Trying to give an encouraging surprise visit to a couple from my home church, which had been at the Mayo clinic, I stopped first at Rochester, calling the local motels to find them. Yet, alas, due to the delays in my own travels, Mr. and Mrs. Robson had flown back to North Carolina that same afternoon. I was told that she had come through her procedure fine and since that was the most important thing, I just went on down the road to Minnesota instead.

Around 5 pm, amidst a foggy dusk, I found the home of John's dad's sister. Aunt Mary greeted me a tad coolly and her husband was not there at all. Immediately, my spirit went on "alert" and I knew that this was <u>not</u> a household friendly to my Jesus. She fed me cold tuna salad and crackers out on her back porch, instead of a warm meal inside her house. The non-verbal cues were surely mounting that John's Aunt Mary was ill at ease having me on her turf! That my presence was unwelcome was coming in loud and clear. I figured she had only allowed me stop there, because she could not think of any way to deny my request to visit, without "looking like a heel" to all the rest of John's kinfolk.

It was not yet fully dark outside, but as she poured her third drink, I suggested that she might enjoy looking at the photos of John when he was a child and teenager. Mistakenly, I had begun to wonder if Aunt Mary's tension could be her worrying about being expected to look at the more unpleasant pictures of his accident and funeral. But, to my surprise, she remarked that I'd better go get dressed for bed, "as you've had a long drive and must surely be tired" and she'd just "scan over the photos" while I changed. Later, I realized that such was her attempt at kindness, to intentionally have me asleep on their den sofa before her alcoholic husband and recently divorced son came home from the races. It would have worked, too, except that the men skipped the last race. Aunt Mary's husband was losing money and her son was eager to get home to have a look at Cousin John's "babe." Both were very drunk.

Being an unusually modest person, it was awkward indeed to see two strange men walk in the house and give me unsolicited hugs, while I was only wearing my nightgown and robe. I had just asked John's aunt directions to any nearby church, so I could attend a service in the morning before driving to my next stop. As the men poured themselves and her more to drink, she laughingly told them what I just asked. They all then cursed and "hee-hawed" about "Miss Goody Two Shoes," going off on a tangent, saying unkind, even vulgar things about Christians in general. Even though my spirit discerned that this was actually a verbal harassment from the pit, their words still hurt my feelings!

Therefore, I turned and walked down the hall toward the den before my tears spilled over. No reason, I thought, to give them anything *else* to make fun of me about! Yet, before I reached the den, their middle-aged son grabbed hold of me in the hall and trapped my body against a doorframe, complaining that, "I wasn't

About Her Father's Business

being very friendly" as he got way *too* friendly with his hands. This gal was not a "happy camper!" Angrily, I pushed him away and fled to the den. His raunchy words and laughter faded towards the bar and kitchen area as I slammed the door shut!

At first I was so indignant I hadn't yet become frightened, but then noticing that my door had no lock on it...sobered me greatly! The Lord brought to my mind the story of Joseph in Genesis 39:12, when he had to "flee" from Potiphar's wife. Believe me, I got the message clearly! Figuratively, it would be better "to leave my cloak" than to lose my character, by staying in that house overnight unprotected. For all I knew, the parents might pass out cold and be unable to offer their help to me, if it were needed. Even if I was over-reacting, it was "better to be safe, than sorry."

Therefore, while they were all getting a huge joke out of "Prim Kim," I dashed with my regular clothes into the bathroom. After locking the door, I got dressed, then, immediately, came out and repacked my one suitcase. Within a few minutes, this gal was walking to their front door, her car keys in hand. They all stopped their banter as I said that, "It seems best that I go to a motel tonight instead, as it appears my visit has made all of us feel uncomfortable." Not waiting for their permission, it still surprised me that none apologized or made any efforts to amend their conduct. Yet, just as the engine of my car started, Aunt Mary came out. She commented that, "Yes, it was probably better this way, as you'd not enjoy seeing three blurry-eyed drunks at the breakfast table just before you went off somewhere to church." She looked utterly miserable being trapped in her sin-filled world and I felt very sorry for her. Yet, for now, neither she nor her men folk were willing to let anyone help them. I discovered out later that the Spirit's warning was not unfounded, as that their son's marriage broke up because "he chased anything in skirts."

* * * * * * * * * *

A few exits down the road, I found a motel with a vacancy. After getting to my room, I sat stunned and motionless for over an hour, just letting God's Spirit minister to my shocked and disappointed state of mind. Those pathetic, rude, ignorant, lost souls! No wonder soft-spoken John was so easily intimidated by them over the years. Yet, those relatives might still be marked for God's grace, someday further down the line; even though, right now, they are lovers of themselves and taverns and haters of holiness. They were in such a sad condition. They knew nothing about prayer, but Jesus had kept John praying for them all these years *and* the Great Intercessor continues to pray on their behalf. Someday, one or all of them might bend their stubborn knee and bow in obedience to His Name. If they do not do so in love before they die, they will surely do so, in terror, afterwards *(Phil. 2:10)*.

After awhile, my brain allowed my body to function again. I sought my Bible and devotional book for solace. Like most people, it always wounds my heart deeply when I feel rejected, or unjustly treated. Scanning the pages of my book titled, <u>For This Day</u>, I came across the following devotion which really uplifted me, putting the whole ordeal back into perspective. From Luke 23:26, J. B. Phillips writes: "When you are attacked for your piety, when your religion brings trials of cruel mockings upon you, then remember it is not your cross, but the cross of Jesus which you carry... Do not forget, that you bear this cross in partnership. You only carry the light end of the cross, it was Christ who bore the heavier end... Remember, though Simon had to bear the cross for only a little while, it gave him lasting honor. Even so, the cross we carry is only for a little (earthly) while, and then we will receive the crown of glory."

Then gleaning from Hebrews 5:8, Philip adds: "The Captain of our salvation was made perfect through suffering. Therefore, we who are sinful and far from being perfect, ought not to wonder or be surprised when we are called to pass through suffering as well. Will the head be crowned with thorns, and will the other members of the body be rocked on the dainty lap of ease? Is Christ to endure the loss of His own blood to win the crown, and then we to walk to heaven in silver slippers? No, our Master's experience teaches us to expect suffering. Yet, He completely sympathizes and sustains us with His power... Remember, to suffer for Christ's sake is an honorable thing...The apostles rejoiced that they were counted worthy to do this... For the Christian, they are the jewels...in his eternal crown" (II Timothy 2:12a).

CHAPTER FIVE

Courting with Honor

The next morning I only drove most of the way through Iowa, and then stopped at another motel to rest. My physical endurance was very low, due to the long miles of traveling, meeting, and adjusting to new people, strange beds every night...plus, that recent "trial." Therefore, I just took an extra day to be alone with Jesus and energize my internal batteries. It seemed best to altar my plans of doing some local sightseeing there, as I needed God's insight and revitalizing to keep fatigue at bay.

* * * * * * * * * *

The next day was an easy drive into Nebraska to see another of John's boyhood friends and his family. The husband, Kyle, had gotten saved at the same revival, but had not stayed close to the Lord. He married a sweet, but non-Christian lady in college and now they had a teenage daughter and son. The wife and son were home when I arrived at 4 p.m. and the husband and daughter came home within an hour. All were very friendly and outgoing and by the end of supper, we would become fast "chums." We did the word-picture flash cards at the table, during dessert, and the teens got a real kick out of being better at the game than were their parents!

It was kind of the Master to grant us all a comfortable rapport early, because once we started looking at the photos, some challenging questions soon came to the surface. The issue of dating arose as I was re-telling how John and I met and had honorably courted. This was a "touchy" subject at that house because the older teenager was being intimate with her boyfriend and her parents felt certain he would make her a bad husband, if they did actually marry.

Kyle's daughter was asked how much time per week she spent in the boy's presence and how much time did she spend with other family or friends doing separate activities without him. (It was sensed that he was purposefully consuming huge chunks of her life, in order to secure himself as the strongest influence in it. His motivation was not out of love or thoughtfulness to her welfare. No, it was feeding his selfish desires and weak self-esteem.)

As an example, I shared how the Lord, in His wisdom, moved John and me states apart, which allowed us to see each other only one weekend, every four to six weeks. It was His warning for us to be cautious and not to overly use each other to fill our own social and emotional needs. It could lead to an overbalanced exclusion of others in our separate lives and would not be healthy in the long run for our own relationship. We were not to lean on each other so heavily, that if God told us not to be mates after all, then we would be unable or unwilling to stop seeing each other. It was not safe to get in the habit of allowing our whole

About Her Father's Business

lives to revolve mostly around just the other person *(Exodus 43:14)*. It would have developed a strong and unhealthy dependency upon each other. We nurtured our romance with one long phone call each week and endless amounts of letters. However, with John needing to concentrate on his new job and me trying to finish college, it was good to not let our relationship overwhelm and distort every other aspect of our lives. Actually, necessary letter writing was a Godsend. Through them, I was finally able to perceive who John *really* was, on the inside, and stopped resisting falling in love with him. Hesitating for months, to even set an official date for our engagement, I felt that John was hiding something from me — that I had not yet seen his "real self." Partly, that was true, but he was not intentionally withholding some dark part of his being. No, John just was not gifted in verbally expressing how he felt about things, especially those that were deeply important to him. Ah, but let that man organize his thoughts and feelings visually on paper, and there was nothing left unrevealed! In addition, we knew it was God's preference that we gallantly "court" each other for a pre-set, extended time frame, not just casually "date."

The term was "old fashioned" to Kyle's daughter, so I explained that "courting" meant that, no matter how often or how infrequently you are able to be with each other, neither of you will "go out with" anyone else. We were to wait until the Lord confirmed our hopeful union or told us to separate, without "muddying the waters," by dividing our attention and affections with seeing anyone else. Honorable "courting" is God's way of training and disciplining His children to later be faithful to our own spouse! Dating, on the other hand, encourages the flipping from one person to another, in rather short order. In addition, many such folks attempt the unwise and futile "emotional overlapping" of trying to develop a romance with more than one person, at the same time. Dating in effect, as it's understood in this generation, teaches young people *how* to be unfaithful and dissatisfied with just one "love interest." In my opinion, it sets them up to never learn the harder work of "hanging in there," even after the first "flutters" have subsided. We need that season of exclusiveness to find out who the other is, whether for good or ill, beyond their attractive outside wrappings. Sadly, very often you will find out that a person is not nearly so appealing or nice "on the inside." Thus, taking things slowly does much in assisting the discovery of such things, before it is too late.

The daughter asked how such advice could do her any good in her own far advanced situation. Hoping this was of the Lord, I told her to test their relationship by ceasing to allow her boyfriend use her for sex and to only be in his physical presence no more than half of the time they were now spending together. She should use some of that recaptured time to be alone and, also, to renew former friendships and family ties. After trying this for one month, she should re-evaluate their relationship and determine if it still has valid merit. If so, continue on the same course until the wedding night; if not, break clean of it and <u>fast</u>!

So far, I had purposefully avoided any condemning or judgmental phrases about the sins they were

About Her Father's Business

committing. You see, if you do not show first that you really care how a person is feeling and, instead, just spout accusations at them, most likely, they will not listen to anything else you have to say. Therefore, now that Kyle's daughter was receptive, it was time to gently tell her of God's "better way," instead of the world's way.

The world says, "Yes, be kind to others and help the less advantaged, *if* it doesn't get your white gloves dirty." Worldly wisdom boasts compromise, not steadfastness to one's convictions. They will agree that purity is nice, but discourage you from being so strict as to deny yourself from "having a little fun." After all, they proclaim, "Everybody does it!" Such cunning advice causes earthly misery, both emotionally and/or physically. It might even lead to your eternal ruin. In following the Lord fully, we must choose to resist the carnal ways of "the world" and leave alone its unsanctified pleasures and false religions. Know for certain that one day all of the world's corruption will be burned up in fire. Make sure you, dear girl, are far from those flames! Yield instead to the Lord's obvious wooing of you to, "Come ye out from among them" (II Corinthians 6:17).

Kyle's daughter was not, yet, ready for a commitment to Jesus. Still, as she got up to leave on a date with her boyfriend, she declared her solemn determination to dare the young man to follow the advice which I had given. During my conversation with his daughter, Kyle often nodded in agreement but, as "head of the household," he surprisingly said little.

Oh, how sad is the state of a backslider *(Hosea 10:5b, 6b)*. His words no longer hold authority and his family respects not his counsel.

CHAPTER SIX

Edify in Christ

After Kyle's daughter was gone he asked, "What was this sabbatical thing you went on just before John's accident?" Therefore, I explained to him that it was my usual one to two weeks of privileged time set aside, bi-annually, to fast and be alone with my Master. While only drinking liquids, I let the hunger pangs remind me to subdue and overcome the cravings of my earthly, temporal desires. And, instead, I'd concentrate on nourishing my spirit with prayer, reading scriptures, listening to sermons or praise music, and mediating on God's Word (Psalms 119:15). Also, the time is used to cleanse my inner soul from any known sins, clinging demonic influences and cease any habits displeasing to Jesus. Using it to completely purify any earthly "yuk" which might have been accumulating since my last sabbatical. The valid truth is that there are times when solitude with Jesus is far more beneficial than human society; that silence and waiting to hear the Lord's voice is better even than speaking in a private prayer language.

As an example, during the sabbatical that was taken just before John's accident, God had affirmed to my spirit that a ten-year-long request had been granted. Lovingly concerned that John would be left too lonely and sad without me, I had beseeched our King that, when our time of parting arrived, to please take him "home" before me. John expressed his gratefulness for that answer the Monday night before he died. Of course, <u>neither</u> of us expected that harsh separation for twenty to forty years! Also, I had sensed that it was *not* the Lords' timing for me to yet stop my six-day fast, as was planned. So, after a great night of sharing and being reunited with John, I was still very much "in tune" with Jesus on the following, very fateful Tuesday morning!

After John had left for work and since it was my day off, I started doing the laundry. Soon a call from school came in, asking if I could substitute for a teacher's Learning Delayed students that afternoon. About forty-five minutes later, the phone rang again. Thinking it was just the same gal wanting to add to her instructions, I was surprised to hear the voice of John's co-worker. He said my fella was not there yet…and that he had seen a bad accident on his way to work! Hoping the truck involved was not John's, I still called our local hospital. Relieved they did not have him there, I was told to check with their staff in Emergency. The nurse would not deny or confirm John's presence there, but had me wait to talk to a doctor. He felt that the accident victim was my Honey, but would not tell me of his condition, and only encouraged me to hurry! Distressed, I reported the news to John's work and then stood to leave for the hospital. Immediately, a paralyzing, knifing panic washed over me! Yet, almost as fast, my "in tune" spirit discerned that this was an attack of "fear" from the evil one, trying to take advantage of the situation. So, I sat right back down and began to pray, pleading for John's protection and denouncing Satan's power over me *(Matt. 10:1b)!*

About Her Father's Business

Before long, I sensed that my Beloved was beyond the need of earthly prayers and that I would be all right. Soon afterwards, I drove to the local Emergency, hoping in my heart that I was mistaken. Yet, by the time I had arrived, God had already begun helping me to accept the upcoming verdict that John was no longer a resident in this world. Our comforting Savior allowed me to remain unnaturally, even SUPERnaturally calm when I was later told the sad news. By then, I would have almost been surprised if it had been otherwise. The Spirit brought to my remembrance a saying that goes, "Death is not extinguishing the light. No! It's just turning off the night-lamp because the dawn has come!" And, after the doctor explained the horrible extensiveness of the injuries, I know that had John survived, he would have been so <u>miserable</u> coping with being very severely paralyzed.

"So, you see, Kyle, it is help gotten through daily devotionals, Bible studies, or retreat times away, that Christians become stronger, more productive laborers for God's service. It is to *our* great advantage when they take time to gather nutrition from His Word and from His exclusive Presence. Our spirits are not nourished enough by just listening to a weekly sermon about divine truths. No, we must also make the concentrated effort to read the Bible ourselves, meditate upon its teachings, and pray. Otherwise, we are not fully digesting and assimilate God's ways…as our own. It is not enough to only desire God's holy wheat, we must also be willing to grind and eat it for its best use in our lives."

Kyle admitted that he had not even picked up his Bible in a long time, so I reminded him that he was losing a lot of precious blessings by his neglect. There is so much value in searching the Scriptures! There may be a promise in the Word that would exactly fit your trouble for that day, but you did not read it, so therefore missed its counsel and comfort. You may continue being sick on some occasion, because you did not examine scriptures which proclaim the healing Christ wanted for you (Jer. 30:17a). Also, beyond just reading, it is extremely helpful to memorize the promises and instructions of God. It seems foolish to me that some people work so hard to remember sayings of famous men or poets, <u>yet</u> rarely make the smallest effort to learn the profound knowledge of God! If we never bother to put the Lord's Truths into our brains, how else will we be ready to have the Spirit quicken a verse or story in our hearts so we are able to solve a difficult problem in life or overthrow a doubt or temptation. Confessing neglect, Kyle vowed to dust off his old college Bible and begin reading it again every morning before work.

Then John's friend asked if I believed in the gift of tongues. Oh Boy! <u>This</u> could be the match to a keg of dynamite, but sometimes, this fool went where even "angels fear to tread!" According to scripture, I explained, the Spiritual gifts are intended to be in operation today, just as they were in the first century church. The "gift of tongues" was only one of several different anointings the Holy Spirit may impart to a believer (I Cor. 14:2). Like me, not everyone has

About Her Father's Business

that particular gift, although we should all be open to receive it, if God wishes to bless us that way. Instead, some may be granted the "gift" of mercy, pastor, helps, evangelist, or still other ones.

In my opinion, it is cruel and unbiblical to expect all Christians, who have been "baptized in the Holy Spirit," to show evidence or "proof" of the experience, exclusively on the grounds of whether or not they can "speak in tongues" *(I Cor. 14:4)*. I have seen untold damage to Jesus-adoring Christians after someone implied that they did not quite "cut it" in God's eyes, because they lacked the gift of tongues. Oh dear, much needless spiritual crippling has occurred over that one issue. Many Christians can exhibit more than one spiritual gift, but each is an evidence of the Holy Spirit in their lives. Some people speak in tongues only as a private prayer language, during their own communion with the Master. Others do not have an inkling of that gift, in any form, yet show clear evidence of the Spirit's indwelling power, by other God-sanctioned ones they do display.

The gift of tongues, I continued, was meant for the edifying of the Body of Christ. Its intent is *supposed* to be encouragement to others in the body of Christ. That is why God decreed that there should always be a "gift of interpretation," following an "utterance of an unknown language." The people hearing the words first spoken can then understand their meaning, due to the inspired interpretation afterwards *(I Cor. 14:13)*. If there are a lot of loud "tongues" being spoken in an assembly of believers, which are <u>not</u> being interpreted, then no one can benefit from the God-inspired words.

People do not understand what has been uttered, including, most likely, the persons operating in the gift at that time. Our God is a God of order, so it is more pleasing to Him if people who are enabled to "speak in tongues" (whether an angelic or an unlearned earthly language) do so only when the gift of interpretation is operating in the gathering as well *(I Cor. 14:19)*.

Also, beware of "false tongues!" They are self-imposed utterances of carnal Christians out to impress others, or a distorted, mock "tongue" from a satanic influence. The interpretation, which follows an utterance, is important for exposing the "fruit" of the words spoken, whether its origins are from heaven, earth, or hell *(Matt. 7:20)*. Kyle pondered this, without any comments.

CHAPTER SEVEN

Mistaken Lights

Next, Kyle's wife asked if the Bible tells parents how to raise their children in safety, considering our society's current dangers? She and her son had been so admiring a new Mormon neighbor's family and their wholesome lifestyle. They had pretty much decided to go to the Mormon Church that coming Sunday and probably join it. She wanted to be taught how to raise her family without, accidentally, turning out kids with low morals or drug problems.

Her motive was pleasing to God, and, yes, the Bible did give guidance on family life *(Prov. 22:6)*. Also, there were many excellent books and videos by Christian experts on that topic, like several by James Dobson of "Focus on the Family." But, many would advise that she was definitely looking to the wrong source by thinking of becoming a Mormon *(II Cor. 11:4)*. They would say that she and her son obviously had no concept of anything amiss with the L.D.S. teachings, wrongly thinking the Utah-based cult was just another Christian denomination! *(For more on what a cult actually is, read such articles as "Marks of a Cult," by Gary Clipperton and "Patterns in the Cults," by Interfaith Witness.)* So, for the next full hour, I explained part of what I had learned about some differences, which were not in harmony with accepted Christian doctrines, yet were taught by the Mormons (i.e.: "The Church of Jesus Christ of Latter Day Saints").

Many such teachings are in total disagreement with the infallible Truths from the Word of God *(II Tim. 3:16)*. Noticeably, each time the Bible contradicts an unusual Mormon belief, *that* is where they claim God's Word was NOT "translated correctly."

Yet, I encouraged, not everyone who joins a Mormon church is unsaved, because they may have learned about the real Jesus elsewhere. Experts say what misleads people is that the L.D.S. church uses most of the same Christian words that the other churches do, yet they apply to those words vastly altered definitions! The dividing trickery is in the use of those false meanings, the difference of which the majority of decent, honorable, pew-sitting Mormons never learn about. *(There are many sources on this topic, but for an easy 'glossary of terms' comparison, look in the back of the book titled The Mormon Puzzle, published by Broadman and Holms, as well as different articles from The Evangel by, Utah Missions, Inc.)*

As ex-Mormons have reported, further advancement, on each rung of the ladder of "works," allows more of the "deeper truth" to be "revealed" to a person by their Ward's bishop, a Missionary, or some other official. *(More about their doctrines can be read in the "Mormons" section of Kingdom of the Cults, by Walter Martin.)* Folks say that many elders in their top Quorum and their so-called "living prophet," know that the L.D.S. church is a corrupt, false-religion. But, the power, prestige and sometimes even good jobs owed to the church, keep them from leaving the Mormon trap. And often, as many have testified, those who do try to leave the L.D.S. church, have to put their relation-

About Her Father's Business

ship with their own spouse and family at risk. *(As clearly shown in the video, <u>The Godmakers, Part I</u>, by Jeremiah Films.)*

At barely 16, I experienced this reaction personally, due to having to leave my parents' home when refusing to attend the Mormon Church, which I no longer trusted. The verdict was to "come back" or entirely leave home! So, I packed my few things and left. Unlike the first three years, my family doesn't hang up the phone when I call or return my letters unopened anymore. Yet, they are still uncomfortable inviting me to their holiday celebrations or to attend weddings or funerals. Most of them are not nearly as strict in their church-life as in prior years. Thus, in their backslidden state (by L.D.S. standards), they are labeled "Jack-Mormons". *(A helpful book for those who will listen to the <u>real</u> truth is, <u>Witnessing to Latter Day Saints</u>, by North American Mission Board.)* It is said that, often the "works" part of the church requirements, wears out the zeal of members fast. Also, as history records show, because their early leaders, especially Joseph Smith, dabbled in occultic practices and secret Mason rituals, the Mormon's foundational beliefs are intermingled with satanic elements! *(One source, of many, is the chapter titled, "Pagan Mysteries Restored," in the book titled; <u>The Godmakers</u>.)*

Having left the L.D.S. church, I am considered an apostate. Other Mormons "in good standing" are taught to rarely, if ever, associate with me. When I was baptized on Father's Day, at the age of 27, for the <u>true</u> Father God, all L.D.S. records of me and my thousands of hours of "merits and works" were erased from their files. To them, I became a non-existent person. Therefore, officials had to again use another "young maiden" to perform the rites of "baptism for the dead" for all of the 43 people I'd already been immersed for "in proxy" when I was 13 years old. To most Christians, several of the distinctive Mormon doctrines and "deeper truths" don't even make logical sense; a few rise from the very pit of hell and are spiritually dangerous! A proven example is that they proclaim *their* "Jesus" was only the first "spirit child" born to their God (who used to be a fallible human on another planet) and to one of his many wives. Guess who was supposedly born second? It was *Lucifer*, Jesus' younger brother. *(An easy source to look at about this is the video called, The Mormon Puzzle, by Southern Baptist Convention.)* I sure don't want THAT Jesus living in my heart *(II Cor. 13:5)*! Even though they produce great-sounding commercials about having "another testament *(gospel)* of Jesus," the Bible tells us to have nothing to do with false prophets teaching "another gospel, another Jesus, or another way!"

As stated in their own L.D.S. books, they teach that all Mormons can themselves "work" their way to heaven and be exalted as a god and goddess when they die, in order to populate other planets that they themselves create (If you recall Satan's fall started when he wanted to be equal in power to God Most High). Their Jesus, God, and Holy Spirit (Ghost) are not a "trinity" of one God, but a separate "council of three gods." Their transcripts prove that early Mormon leaders taught that the sacrificial blood of their Jesus only covers <u>most</u> of their sins. That for them to be forgiven and make amends for really bad ones (like apostasy from the L.D.S. church), they claim that the person can only be cleansed by the "shedding of his own blood," via "Blood Atonement." Literally, that teaching means that he needs to die or be killed, in order for his soul to be "saved." And, reliable facts gathered, show there are a mysteriously high percentage of ex-Mormons, in strong L.D.S. controlled areas, who have suspicious auto or shooting "accidents," or who just disappear and are never seen or heard from again. *(Related, actual testimonies are numerous, so view the Godmakers – part II video.)*

There were more questions asked and answered that night about Mormons, but I felt nudged to get their "saucer-like" eyes focused back onto the One True God. Kyle's wife and son were told that the Persons of the Trinity never act apart or with more importance than with the others; they co-exist and are co-equal *(John 1:1, Romans 8:11a, II Cor. 3:17, John 6:63).* Not from Creation to atonement, nor as their work on our sanctification is still being done, have they worked independently of each other (You might want to look up: Jude 1: 21, I Cor. 1:3, John 10:38b, and I Peter 1:2). They are as united in their deeds as in their essence; the Triune God is One! We talked about many aspects of God's character and what our Lord of heaven and earth expects from us. Indeed, how sweet and precious it was to, then, have all three of the family members present, bow in prayer and each commit or re-commit their lives and hearts to the One true Jesus, the Lord God Almighty!

Kyle's son was very excited. He marveled at the Lord's timely intervention of sending me to their house only four days before they would have surely joined the Mormon Church *(Col. 1:28)*. He and his mom took down the Bible references I gave and other resources suggested. But, still the lad was eager to "do something, anything for Jesus now!" His emphatic words reminded me of Ecclesiastes 9:10, which states, "Whatsoever thy hand findeth to do, do it with all thy might." I explained that such refers to works honoring God that He <u>wanted</u> the boy to do. There are many things his heart and mind may think of to do, which may actually *not* be God's will for him personally, and should be left for someone else to accomplish. He must always ask Jesus whether he ought to go "to the right or to the left" before jumping into anything.

Even so, one small good deed well done is far more valuable than a hundred unaccomplished opportunities that he never quite got around to doing. So, do things day by day in your current life and sphere of influence, which please God. He will prepare you for mightier deeds, as you show yourself faithful to the smaller tasks that He gives you now *(Luke 19:17)*. The only "time" we can count on having is the present. Don't wait until you are older and more mature to start serving God; start bringing forth "good fruit" in your life now ! We honor Christ by the little things we do today, not by the great feats we <u>intend</u> to do for Him tomorrow. The Lord will surely bless you as you wait on His further instructions and, in the meantime, be faithful in the tasks at home and school He gives you to do now.

About Her Father's Business

Soon thereafter we all went to bed, as it was almost one o'clock in the morning. All were still asleep the next morning, except Kyle, when I had to begin my travels again. He gifted me with a "prayer-covering" for the next leg of my journey, and said he'd write to let me know how they were all doing, once I got back home.

Therefore, as of Kyle's last report, his family is now attending a local Pentecostal Church. His teenage son is planning a summer trip to Jordan with their church youth group. And, his daughter broke off the relationship with her boyfriend and has gone back to college. Kyle didn't mention if his daughter had also submitted to Jesus, but she does not seem far from there.

* * * * * * * * * * *

For more information about the REAL doctrines of Mormonism, research the following:
Cults, Chaos and Conflicts (#7), by Guy A. Davidson
Misguided Lights (Chapter Two, Sandra Tanner), by Stephen M. Miller
Is Mormonism Christian, by Gordon H. Fraser
A Closer look – Mormon Concept of God, by Home Mission Board, SBC
Mormonism, by Jesus People USA – printed by Cornerstone
God's Word; Final, Infallible, and Forever, by Floyd McElveen

Kimberly Rae

<u>A Biologist Examines the Book of Mormon</u>, by Dr. Thomas Key
<u>Witness Effectively to Mormons</u>, by John L. Smith
<u>Child Abuse, Cults, and the Law</u>, by Michael J. Woodruff

CHAPTER EIGHT

A Form Loved

My next stop was at the home of Fred and Linda in Fort Collins, Colorado. They were Christian friends John had previously worked with in the higher elevated town of Gunnison, where he lived during part of our courtship. The couple had visited us once in North Carolina, when their first son was a baby. Now they had four sons from ages 9 years to 6 months! It was a tremendous relief to be under the roof of an already believing household again. The Lord, I thought, would now be giving me a bit of spiritual rest and recuperation here. But, this trip was a mission on which I was to mostly give, not receive.

We long visited over the photos of John's life, the accident, the funeral, and why his ashes were being buried in Colorado. Fred and Linda's sons had nearly insatiable questions and were not self-consciousness to ask just about anything! Several times their parents were aghast at their boys' tactless inquiring into rather "delicate" matters. But, God's grace was sufficient for me entirely *(II Cor. 12:9a)!* By that time, I'd gone through the photos at enough households to not be so disturbed or saddened by their viewing. I had even begun to know when most folks would raise a question or need an arm of comfort, as the pictures sometimes brought on a resurgence of their own grief.

So, when one of their sons asked, "Was Mr. Thomas really squished?" I was able to calmly tell the details of John's accident and injuries and how my husband was trying to help a stranger's car get unstuck from a snow pile. John was kneeling on the ground, to hook up his tow chain from his truck to the rear of the fella's car, when another driver came over the rise behind them. Being unable to stop his car on the icy road, it slammed into the back of John's truck. The resulting force caused its front-end to, literally, "crush" John's middle section. The collision smashed over 4" of his vertebrae, burst his aorta and collapsed his lungs; as it pinned him against the trunk of the first man's car. Just before the impact, John must have felt some instinctive inner warning or perhaps the God-sent vibration from the ground, because he popped his head up suddenly and began looking ahead and side to side. But, he had not yet turned to look behind him before the accident occurred *(Col. 1:28a)*.

Later, the hospital doctor said it was a blessing that John had lifted his head and upper torso at that exact instant. Had his body still been pointing head first, towards the undercarriage of the first car, it and his upper portions would've been utterly mangled. Then, I would have had to identify his form by recognizing some other undamaged section of his body (How merciful was God to help me to avoid *that* kind of gruesome ordeal). The doctor said that John probably felt no more than a flash of stunned surprise, before his body went into immediate, numbing shock due to his massive internal injuries. His strong heart pumped the last of his life's blood into his chest cavity for only a moment or two. Then John's eyes glazed over and closed to any sight of this earthly side of the veil. Mr.

Gerald, the man John had tried to help, said that the expression on John's face never registered even a faint glimmer of pain. He just rested his now bruised cheek on the frozen ground and "went to sleep" as John's immortal spirit left his mortal shell *(Job 14:12)*.

Another young boy asked, "Was he scary dead?" So, I gently talked them through the hospital experience and what things were like for me identifying my husband's corpse down in the morgue. Upon entering the hospital, I saw John's boss there. It was one of his other employees who had first called to alert me about the accident, thus Tom rushed to meet me in the Emergency Lobby area. When John's boss smiled at me, I had a flash of hope that he had some good news to tell me about John's condition. But, actually, the kind man had been told nothing as yet. He wasn't the "next of kin," so Tom was just relieved to see me arrive, so that we could now find out what was going on. We were led into a small room and told to wait for the head doctor. Within a few minutes, a doctor, his medical assistant, and a police officer entered our room. The doctors sat down, drew their chairs near, and leaned towards me. Tom and I were about to gently be told that John "didn't make it" *(Ps. 4:8)*.

Just then, the door opened and my school principal and supervisor (who were also co-pastors from our church) walked in. Tom had already called the Christian school, where I worked, and told them that John had been injured in a bad vehicle accident. John's boss had phoned out of concern for me driving to the hospital alone and upset, especially when I'd not arrived as promptly as he'd expected. Therefore, the Lord had arranged for those kind men and other school friends, to immediately join me at the hospital. Still having trouble absorbing the news myself, I turned to inform the new arrivals that we'd just been told that my Honey was dead. They were all stunned and gallantly fighting tears. My own heart was painfully constricting, but I felt a bottled tenseness inside and my own tears were not yet able to release. Instead, I felt the need for more information, further details, and some answers about what had happened. Therefore, to help my befuddled mind to focus, I forced back the surge of screaming emotions. Most urgently, I wanted to know if John had suffered much pain or for very long, and was reassured that he didn't. John would have felt so awful if he had been the cause of harming someone else, so I asked if others were hurt in the accident. They told me that only slight injuries had occurred to the man driving the second car. Then, the police officer explained the fatal incident step-by-step. Reality, at its cruelest, had struck.

Afterwards, perceiving that the doctor and his medical assistant were expecting some type of "female hysterics," I reassured them that I was alright. Then, they informed me that the assistant had prepared a hidden syringe, in case I became too overwhelmed by the shocking news, and needed to be tranquilized. But, since it did not appear necessary, the policeman and assistant soon left the room. Feeling sorry for these professionals, whose job often required them to deliver sad and painful news to strangers, I asked the Lord to extend an extra measure of His grace to them. Theirs is a noble, yet sometimes heartbreaking occupation.

Next, the doctor told me there was a very unpleasant task to which I must attend. He explained that the reason the hospital had not called me themselves, was because John, at the time of the accident, had no identification on his person. By law, the hospital can't inform the next of kin, until they are certain of the identity of the deceased. The police had traced John as the owner of the truck, via its license plate. But, they had no confirmation that the man lying dead on the ground was the truck's owner. He had no picture on him, nor did anyone else at the scene know who he was. I remember thinking, "Well, that makes sense." Slender John didn't like sitting on his bulky wallet, so he'd often lock it inside his briefcase. The authorities had no right to pry open the lock. So, the briefcase was still in the cab of the truck, which currently sat at the salvage yard where it had been towed. The problem now, the doctor explained, was that I had to go down to their morgue and visually identify the "John Doe" being refrigerated there. They needed to be certain that the body actually did belong to my husband, John L. Thomas.

When John's body arrived at the hospital, the doctor immediately concluded that his remains would "harvest" a bounty of organ and tissue donations. But, without permission, his medical team could not remove any of them. The longer the time span, I was told, between death and the removal of viable organs, the greater was the risk of an unsuccessful transplant operation. That is why, when I called the hospital earlier and asked him, "Should I bring fresh clothes for John?" the doctor just advised me to "not delay!" His comment had temporarily given me false hope that my husband just might be still alive. But, in fact, the doctor only wanted me to get there quickly, so as to have as little further damage to John's organs and tissue as possible. He was hoping to be informed that John did want to become a donor. This was indeed true, because as a couple, we had both discussed our desire to help others by donating our organs after death.

So, although I'd been practically expecting the "death verdict" and was depending upon God's sustaining grace to cover me in *that* situation, I was *not* expecting the forced viewing of the unprepared, slightly bloodied corpse of my Beloved. Wanting to get the unpleasant task over with before getting too nervous, I asked to be taken to him as soon as possible. Following the doctor to another area, I silently prayed for Jesus to give me courage *(Joshua 1:7a)*. Answering swiftly, He provided me with a compassionate, female Medical Assistant who was also a Christian. She escorted me down two flights of stairs, along the morgue's echoing, lifeless halls, and into the tiny room where my Honey's form lay on a table, draped by a sheet. The assistant had only just taken his body out of the cold locker before we'd come in, so John's skin (now devoid of his former red-rich blood cells) had lost its accustomed pink, ruddy color. Instead, it was mostly a bluish hue with small, yellowish splotches.

My first two thoughts were, "Yes, that is my very own John and, yes, he <u>really</u> is dead." There was, obviously, no life within that cold, still body. After

About Her Father's Business

being reassured that I'd be okay, the assistant left me alone with the remains of my "dearly Beloved" and softly closed the door. At first, I just sat in a chair nearby, sadly but endearingly gazing at my Honey with teary-eyes, but without any hopeless sobbing. Softly talking out loud, I just expressed to my Master the impact of how I was feeling inside. After about 5 minutes, I felt the urge to draw close and be near my husband's form. Being a logical person, I was not the least bit afraid of John's dead body, even its odd coloring was no longer objectionable to me *(I Cor. 15:44)*. After all, it still had the look and shape of the earthly vessel God had given to my devoted husband. That skin still covered the man my heart adored. During our years together, he had wonderfully loved and protected me from any harms or fears along life's pathways.

For several healing minutes, I actually enjoyed intently gazing and purposefully searching his features to permanently imprint and cherish them in my memory. How well I <u>still</u> remember John's boy-like smiles, twinkling, hazel-blue eyes, and deep, contagious laugh when he got really tickled about something funny. Yes, even alone in the morgue, I did not feel desolate; Christ's nearness was warm and close *(I King 8:57)*. He had not abandoned me in my time of dire need, but instead, had gently showered His sense of love and peace onto my aching, troubled heart. In a few minutes, I began to feel an obligation to get back upstairs to the caring friends waiting there, as did not want to cause them unnecessary worry. Yet, I could have easily, comfortably stayed with my husband's form longer. It had been sweet recalling fond memories, while trying to accept that, this was the beginning of our "good-byes."

When Fred and Linda's five-year-old son asked, "Did you touch him?" Yes, I admitted, on more than one occasion. The boys wanted me to explain how John's skin, hair, and body felt. So, they were told that while I was still in the morgue, I finally did feel at ease enough to touch John's lifeless body. The texture of the skin felt like cool wax and not very pliable. But, his hair didn't feel or act any differently. It was soothing to again stroke the silky, fine, reddish-blonde mane on the top of his head, then to softly run my fingers across his darker, coarser, barely silver-streaked beard as well as stroking the soft, short hairs on John's arms, hands, and chest. Folding the sheet back a little at a time, I gathered the nerve to view his damaged area. I was so very thankful to have already known that John had not felt pain or suffered after the impact. Even more, I knew that our Creator God would mend and rebuild John into far better condition in heaven! Those thoughts kept the sight of his body's wounds from being the least bit "yucky" or disturbing to me. Praise our Mighty God! Later, the Master even fortified me enough to instruct the funeral "artist" to part John's hair on the other side and change his facial tones to better match his former natural skin color. Also, to "puff up just a bit" John's uninjured cheek, to more blend with his now slightly swollen other side. I was hoping to avoid upsetting other people, who viewed John later, if they could be prevented from noticing the small damage to that part of my Honey's face.

CHAPTER NINE

Helpful Saints

Fred and Linda's family asked me to share more. So, I told them how all the people who had come to the hospital also followed me home *(Ps. 119:173)*. They began helping me to sort out what to do next. One "sister," Mary Ellen, even drove my car, so I would not be at risk while feeling so scatter-brained and stressed. I even remember teasing her (not seriously) that I could now go substitute for her at school as planned. Instinctively, I sensed that doing something totally unrelated to John's death was a form of escape, realizing that the decisions and tasks I'd have to undergo back at home would be most unpleasant. Admittedly, this wife (new widow) wanted to delay having to so openly talk about and blatantly face the reality of her husband being gone. But, Jesus supplied me with a logical mind that He had disciplined and trained, so I had to submit to the ordeal ahead.

Different people, especially John M. who was my principal, expressed their knowledge of the next several steps needing attention. There were decisions I'd have to make within the next few hours, as well as other stressful matters to resolve over the next couple of days! Things like where to hold the funeral, which day, what time, who would conduct it, which people should be called, whether John would be buried or cremated, how much his funeral would cost, and many other related topics. Beginning to feel confused and overly pressured, I was near to tears. Concerned that I'd give a wrong answer, just to be rid of that particular question, I requested to be left alone for a little while to be allowed to go upstairs to our Prayer Room and have the undisturbed time to talk privately with my God. He needed to tell me what I should do in each situation or I'd be sure to make some wrong choices I'd probably regret later. Asking for the "most urgent" things on which an answer was needed, I excused myself to go upstairs. Within about twenty minutes, Jesus had given me clarity and peace on each topic so I could then relay His direction to my friends *(Ps. 119:165)*.

John and I both had left detailed instructions for each other in case of our "absence." But, sensing that I was not yet emotionally ready to handle seeing my love's handwritten words, I'd asked one of my co-pastors to read the parts in the folder that held John's instructions and requests. Now, though, actually dealing with a spousal death, I discovered that there were still *many* other choices to make about things of which neither of us had even a clue. On several of these decisions, I had no vague opinion, much less a firm conviction, of what I wanted or what John would like to be done. How gracious and loving is our God who sends human "angels" to minister His love and wisdom during the harsh complexities forced on those in sudden bereavement *(Matt. 5:7)*.

For example, people turned up to retrieve John's truck from the salvage yard. They cleaned it and tried to pull out the dents (at the front and back ends), as much as possible, before bringing it back to our house. Philip, another brother in the Lord, plowed the snow

About Her Father's Business

out of our driveway to better fit the cars belonging to the people coming to visit and help. One gal even finished my interrupted task of washing the laundry, so I'd not have to handle John's clothes too soon. Three ladies took turns staying constantly with me, day and night, until John's parents arrived from Colorado. Mr. Daniels, our neighbor, even volunteered to meet John's parents at the airport for me, then delivered them back again a few days later. The day my in-laws had arrived, Linda-Sue, a dear Tennessee friend and her devoted husband, drove through those long, treacherous miles of snow to be at my side. When she and I were able to be alone, my intercessory "sister" prayed long and tenderly for me as she held my hands. Having no one from my own blood-family there to uphold me, the Lord provided her and a few other close friends nearby, to "fill-in" as my family!

Debbie, the gal from church who had mostly stayed with me, became the wisely appointed "overseer" of tasks to be done and appointments to be kept. She answered my frequently ringing phone, kindly talking to worried callers and becoming a wise "buffer" to help preserve my depleting emotional and mental energy. Debbie even did the most unpleasant and sad job of calling our friends nearby or out-of-state to inform them of John's accident. She went with me to the funeral home to assist in "making the arrangements" and to be sure that the Funeral Director didn't pressure me into spending more funds than I could reasonably afford (Or, more than my frugal John would have wanted me to spend). Debbie was with me as I had the unprepared shock of following the Director through a door to view the two casket choices I'd requested to see, only to be hit smack in the fragile emotions by a huge roomful of open caskets! Starting by the entrance with the most elaborate and expensive ones, then walking down row after row of styles and models towards the back, until we reached the ones displayed that I could afford. Even in my dazed state, I discerned how other new widows could be psychologically "tricked" into buying a far more expensive casket. They, too, would be paraded through this degrading experience of seeing what their finances could allow, in comparison to the many finer, costlier samples. Dear Jesus, please protect those grieving widows! Also, send them a solid friend or family member to help walk them through that experience, like You thankfully, mercifully had provide for me! As confusing and stressful were those awful days, my spirit continued to sense that Jesus never left my side. Often, I'd feel His closeness and direction from loving, caring members of "the family of God" that He sent to emotionally "cuddle" me.

Fred and Linda's boys were amused at me being so perplexed at first, about how friends and neighbors kept showing up at our home. Often, they arrived with food and without calling ahead, but would just come on over for a visit. Finally, I asked Debbie why people were seemingly "coming out of thin air" and stopping by the house so unexpectedly. John had even invited several of them over for fellowship in the past, but most seemed unable to fit our companionship into their busy schedules. Yet, then when he was not even here to enjoy their visit, folks kept "coming out of the

About Her Father's Business

woodwork." It was as if they were attending a sort of food party, although I was certainly in no condition to entertain them. To me, it actually seemed insensitive of them and invasive to my privacy. It robbed me of feeling that my home was still a peaceful, safe place of needed solitude. Admittedly, though, each one arrived with friendly sympathy and an obvious willingness to be of any help. Debbie informed me that such "visits to the bereaved" were an accepted, accustomed, and even expected way of people displaying their supportive caring. This was how folks showed their concerned desire to be of some help to someone who had just suffered a death in the family *(Rom. 12:15)*. Dumbfounded and embarrassed at my gross ignorance on the matter, now I knew *why* people just kept showing up. They were trying to communicate that they cared and were hurting <u>with</u> me! And, from then on, I welcomed their unplanned visits!

Having been reared in a rather cold family environment, one that moved around as much as two or three times a year, I'd never experienced this kind of sympathetic undergirding. We had rare interaction with even other family members and never stayed in one location for enough months to really establish close friendships. I had no idea that it was the "proper conduct" to go visit a bereaved family. Nor, that folks would usually bring over some helpful food item to lessen the burden of cooking for guests of undetermined numbers. It was a humbling revelation and difficult to absorb that so many people actually cared that I was in emotional pain. Except for John, and a sampling of such caring after my tumor surgery four years earlier, these kinds of endearments had seldom come my way. And, what a relief it was to no longer be the only person unaware of the "expected behavior" going on around her!

Next, the boys were sorry to hear how hopeless and sad John's parents felt when they first saw their son's body. Fred and Linda remarked that it was kind of me to have requested that John's casket be closed at the funeral before his parents and I entered. We were instructed to sit in the front pews of a roomful of people, most of which Jake and Paula had never met. So, I was trying to reduce the distress John's non-Christian parents as much as possible. Yet, after the funeral helpers had folded and given me the United States flag, which had been draped over John's casket, and the service was almost finished, the attendants re-opened the top part again.

That way, his parents and I, then any others who wanted to, could file past John's body one last time to mentally "let him go."

I was led up to him first, but felt that the attendant was whisking me past my Beloved too fast! So, taking my hand off the man's arm, I stepped back one pace to draw near to John instead. Through loving eyes, I gazed at his handsome, rugged face once more. Ignoring how shocked some people in the audience might be, I reached out to touch John as naturally as I'd done so many times before. I felt so proud and impressed, because he looked rather sharp indeed, clothed in his fancy shirt, tie and tweed jacket. Thus, quite comfortably, I placed my hand on his chest and stroked it a time or two, then moved my fingers up to his jaw to caress his trim, manly beard and cheek before having to leave the room…without him *(Prov. 10:7a)*.

It was a relief that this last sight of him no longer tore at my heart so. Unlike the very first time I'd seen him at the Funeral Home and received the cruel shock of seeing his complexion in artificially made up tones of life and vitality, and for a fleeting moment thought, "Oh! It's all been a horrible mistake! My John is not dead; he's only sleeping!" Then awhile later, breaking down briefly into deep sobs, as I asked Debbie, "Who will put their arms around me and hold me now? I don't want to cuddle into anyone else's embrace." Only John had ever cared enough to patiently learn how to surround me with his "arms of protection." Thus, causing me to feel feminine and dainty. He'd gently comfort away all those residual childhood fears and nightmares and vanquished my adult worries and prior years of loneliness. For a lovely season, the Lord had given me John, and <u>that</u> blessing would endure through all the seasons of my life!

CHAPTER TEN

Be Not Afraid

The most complex question to answer came from Fred and Linda's oldest son who asked, "What happened to your husband's body after you let them burn it?" Behind each of the boys' questions, I sensed that lad's hidden fears and potential nightmares about the topics asked. So, intertwined with answers, I tried to filter in the comfort and reassurances of Jesus. Trusting in our holy and wise God, I explained, made accepting every part of John's death, "Ok, not fun, but okay." Then the nine-year-old was told that being cremated didn't hurt, even in that intense heat, because a lifeless body *feels* nothing. And, John's "new" body will be put all back together again, in even better shape by God's creative power. After the funeral, John's parents and I searched the local stores for appropriate urns. So that, once the cremation was finished, the Funeral Home could divide and share the remains of John's ashes between us. That way, each of us could have a small portion of him to keep near.

Then, about three months later, I went alone to a favorite spot of John's on a lovely mountain overlook. And, in just the company of our Creator and the morning's dawn, I scattered my portion of John's ashes over the landscape he'd learned to love so much in his last years. The scene reminded me of a conversation we shared the night before he died. Even after several years away, John still so missed the majestic views of his beloved Rocky Mountains. He was eagerly looking forward to summer and our vacation plans see them again, while we visited his family and friends in Colorado. Yet, John was also extremely content living here. So, I'd teased him that it must be his spirit "longing" for its "heavenly mansion," which surely had a wonderful view of God's holy mountain, that was actually pulling at his heartstrings *(John 14:2)*. Bemused, John agreed it just might be so! One day later, that jest became sadly prophetic.

The scattering of John's ashes was done so that his parents could legally bury their part of them in a beautiful military cemetery, near their home in Colorado. But, only if no other part of his remains were kept or buried any other place, could John be interned at that cemetery. Now, I knew where my Honey's spirit *really* was, and that I'd see him some day in Glory *(I Thes. 4:14)*. But, John's non-Christian parents didn't have that assurance. So, I realized that they needed the additional comfort obtained by having a tangible place to "visit John." *(I Thes. 4:13)* Thus, as it seemed the kinder thing to do, I agreed to just "let go" of my portion of his ashes.

Next, Fred and Linda's seven-year-old asked, "Do you ever get scared?" So, it was time to explain that such didn't happen very often anymore, but when younger, I *used* to have <u>lots</u> of bad nightmares. Even after John and I were first married, I'd have three or four of them a month. But, as my trust in him *and in Jesus* grew, so did my inner security and feelings of safety. To help bring me out of a bad dream, John

About Her Father's Business

would speak softly to me until I again realized where I truly was. Then, he'd enfold me with his long, warm arms until my whimpering and trembling stopped and I could drift back into a peaceful slumber *(Ps. 4:8)*. After a year or so, I only had a nightmare once a month or less! And, even it was usually brought on by some unusual physical discomfort or an emotional distress I was feeling before going to sleep. The Lord continued to use John to heal my "inner man." Except for the increase of the bad dreams around the time of my last major surgery and recovery, those subconscious, terrifying childhood re-enactments only surfaced a couple times a year anymore.

Admittedly, while John's parents were still with me after his funeral, I had a nightmare. Yet, as I called out in panic, John's father "just happened" to be walking by the bedroom door. As he emerged from a late night bathroom trip, God had Jake right there to overhear my cries. John's father spoke calmly to me from the doorway. His own voice being very similar in sound to his son's, brought me out of the imagined terror. Although I was in no physical pain and could even "hold it together" during the day (trying to not further burden John's parents), that nightmare caused me to realize that, in my emotions, I was hurting deeply. So, after softly crying awhile, I prayed to Jesus to be the "guard of my dreams" *(Num. 12:6b)* and my Comforter *(John 14:26a)*, to override all my new insecurities from having to now face life again without John's protection. Jesus honored that trusting request. I am not afraid to be alone at night and *rarely* experience anymore bad dreams. Praise His name!

Fred and Linda's young boys were then reminded about the three faithful men who went into the "fiery furnace" yet came out unhurt, because Jesus had walked in there with them. Well, since John's injured body was already dead, it would not ever "walk out" to life on earth again *(Col. 1:28a)*. He will never come back to our mortal side of existence. But, those he loves "in Christ" will join him one day heaven! And, as it says in Hebrews 2:14, we should all look forward to that wonderful day of reunion. When our hearts live near to the cross of Calvary, we begin to feel pleased for saints who have already died. They who, like John, were "homesick for heaven" welcomed that final, cold embrace with intense delight. Death is not banishment; no, it's a return from the exile of living on earth among aliens. The distance between already glorified persons in heaven and militant saints here on earth seems great, but it really, truly isn't. None of us are far from home; a God-chosen moment will bring us there instantly! When our eyes close in death on earth, they next open to eternal life in heaven! Death is only a Jacob's ladder whose bottom rung is in the grave; yes, but whose top reaches straight into the everlasting joy of Glory. So, it's good to look forward to being with our Bridegroom. Any delay just allows us more time to bring as many fellow "guests," as God grants us the opportunity to invite, to the wedding banquet. Eagerly waiting for our turn to go to heaven is sort of how a young child feels waiting for Christmas morning to arrive! We like living here on earth, in between, but oh, we certainly look forward to Christmas!

About Her Father's Business

After this, their five-year-old son turned to his parents and asked if he could make sure that he'd see Mr. Thomas and Jesus someday, too. His Daddy explained about giving one's heart to the Lord and then helped usher the third of his young sons into God's kingdom! Oh, it was a very precious sight.

CHAPTER ELEVEN

Prayerfully Arrived

Early the next morning, I traveled south to the Denver area. First, I drove to their military cemetery to see the John's burial site. Using a photo his parents had sent, I was able to find the spot. Surprised that his marble headstone wasn't erected yet, I still placed a pretty flower arrangement under his name. I wanted to be alone the first time I saw where John's ashes were buried, without having to share the moment with his unbelieving parents. The acres of perfectly lined headstones astounded… and saddened me. So many thousands of men gone, meant so many more broken hearts. Feeling a bit cast down, I did not stay long.

After a short drive, I was able to find and visit Dinea. John and I had been privileged to get acquainted with this sister-in-Christ a few years ago. Having been out of the USA for over two years, Dinea was now on furlough from her own "missionary" work in China. We gals had a grand time of fellowshipping in the Lord together. She treated me to lunch and afterwards we each prayed long and hard for the other. No one who takes and uses prayer seriously will ever have to moan about their leanness of soul. Lack of time with Jesus in prayer, is the cause of our inner spirits being underfed, dry, and parched. We two gals knew that "wrestling in prayer" *(Eph. 6:12)* made us stronger, kept us living near the mercy seat of God, and increased our assurance in Jesus' love. When Christians only spend a little time conversing with their Master, it causes their faith to become shallow, overrun by many doubts and fears, and lacking the joy of the Lord. Prayer, private devotions, and close fellowship with Jesus are attainable by any Believer! Nothing earth can offer compares to the holy calming of a troubled heart that, through fervent prayer, "leans on the bosom of Jesus" *(John 13:23)*. Another pleasant tool to strengthen our spirits, as we abide in Christ, is giving Him praise! Psalm 66:2 indicates that praising God is <u>not</u> an option for His children. Praise is the Almighty's rightful due and every Christian's a responsibility. We are to cultivate a grateful heart and praise the Lord *all* of our days, no matter what each day (whether good or ill) brings our way. If we do not praise God, we are not bringing forth some of the "good fruit" our good Husbandman has a right to expect from us. So, we need to make our praises and our songs of praise become acceptable gifts to our King! Dinae and I shared a wonderful time of just basking in His Presence together.

* * * * * * * * *

Around 4 p.m., I drove to the suburban home of John's parents, Jake and Paula. They were glad to see I'd arrived safely, but were noticeably less warm than when they had stayed with me during John's funeral. Perhaps Jake's sister, Aunt Mary had called to justify the unpleasantness I'd experienced at her home? No, the coolness was caused from John's folks not being at all happy over the conversions of Paula's Illinois

About Her Father's Business

relatives. Aunt Joyce, I was told, had been making a "pest" of herself by calling and pressuring them to believe in Jesus. John's parents were "on guard" at first, lest I try "preaching" to them. Their stiffness dissolved, though, when reassured that I would not "cram my religion down their throats!" Dear Lord, spare the unsaved loved ones of tactless, brand new believers who, in their zeal and enthusiasm, are prone to apply pressure beyond Your wisdom and simple good manners. Sometimes, such behavior can do much accidental harm to the Kingdom in "turning people off" to the gospel. But, God bless their boldness and gumption anyway! At least, they bravely encroach upon the enemy's territory!

John's parents let me settle into his former, boyhood bedroom; then we departed for the airport to meet their second eldest son, Jim. This sibling had been a Christian for about two years, but only after John's funeral, had Jim mustered the courage to tell his family of his own conversion. Jim had, fearfully, been remembering how each of them, for years, had meanly teased John for being a Christian. Jim hadn't wanted their taunts or rejection directed now towards him. But, after learning how John's faith-filled life had affected people in North Carolina, Jim boldly wrote his parents. Now they knew that John wasn't their only son who believed in Jesus! Yet, this was the first time, since he had proclaimed his stand in Christ that "Timid Jim" was seeing his parents and siblings face-to face. Thus, for extra moral support, Jim had asked me to already be at his folks' place by the time he arrived. Jim wanted to get past the hurdle of meeting his folks, "as a Christian," prior to having to also face his siblings, Cindy and Dan. So, he'd planned his flight from Texas to arrive the day before them *(Matt. 5:9)*.

Yet, in answer to prayer from the both of us, Jim only experienced one brief negative comment the whole time he was there. God showed His faithfulness again! Also, we suspected that while I was there, John's family knew *not* to downgrade our God! Maybe it was just out of plain, human decency (due to the Memorial Service), but they gave his widow a bit of leniency in expressing her "particular" beliefs discreetly. It was a huge relief and blessing that God managed to work things out peacefully; we were very grateful *(Matt. 19:26b)*.

For the most part, John's siblings came for the Memorial Service at the request and on the funds of their parents. None really wanted to go through this morbid ordeal, but didn't know how to get out of it without hurting their folks. It had been impossible for them to really "connect" with the loss of their oldest brother last January. None of them had come to John's funeral or seen any of the pictures of it yet. But, their attitudes and perceptions were about to change.

Late the next morning, after we'd gotten back from the airport picking up Dan and Cindy, I was finally able to get the family together to view the photo albums. The first was of John's childhood, young adult milestones, and our first three years of marriage together in Colorado. The second was a collection of good pictures to unfold John's North Carolina years, the accident, his work-related "awards," the news articles, Resolutions decrees, and the funeral photos.

About Her Father's Business

That session took about three hours, with each member reminiscing over their prior shared lives together. His siblings were awestruck over how John had turned out and blossomed while away from them. For the first time, John's death became a true reality to his siblings and caused feelings of grief and remorse to surface. Expressing regret about their prior reluctance to even come to Denver, now for John's sake, they wanted to be really supportive.

At first, none of his siblings wanted to see the burial site. Because of John's headstone not yet being in place, his siblings had been relieved that viewing it wasn't part of the Memorial Service. Yet now, before it got too dark, they each wanted to take a drive over to the cemetery to sort of be <u>near</u> their eldest brother! As they hurried to get ready, I called the cemetery's office. John's parents kept getting vague answers to their questions, but as his widow, they hoped a call from me would carry more weight. Although, possibly still in its crate, we wanted to check if John's headstone might actually be there. If so, could it be arranged for his family to see it that night or after the service? But, I was told to call back tomorrow, when their computer would be back in operation, as the office was now closing. We briefly visited John's gravesite anyway.

During supper, Jake and Paula revealed that they had already granted me their permission to use a couple of minutes to add something about John during his ceremony. Now, each of his siblings also requested time to say a few words about their brother, too. His parents were very touched and, right after the meal, each offspring wrote down what they wanted to express.

John's siblings didn't come with clothes "fittin" for a loved one's Memorial Service, and only after seeing the photos of his funeral, did they realize how ill-prepared they were. So, his siblings now called several of their parents' neighbors, successfully borrowing long pants for Dan and Jim, plus a dress for Cindy. It had now become important to them to show more respect, in the attire they wore, to John's service the next afternoon *(Num. 23:10b)*.

Late that night, his parents and siblings decided to stay up visiting over shared memories and trying to get reacquainted as a family unit again…minus one. They needed that time of bonding. So, in order to allow them more privacy, I went up to John's childhood bedroom to update my journal and write letters. None of us slept much that night.

CHAPTER TWELVE

Memorial Service

In the morning, the guys washed cars as the gals prepared the luncheon for guests who were coming back to Jake and Paula's after the ceremony. It was a cloudy day but we decided to leave early to allow John's siblings to put flowers at his gravesite. Their Aunt Kathy, a close family friend, came to help out that morning. When cars were being loaded up to leave, John's siblings got into their folk's car and it began backing out of the driveway. None offered to include or make room for me. I was pleased that John's kinfolk were feeling like a "family" again, but it did hurt a bit to be so completely left out of their fellowship. It reminded me how John once told me that his parents' "pet-name" for his three younger siblings was "The Three Musketeers." They were all so lively, sharp, and full of mischief. John said their threesome often made him feel like an outcast and gave him the clear message that they were "a team" which he wasn't considered bright enough to join. It seemed to me that his parents forgot that they had birthed four, not just three children. But, now I had a taste of how "left out" my Beloved felt within his own clan. It's easy to understand how Jesus' love won John's heart in his late teens. Belonging to the "family of God" helped defuse his loneliness by the warmth and acceptance of the other saints *(Eph 3:14-15)*. Now, myself being the "odd man out," I asked to hitch a ride with Aunt Kathy.

We shared richly sweet memories about John on the way.

Earlier, I had called the cemetery and was told that, although John's marble headstone had left the mason's, it had not yet shown up as an arrival on the office computer. They figured it was somewhere still in transit. But, a surprise was soon awaiting all of us and I just know it was a special gift from God!

You see, the Director who had to tell me that John's marker hadn't arrived yet, felt awful about the delay. Soon thereafter, he was in the staff coffee area lamenting to his co-workers, explaining how he had to "tell the young Thomas widow" that we didn't have her husband's headstone. It wasn't here for her to even look at, before she had to drive all the way back to North Carolina. Well, the maintenance and grounds supervisor was also nearby getting coffee. He overheard that one sentence and it began "ringing bells" in his head! The prior Friday, a shipment of finished headstones had arrived. But, he thought the one for "Thomas" had an incorrect date chiseled on it and had sent a message back to the company for confirmation. Therefore, he'd not let his men put the headstone in place, waiting to hear back from the mason. So, without telling anyone until later, that supervisor went back to his shipping department and was pleased to find a note of verification that the dates were not a mistake. Thus, he sent the paperwork to the front office and quickly sent his crew to dig the hole and put John's headstone in place.

So, when we all arrived about an hour later, there to our delight and amazement was John's upright,

About Her Father's Business

officially engraved, white-marbled headstone! It stood tall and straight, just like a proud soldier "at attention," decked out in a brand new uniform! We were all so very pleased and took some nice group photos, then piled back into the same cars to drive where the Memorial Service was to be conducted.

Yet again, when John's family were mingling with friends at the procession site, and it became time to get into the cemetery limousine and other cars following, I had to "bum" a ride from strangers who had room in car number three. The widow of the deceased was supposed to be in the lead car with his parents. But, John's family just didn't think to include me. To their embarrassment later, even the cemetery "Greeters" thought that John's sister was his widow, as she'd been riding in the limousine. Oh well, non-believers are sometimes a strange breed.

For use at the service, I'd brought a framed, enlarged photo of John smiling. Knowing that many of his parents' friends and neighbors hadn't seen him in ten to seventeen years, I thought they would appreciate a current picture of John on which to focus. In Jim's opinion and mine, Jake and Paula's misinformed choice of using a female Christian Science "pastor" was a real dud *and* an insult to John's memory. But, she didn't get to talk nearly as long as planned, in order for John's siblings and me to have our few minutes each to speak *(II Pet. 2:1)*.

After Jake and Paula thanked everyone who had come, I rose to speak first. "You're going to hear some nice things about my husband from his siblings and me. Believe them; they are all true…and much more.

It has been a privilege being the wife who was loved by John Thomas. If God had given me a choice between these two following lifestyles, I know which one I'd choose. In one, He'd let me be born in a good, caring family and have close, dear friends all of my growing up years, marry early to a decent, if not overly exciting man, and have a mediocre, but long compatible 50 years together. It would even be filled with healthy children and grandchildren to love and nurture, who would remain supportively near me, even after that husband died. Or, I could choose to be born into an abusive household, move around so frequently that I'd never know close, lasting friendships, be forced to earn my own living by age sixteen and rarely go on dates because of painful experiences of betrayals at seventeen and twenty-eight. Until, God finally allowed me to be joined in a Christ-honoring marriage. Yet, by then, I'd be almost 31-years-old and it would already be too late for my body to birth any live children for us. But, I'd be given a good, noble, and godly man, who would cherish me and be ever thrilling to me, in whose arms and under whose tender care my faith would continually grow, causing all of my prior hurts and disappointments to be utterly erased. Yet, we could only share our affectionate devotion for fifteen years, before it would be required of me to be alone again. Well, folks, now that I've had the beautiful experience of receiving John's love, I'd not hesitate an instant before begging the Lord to 'give me the good one!' He would be MORE than worth all of the trials before and all of the lonely years after."

Next Jim, with obviously shaking hands, limbs, and voice told how John was an example of integrity and had a faith worthy to follow. And, these past two years, *he* has done so! Jim read the 2 Thessalonians 2: 13-14 passage with a chocked voice and paused often to regain his composure. Yet, clear was his message that John was a "brethren beloved of the Lord." Later, Jim played a medley of praise songs on his guitar as people shook hands then departed the service. John would have been proud of this younger sibling and "brother-in-Christ."

Next, Dan read several instances where he now realized that his oldest brother, John, had "paved the way" most of their growing years. John often had to be the first one to accomplish things. Because John was the oldest child, he had to face life's milestones before the rest of them. Dan said he had "cruised through" his own childhood, teen and early adult years pretty much unafraid. He figured if John, his slow-thinking older brother, could start school, ride a bike, learn to ski, attend high school, go on a date, get a job, travel with the army, and even get married, well, then Dan could surely manage those things as well...or even better! John had given this younger brother an ingrained courage, because nothing appeared too difficult to tackle. No hurdle was too high to reach, if John had managed to scale it first. Dan said he now felt sorry that John had to "do all that new scary stuff alone;" including how, even with his death, John continued to "blaze the trail" ahead. Yet, Dan guessed, this was one task John wasn't a bit afraid to do. He said, with John no longer here, *he* had begun to feel the weight of being "the big brother" now. Dan hoped he'd be even half as good at assisting his younger siblings over life's rough spots, as John had been for him.

By now all of John's family was crying and Cindy could only hug her two remaining brothers. Admitting through her tears, that she just wasn't able to say anything to the crowd, except how proud she felt of all three of her older brothers! The service was soon over, and folks began departing for the reception luncheon. Again, Aunt Kathy had to give me a lift and I began to suspect that God was forcing us to be alone…for His own purposes.

CHAPTER THIRTEEN

You Are Valued

At the reception, before we began eating, a guest asked if a prayer should be said. Jim suggested to his parents that "maybe Kimberly would do it." Willing to bless the food, I was eager to also have the opportunity to use a couple of sentences to remind people that John was alive and would be highly welcomed in heaven *(Luke 18:1b)*. While his family was visiting with all the other people, I sat in the corner with Aunt Kathy, the only other person I knew. Since the service, she had been exceptionally quiet and sad looking. So, I asked Aunt Kathy what was troubling her and if she felt like talking.

Instantly her floodgate of questions poured out! Did I feel incomplete now that I was only "single" again? What was her personal value? After all, once her elderly mother dies, Aunt Kathy wouldn't have anyone who needs her. Having never married, she had no children to remember her legacy and wondered if she would be worth anything to anyone. So, I began, "Well, dear, without John, I no longer have anyone who really needs me and have never held a child of my own in my arms. Do you now think of me as someone with no value or worth?"

"No, of course not!" she exclaimed.

"Thus", I replied, "neither are you some worthless cast off."

In God's eyes, I explained, we both have enormous value! We are very loved and dear, fully complete and whole persons in His sight (Colossians 2:10a). Before ever marrying John, I had come to the truthful, healthy conclusion that I was of special esteem to the Lord. It did not matter if I was married, single, young, old, ever a mother or not! He feels the same way about you, too. Just let yourself believe in His wholehearted approval and receive His affectionate embrace. You will FEEL valuably loved, if you choose to become part of those who are each part of the lovely "Bride of Jesus" and in whom He is well pleased *(Rev. 21:9b)*!

Aunt Kathy was very near to stepping onto the Kingdom's soil, but asked one more question: "If I believed in John's God, would that mean I'd get to see him again" (*I Cor. 6:17)?* She elaborated that she'd always had a tender and extra affectionate spot in her heart for that boy. They were often on the same "wave-length" and Aunt Kathy loved John like the child she never had. She'd perceived that John had a more sensitive nature than his siblings. Observing how unfairly his family sometimes treated him, she'd tried to encourage them go easier on John. Finishing, she added, "Today, while you spoke, I realized at least one other person honestly loved John, perhaps even more than I have all these years. So, I'd like to know, as I get older and closer to death, that I'll end up being with you and John. Then, I could be happy and look forward to my last years here. I could stop grieving so much over John's death, if you could just tell me for sure, that I'd get to see him again."

About Her Father's Business

Therefore, I quietly shared with John's "aunt" the gist of Isaiah 65:17, 19, reassuring her that in Glory, we feel no separation and there is no more cause for grief. There are no broken relationships or friendships, no sin, no hardships, or ever any reason for sad tears or to feel alone or afraid. We will all feel cherished and blessed because our loving Father resides there with all of His redeemed children. It is never too late, I told her, to become a daughter of the Most High God and know the confidence of eternal life enjoyed with those we love, even if they have gone "home" before us. So, while the shallower, worldly "chit-chat" of people nearby drifted around us, Aunt Kathy prayed and became a "born-again" child of God *(John 3:13)*. Now, she and John are truly related in Christ Jesus! When I got back to North Carolina, Aunt Kathy had written to say how much better life looked to her now! Also, that she had explained about accepting Jesus' gift of eternal life to her ailing mother, too. They had prayed together and, at over ninety-years-old, Aunt Kathy's own Mom had become "a new babe in Christ"!

* * * * * * * * * *

Deciding to leave early the next morning, I wanted to give John's family one full day alone together before his siblings had to fly to their separate homes. Also, my aim was to be in Durango by that evening, to keep the reservation I'd made on John's and my honeymoon suite. But, on my way through Colorado Springs, south of Denver, I paused for awhile to drive around the complex of "Focus on the Family." Also, it had been planned that I stop, about noon, at the home of a Chuck and Joan; an older, precious Christian couple. John and I had known them from our former church up north, close to where we'd lived the first three years of our marriage. Chuck was now pastoring a small Methodist Church, near the foothills of the mountain pass I'd have to cross to reach Durango later. So, it was really neat making this route connection.

After touring their sweet, historical church building with Chuck, I then showed them both John's photos and such. We talked deeply of the need of always staying close to Jesus. They showed pictures of their grown kids and new, young grandchildren. We rejoiced in how the Lord had brought Chuck through cancer and was bringing me through the loss of John. Joan fed us a tasty lunch, and afterwards, they lovingly prayed over me before I left. They commented how blessed they were to see that, after all these years, John and I still stood firm in our faith. Jesus was being reflected through even this time of trial, due to my desire to forgive others and to live in His peace. I felt humbled, yet highly honored by their words *(Acts 4:13)*. We should always strive to be Christ-like and have people sense that we have "been with Jesus" and are His. But, wanting it to be so, and sometimes finding out that it was actually being accomplished, was a real treat! We parted with the greeting, "See you in Glory, if not before!"

(*Note: A few years later, the cancer returned, taking Chuck "home.")

CHAPTER FOURTEEN

Reminiscing and Praises

Traveling over the mountain range and through such lovely country, it was easy to find things to praise God about. Even the shaggy buffalo and curved-horned sheep were a delight to behold, as I'd forgotten about those things being part of Colorado's charm. Nearing the higher elevation of the Pagosa Pass, more ice-crystals were in the heavy rain drops. The drive was very safe, but it brought to my remembrance other occasions, years ago, that death almost claimed me on the lonely, icy roads of Colorado.

The first time, it was late evening and I was on a long stretch of deserted, unlit two-lane between the towns of Rifle and Silt. Driving next to the mountain, I came upon a slightly curved incline. My car hit a patch of sheer ice, and without making the turn, headed straight towards the cliff on the opposite side of the road. In those long seconds of speeding towards the black void, this new babe in Christ screamed out "Jesus, help me!" *(Isa. 58:9a)* Within a heartbeat, my car slammed to a stop, like I'd hit a solid wall at the very edge of the drop-off. Only by looking behind me, could I see any ground anywhere! It took all of my courage to shift the car to reverse; praying out loud and hoping the movement didn't plunge my teetering car over the brink. Inch by scary inch, the Lord helped guide my skating retreat, until I was hugging the mountainside of the road again. After sitting and shaking with relief for awhile, I noticed my chest hurt and my palms were bleeding. That's when I realized that the impact of my stop was so forceful, that my upper body had been thrust bruisingly into the steering wheel and several of my nails had broken off, imbedding into the meat of my hands.

Curiosity soon outweighed fright, though. So, climbing out of the car, I progressed carefully, step by tiny step, over to the spot where my car had stopped. There was no visible gravel at the edge, which my tires could have grasped hold of to prevent a certain plunge over the edge. Instead, obvious tracks from my tires were shown extending right to the very brink, less than a breath away from that hollow darkness below. The "invisible" wall that stopped my car, I knew, was really the mighty hand of God! Perhaps, He'd even used a pair of strong angels, impassively hovering shoulder to shoulder at the top of that gorge, to defeat another of Satan's attempts on my life!

The next scary incident happened the following Christmas season. Although I'm <u>not</u> the "shop 'til you drop" kind, most of the local, mountain gals were. They enjoyed doing their holiday shopping in the much larger city of Denver, as it offered a huge variety of stores. My Christian friend from work, Sue F., wanted to indulge in a full Saturday traversing the shops there and I offered to drive. So, with her young daughter along, we gals set out early on the 3-hour one-way journey to the "metro!"

After a fun day of good bargin hunting and an early supper, we headed back towards home. Weary, each of us were relieved to be getting away from all of the

About Her Father's Business

big, noisy crowds. Sue's youngster quickly fell asleep across my back seat and we ladies were soon fighting drowsiness. Without other cars on the roads nor any street lights, it became VERY dark traveling along the different mountain ridges. About halfway home, we had to climb, then descend, steep Vail Pass.

It had been snowing lightly since departing Denver, thus a big snowplow was scraping the road a short distance up ahead. Its yellow flashing and rotating light reflected over a huge area of the gleaming ice and snow clinging to the pavement and on the sides of the mountain. Soon, I'd become entirely mesmerized; as if asleep, yet sitting up and with my eyes still open. The white, fluffy snowflakes swirling out of the pitch dark and brushing against my windshield, as well as the pulsating, yellow light ahead, had become eerily hypnotic!

The road's incline had been straight, but it started tilting sharply downward as we neared a long, steep curve. Sue, half-dozing, suddenly felt apprehensive about how fast the car was going. Warning me aloud, she touched my arm. Startled, but brought back into alertness, I knew we were in big trouble! By then, the car was streaking downhill at more them TWICE the safe speed for such wintery conditions. We both knew the danger of skidding off the road if the brakes were stomped on too hard, too fast. With murmuring pleas to God, I fought the fear and strong impulse to do so anyway and, instead, managed to repeatedly pump the brakes slowly.

As we fought the decline's pull, it seemed MUCH too long before being able to discern that my car was slowing down again. We entered the threatening curve faster than hoped, yet our tires still clung to the road enough to propel us safely through the other half of the arc. Had Sue ***not*** have brought me back into awareness when she did, there is little doubt that all three of us would've plunged over the ice-glazed, cliff edge of that curve! With our adrenaline now surging, we gals were thankful for our safe deliverance and praised the Lord for His "divine intervention." Needless to say, we had no trouble staying fully awake and talking the rest of our drive back home.

After that experience, I wisely never ventured out on long, nighttime, drives over mountain passes "just for fun." On the rare occasions that required driving some distances on wintery roads, I did so without undue fear, yet with respectful trepidation. No longer did I foolishly think that accidents could "only happen to other people." Now, I knew that the mesmerizing affects of snowy conditions really could (whether by Satan's design or just human fatigue) claim <u>anyone's</u> life.

The final occasion, five years later, happened on my way to see John, when he worked in Gunnison. Almost there, after driving nearly ten hours from Arizona, it was another dark, snow-packed evening. Coming down an average decline of gently curved road, I had no clue that it was totally ice-glazed. To avert a large rock, which had rolled from the mountain side of the road onto my cliff-edge side, I swerved impulsively. Momentarily, I'd forgotten the 'Cardinal Rule' to, "Never, ever make a sudden move" while driving in icy conditions! Immediately, my car was skidding sideways the short few feet to the cliff's edge. Thinking that, "This is it!" and peacefully accepting the inevitable, I only said, "Thank You, Lord that I belong to You." But, even as I felt my car begin to dip over the edge, an enormous updraft and gust of wind hurled me back onto the road. It kept pushing my car across both lanes, until it buried me in a soft "puff" of plowed snow against the side of the mountain! A man driving up the road saw what happened, stopped his car and scooped away enough of the snow on my windshield to see if I was still alive. Yet, both my car and I were utterly unharmed! The only indication that anything out of the ordinary had occurred was that the impact had popped off my oil cap (The next day, John found it wedged in another part of the engine). The man helped shovel me out of the snow bank and watched in amazement, as I just "tootled on down the road." He told me the gorge was so deep and treacherous at that curve, that no one could have rescued my dead, frozen body until the spring thaw. Cringing, I thought of how frantic John would have been, had I never shown up. For months, no one would have known what had happened and why I'd disappeared. When John did find out, he would have felt so guilty, remembering that I'd been on my way to see him. Praise God for His bountiful mercies *(Ps. 89:1)*. Except by divine intervention, most likely utilizing His angels, I truly believe that this gal would long since have been just another road statistic. How sad that we often take for granted our safety and good health. Oh Lord, help me to not be a complainer in the midst of so much undeserved grace and forbearance.

CHAPTER FIFTEEN

Down Memory Lane

Finally entering Durango near dusk, I was not exactly sure if memory could locate the fancy Strater Hotel. But, having to stop for their narrow-gauge train to pass, I took a picture of it. Low and behold, captured in my viewfinder was the roof-sign of the very hotel needed. God's Spirit did neat things like that, guiding me to places and people all along my travels *(Ps. 46:14).*

Checking into the beautiful 18th century, refurbished hotel, I went upstairs to where John and I had spent our wedding night. It was one of their "deluxe rooms" on the second floor. The Lord made it possible for that same suite to be available by the time arrived (I didn't want to sleep in any other room; just "ours!").

For each of our first three anniversaries, we'd made it our own tradition to drive to Durango and eat at a favorite oriental restaurant Saturday night. The next morning, we'd enjoy the Strater's marvelous Sunday Brunch before driving back home near Cortez. This time, wanting to sort of "relive" our precious memories, I bought take-out food from the same Chinese place. Alas, I just wasn't brave enough to actually eat there at "our" table alone. Back at the hotel, I wrote on a page in the room's Guest Book, explaining our visit first and why I was here without John now. John and I had written in that book on our wedding night, too. The suite was more lovely and elegant than I'd recalled.

It was good to take pictures of it this time. Even the old-fashioned, claw-foot bathtub had a sweet memory to go with it.

You see, I was awfully nervous on our wedding day. I had literally worried myself silly over the upcoming wedding reception, if my mother would behave, and, oh dear, the wedding night! Bathing before slipping into my gown, I could not keep my hands from shaking as I tried to shave my legs. After two or three "nicks," I just gave up! I consoled myself that John was a "gentleman," and he wasn't going to turn into a "beast" the minute we closed the hotel's bedroom door. Surely, if I explained my dilemma to him on the drive over, John would be patient enough to let me take a hot relaxing bath there. Then, being calm enough, I'd be able to shave my legs smooth. *(After all, on her first night as a new bride, no gal wants to feel like a "prickly pear!") Due to some childhood imperfections on my body, I was already apprehensive, so I didn't need anything else to fret over. What if John decided that he thought I looked better with my clothes on than off? But, I shouldn't have been concerned, as my inexperienced groom was still completely male, and slight flaws didn't lessen his enthusiastic amour in the least. If only in Jesus and John's eyes, this vessel was lovely in their sight. Also, he was more than a gentleman while I was taking a bath. John even took a long walk around the hotel, just to give me more privacy and help me to feel less self-conscious. It was always his details to the small things that endeared him to my heart over the years.

About Her Father's Business

The reason for staying at the Strater Hotel was to allow myself to fully give in to the sorrow of losing John, along with our shared hopes and dreams. It was time to start bringing a "closure" to that chapter of my life. But, although it was a healthy thing for me to do, oh, it was so terribly hard going "down memory lane" alone *(Eccl. 3:4)*. By the next morning, being so downcast and heartsick, I was tempted to just leave. Although intending to skip the included Brunch, I still wanted to just "peek" into the dining area. Would it still look as I'd remembered? Then, near the entrance, who should walk by, but the very waitress that had served John and me for all our Sunday Brunches there! Taking that as my Lord's confirmation that He wanted me stay, I went inside, trusting Him to help me swallow and keep down the meal.

The hostess seated me at a small table and, of course, who was assigned to work that area? You guessed it, that older waitress, Leona, we knew from before. Mentioning that I recognized her, even after 10 years, she claimed to remember us, too. Leona recalled that we always came in on the Thanksgiving weekend and that my John looked sort of like a blonde Abraham Lincoln. Also, that we always asked her to take our picture. Well, with that, I whipped out my camera and she did the honors one last time. To not upset her, I only explained that John couldn't join me on this trip, so I was "reminiscing" for us both, before leaving Colorado.

Looking back on that incident now, and remembering how much I enjoyed the food, the elegant old fashioned decor, and the live soft piano music, it makes me wonder if the <u>real</u> Leona was actually there. Or, had God sent an "angel in disguise" to lighten my heavy heart? Guess I'll have to wait until glory to find out for sure, but it's a nice thought anyway *(Heb. 13:2)!*

* * * * * * * * * *

Next, I drove through a small town in Colorado where John and I lived in our first home. Slowly cruising the familiar, tiny streets and short business area, it all felt different, even though very little had actually changed there. Guess all the changes were riding in the car with me.

From there, I drove downhill to the larger town of Cortez. It had REALLY grown! It was a struggle locating and recognizing places I wanted to see. Finding a motel, I checked-in, slightly unpacked. Then, I phoned a couple from our former church, in nearby Mancos. Before leaving on this trip, arrangements had been made for me to visit and share lunch with them.

CHAPTER SIXTEEN

Grief Expressed Becomes Less

With the passage of ten years, kids in a household can sure grow up fast! The four-year-old "baby" was now a strapping 14-year-old young man and hardly recognizable. Two of his older siblings were married, with small children, and the other one was off serving in the Navy. The parents, Mark and Terri, who I'd arranged to go visit, seemed to have barely aged at all. But, it soon became apparent that God had a main reason for prompting me to stop at that home. Their only daughter, Mona, had unexpectedly arrived two days earlier with her four little children in tow. She was in shock over being deserted by her older Vietnam Veteran husband, because of his obsessive attraction to a girl in her late teens.

After hearing some of her tale, we conversed, and then prayed for awhile. The Holy Spirit enhanced our understanding, revealing that her husband's reasoning powers had long since been satanically affected (Ezek. 18:12). The use of drugs and the trauma of his war experiences had caused him to often behave in unstable and irrational ways. The Lord opened Mona's eyes to see that ever since she had met her husband, he had been mind-manipulating her and had steadily increased his control. Lately, he'd gone on to "fresher" pastures when she refused to participate in any type of "threesome" arrangements. Mona realized that, had she kept her eyes on the Lord more firmly, she would have never been tricked by her husband's "phony charm." She cried out, "How can I return to Jesus? I've strayed so far, I don't even know how to pray anymore."

I agreed that when Christians choose to sin, they seem to do it with an emphasis! But, being forgiven and coming back into fellowship with the Lord God isn't difficult *(Ps. 86:5)*. Just think back to where you seem to have lost His close company and that's probably the place to begin finding it again. It might have been a blatant sin, lack of prayer, neglecting the food of Scripture, or just moving ahead without or even contrary to His direction for your life. Our prayers don't have to be eloquent or professionally worded, either. As Richard Foster has said, "When we stumble over our words, the Spirit straightens out the syntax. When we pray with muddy motives, the Spirit purifies the stream. The point is that, we do not have to have everything perfect when we pray. The Spirit reshapes, refines, and reinterprets our prayers, so that they are always understood by the Father heart of God."

From there, we adults discussed the possibility of Mona's husband "mending his ways" and going with her through Christian marriage counseling, the only kind to help rid her husband of demonic influences. Alas, the prospect looked grim of improving or even salvaging their bad marriage. But, the family could do their part by being available to communicate and by praying for his change of heart towards his family and towards God! In the meantime, we thought it to be wisest for Mona to obtain a legal "Separation." That enabled the law to assist her in acquiring financial support from her husband. Such could be revoked easily, if they did

About Her Father's Business

choose to renew their marriage commitment. Yet, it would also make a divorce go more smoothly, should that be the eventual and unhappy conclusion.

Discouraged about her current poor judgment of a man's character, Mona was feeling like a "loser." Even if she did become single again, avoiding another "rotten apple" was a concern, especially now that she had young ones to protect. Mona asked, "How could I ever get a "good" man? How can I know which one to trust or depend on?" So, going over thoughts about dating versus courting, I shared much of what had been explained to Stan's daughter in Illinois. Also, other qualities advisable to look for in a fella were his "stand in Christ" and how he currently treated his own mother and siblings. In my opinion, it was best to first be true friends before getting deeply romantic. Although, I teased, maybe John and I remained "just friends" a bit longer than most! We had known each other for over five years before ever going out as a two-some. Much later, John confided that, although I wasn't aware of it, he had been "secretly" courting me already for two or three years! How? Well, bashful, quiet John would make a point to say something nice or interesting to me every week at church. These were comments and questions he had practiced in front of the mirror beforehand, to make sure they came out just right. Praying that God would give him just such a lady, John decided to stay nearby, in case I became available.

Each summer, we always played on our church's volleyball team. Not once failing, John, purposefully, arranged to be on my side of the net. He wisely hoped that I'd get to feeling comfortable in his presence and with the idea that, if I ever needed a friend, he was "on my side." His clever plan worked, too! Later, in a time of great disappointment, I trusted in his friendship for help and he greatly lifted my spirits again *(Prov. 18:24b)*. Soon after that, we began to officially start "courting" and became each others' "lady" and "gentleman friend!"

"Oh," Mona said, "I can't imagine your John ever letting you down!" So, to illuminate the reality of any type of relationship, I mildly contradicted her. Actually, in small ways, we did disappoint each other at times. But, a wedge was never put between our love and respect for each other over those little incidentals. Yet, there was once that the Lord allowed a testing of the endurance of our commitment. And, it was only through our joint "love of Jesus" that we were able to weather the storm, *(Isa. 25:4)* emerging more strongly-bonded and closer than before.

The crisis in our own marriage occurred after the death of our only child. By now, I don't think John would mind, if I shared the incident. The kindly viewpoint of our Father in heaven affirms to all of His children that a person's grief must be expressed, not unhealthily suppressed.

You see, chances that I'd ever conceive again were so close to impossible that we entered our marriage expecting to adopt children. Yet, John and I never used any "precautions," just in case the Lord chose to intervene! After we had been married for nearly six years, my normal cycle was unusually late. Trying not to get overly hopeful, John told me not to mention our excited suspicions to anyone yet. We were still fairly

About Her Father's Business

newcomers to North Carolina, getting acquainted with folks at our jobs and settling into our new house. John reasoned that, if this was a miracle from the Lord Jesus, GREAT!; yet, we shouldn't get ours or others expectations up too high. This seemed logical, so I agreed.

A couple weeks later, mild morning sickness began! We made an appointment and met with a doctor two days later. During the time we waited for the pregnancy test results, he reviewed my medical records. When the test came back positive, John and I were elated, but the doctor sure wasn't. He warned us that due to the reason of my prior, very early miscarriage, the chances were extremely high of this pregnancy going the same way. Even if I made it into my second trimester, my damaged uterus would never be able to carry the baby to full term. At best, if my pregnancy lasted into the sixth month gestation period, we would be looking at a risk-filled and early C-section. He predicted that a premature birth, before that stage, would most likely not survive.

With this prognosis of "doom and gloom," John continued to hold firm to his resolution that we not share the news with anyone just yet. It'd be smarter to wait awhile longer to "see what would happen." Yet, due to his decree of silence during those first six weeks of pregnancy, I sadly missed out again on the joys most women experience in proclaiming their news "of a baby on the way" to family and friends. Then later, we both missed out on people's help to lift our burdened hearts, after we lost our child. Nobody had even known I'd been expecting.

Another month passed and I was still pregnant! By now, we had decided upon names we liked for our tiny daughter or son. John was even starting to feel confident enough to tease that he could tell I was just barely beginning "to show!" Our baby was growing at a normal rate and we were so excited! Having just bought a few items for infants, we were nearly bursting to tell folks about our "miracle baby!" Still, methodical and always careful John felt that we should hold off one more month, "to be on the safe side," before telling people of our pregnancy.

Feeling the first "flutters of life" just days before attaining my fourth month, we both danced a sort of "praise and hallelujah polka" right in the kitchen! And, in less than a week, we were going to "shout to the housetops" about our wonderful news! But then, only a couple of days later, the movement, and the morning sickness suddenly stopped. The doctor arranged to see us for an appointment and confirmed that he could find no heartbeat. Devastated, we asked him, "What went wrong? I had been feeling fine: no pain or fever this time. I had not overly exercised or exerted myself in anyway. I was eating the types of healthy foods I could keep down. So, why did our baby suddenly die?"

The doctor theorized that, probably, our baby's placenta had attached itself too near a scarred area in my uterus. As our baby's weight increased, the placenta didn't have enough healthy tissue on which to cling. Slowly, it tore away from my womb's lining, thus progressively cutting off our baby's nourishment and oxygen supply. John and I were so heartsick. Our baby's tiny body was still inside me; I still looked

About Her Father's Business

slightly pregnant, but actually, our sweet infant's spirit had already gone away. Not knowing whether my body would eventually miscarry on its own, or if labor would have to be induced, the doctor sent us home to wait and see. After a disheartening and dejected week of only slight spotting and mild cramps, a suddenly intense fever scorched through my body over the Labor Day weekend. The doctor insisted on an immediate D & C procedure (Dialation & Currettage) done to "remove the fetus"....the last earthly remnant of our own tiny child.

During the whole painful ordeal I was awake, shedding silent, unceasing tears *(Ps. 143:4)*. Partway through the "extraction," the nurse exclaimed, "What a pretty little face she has," before the doctor sternly "hushed" her. That's how John and I learned that we'd almost been parents of a little girl. Already, we had been calling our child by his or her intended name. But, indeed, this was a harsh way for us to find out that it was dear "Baby Kimberly" I'd been carrying and which had been growing inside of me. Yet, at least, for a few short months her anticipated arrival had been a bright "ray of sunshine" in our hearts. **("Pen Name" is to honor her memory.)*

To become a mother had been a fervent desire in my heart, every since I was eight-years-old. To have the privilege of giving a baby of my own a childhood filled with innocent laughter and full of loving security. One of nurturing and safe from harm by other adults. A childhood better than my siblings and I had ever known. Yet, John probably wanted the blessing of children even more! And, for weeks, we had already loved the personhood of our unborn child.

After being wheeled into post-op and left alone, I just stared numbly at the ceiling. My inflamed and sore insides, were now vacant. My emotions felt bruised and empty, too. Most hospitals are rarely geared to deal with the grief of a miscarriage. They gave neither our baby Kimberly her due merit, nor us any supportive information on how to mourn and grieve healthily. We never knew if our little daughter's body was perfectly formed or misshapen, whether she had John's reddish hair or my browner tones. We never learned the coloring of her eyes, or her weight or length. Our daughter was never granted a birth certificate or a funeral. We never got to hold her in our arms, nor let her tiny ears hear our voices speak of the tender love held deeply in our hearts for her. But, oh, we had so wanted to!

In awhile, the nurse came in and said I could go home. Teary-eyed, John was waiting for me down the hallway. When he got to my side, we held each other and just wept. Wordlessly, we walked out of the Maternity Ward, past the window of cooing bassinettes and beaming new parents, and to our car, that now, would never use the baby seat we had purchased. Even as solid Christians, our mutual pain over leaving the hospital without our longed-for baby, was shattering to us for awhile. We thought *that* was our time of crisis, but actually it was only just beginning.

People grieve differently. For me, it was comforting to talk about our lost baby girl. But, John hurt to have the topic brought up. Soon, he didn't want me to even mention Kimberly and insisted that we not tell others about her. Beyond dealing with his sadness, John felt disgraced and shamed by "the failure." Although not outwardly unkind to me, my usually gentle husband began to be verbally cutting and unreasonably critical. It seemed like I just couldn't do anything to please John anymore; plus, he was now so easily angered. Late one night, his emotions finally exploded and John admitted that he felt it was *my* fault our baby died! It was, after all, my womb that couldn't hold her, due to a violent childhood injury that had caused damage to what should have been the safest place on earth for our daughter to grow and thrive! Probably deep inside, even John perceived that he was acting irrationally. Still, the accusations wounded and sliced at my heart. The enemy used my dear husband's disappointment and unvented bereavement to heap loads of undeserved guilt upon me *(Rev. 12:10b)*.

Soon, except for short prayers at meals, John stopped wanting to pray with me. Aware that we were "slipping under" spiritually, I agreed to start attending a lively and more upbeat, yet Bible-centered church in the next town. The change in worship environment, I hoped, would help us to win this battle of an attack from the pit *(I Tim. 6:12a)*. Within a couple of weeks we found out that one of the elders from that church, Bob R., was a Christian Counselor. Even though I still loved John, by our first meeting with the counselor, I was distressed enough to agree with my husband that, "Yeah, poor John got a raw deal when he married me."

Yet, within just a few sessions of counseling, praise the Lord, our marriage began to get back to normal. It even progressed to a better, more accepting and grace-filled condition. It is doubtful that John ever told the elder why our "crisis" had started. But, the God-centered therapy helped teach John to more constructively vent his frustrations and disappointments. We were assigned the task of writing weekly "love letters" to each other. Before long, my sense of inner value was restored and my kind Beloved resurfaced! John eloquently reaffirmed his true devotion towards me. Through those sessions, the Lord clearly reminded John that he'd not married me to get a "baby factory." He married me to be his wife, and had promised to be the one to cherish, protect, and care for me all of his days. John felt sincere and terrible regret over the damage he allowed to happen to our union…and to me.

Still, for the rest of his life, John never lifted his ban for us to not tell others about sweet, Baby Kimberly. In the years since, I did accidentally slip and vaguely tell a couple of close, dear friends about my lost child. But, now, due to my own fresher experiences with the pain and grief of losing John, it no longer seems emotionally healthy to keep our daughter's brief life and early September death a secret. As I profoundly learned, while recovering from tumor surgery four years ago, we "soldiers of Christ" cannot stand against life's storms and Satan's many darts alone *(II Tim. 2:3)*. We need to reach out to each other in prayers, mutual support, and encouragement. We also need to forgive others quickly, completely, and permanently… and learn to do the same for ourselves. Forgiveness is

About Her Father's Business

not really forgetting; except with God. Sometimes it is wise to remember the bare, unemotional facts, in order to prevent future wounds from the same people. But, it is graciously dealing with the past, so that we no longer want to punish those who have hurt us. That alone is God's responsibility *(Romans 12:19)*!

Before leaving Mark and Terri's place, I led us all in a "prayer of agreement" that Jesus would guide Mona back to Himself completely and "break any satanic hold" upon this young mother, including, any "generational curses" *(Ezek. 18:20a)* her husband's influence or ungodly lifestyle may have inflicted upon Mona's four young children. Although their marital problems hadn't stemmed from disappointments over a *lack* of babies, they had major discord regarding fidelity and drugs. Besides, there would be additional conflicts now about the God-honoring values Mona wanted to teach their children *(Deut. 6:6-7a),* ones that "the enemy of their souls," did not want them to learn *(Lam. 1:16c)*!

Obviously, I got back to my room in Cortez late that night. I was rather emotionally drained, yet, pleased to have been of use to my Father. And, He granted me a deep, restorative sleep.

(For more information about how "the serpent" disrupts marriages read the sermon, "Satan Seeks to Devour You" by David Wilkerson, in the Times Square Church edition 12-27-199.)

CHAPTER SEVENTEEN

Unfriendly Territory

Leaving early the next morning, I began a long drive to see my former pastor and his daughter. When I'd attended college in upper Arizona, Don H. shepherded and "fed" his flock well. It was so pleasant being in a Christian home that was not in the midst of some crisis. We three had sweet, refreshing fellowship-in-Christ, praying for and ministering to each other. Later that day I had to enter an "enemy zone." So, this time of "fortifying the spirit," was greatly appreciated!

Now being semi-retired, Pastor Don had lost his life's companion about four years earlier. So, he could relate to my confession of frequently longing, those first weeks after John had died, to also be taken to glory… rather than being left here alone. But, as it states in II Tim. 4:8, I had the reassurance that, when my time did finally arrive, there was a crown in heaven reserved for me, one that even an arch angel could not wear! No, it would fit no head but mine, and already written on the doorpost of one of those heavenly mansions is my own name! Just think, when all the saints are gathered in, there won't be any vacant homes or thrones around our King!

Because of the pastor's advanced years, we could talk comfortably about the anticipation of us someday "going home" to be with Jesus. In a few more years, soldiers like him who have long "fought the good fight" *(I Tim. 6:12)* will be finished with earthly conflicts and enter into the "joy of the Lord" *(Matt. 25:21b)*. Both of us realize that God, in His wisdom, has chosen to not yet take us out of this world. We are to stay here awhile longer, as helpers to others, even if we don't see the advantage of remaining here for ourselves.

Too many Christians often want to die when facing a rough trial. When asked why, they will usually say, "Because I want to be with the Lord." Yet, too often, the longing to depart is more to rid themselves of enduring what God has allowed to be laid on their shoulders. Otherwise, they'd feel the same yearning at times when they were not being "tested" and under uncomfortable pressure. Admittedly, though, to "be with Christ" *(I Phil. 1:23b)* is far better! But, the wish to die, just to escape troubles is a selfish one. Our desire should be to glorify God in our lives, for however long He pleases to keep us earth bound and to humbly submit to His divine wisdom in determining when we have suffered or even lived here long enough.

Pastor Don made one comment that really touched and ministered to me. He said, "Isn't it hard when people stop letting you talk about your lost loved one? Almost as if, that person had never even existed? Well, remember, dear, Jesus has never forgotten them. Sometimes, it's real nice to enjoy a long, reminiscing chat with Him about them."

Before I left the next morning, he prayed over me with concerned tenderness. Beginning my drive to southern Arizona, the Spirit reminded me of I Thes. 5:12-13, where the apostle is imploring Christians to pray for all "ministers of the true gospel." Those men are the "officers" in Christ's army and are more

About Her Father's Business

frequently targeted by the devil and his demons. Their duties sometimes involve temptations and burdens that most lay-persons never encounter. They more often have to hear about sad tales and observe backslidings, which can grievously wear on their souls. We need to remember to intercede for those in direct ministry. They are only human, too; yet, their load and responsibility to God is much heavier than ours!

* * * * * * * * * * *

While driving through colorful scenery, I prepared myself to be spiritually dressed, "in full armor" *(Eph. 6:11)* before arriving at my Mom's house. It is difficult to expose unlovely things about the woman who gave me physical birth. For, you see, I still love her very much, which makes her "affliction" all the more painful to witness. Yet, it must be done, in order to explain Mom's sad and unusual "spiritually captive" state.

In addition to her decades of unquestioning loyalty to the occult-rooted Mormon church, Mom had also spent many years dabbling in witchcraft, séances, and hexes. In the past, she'd make use of milder illegal drugs or purposely misused prescription medications. Thus, she opened the door for evil to harass and cling to her soul in demonic oppression *(I Tim. 4:1b-2)*. This condition intensified, until it caused her to be a very complex, even "split" person. You see, there is the sweet, loving, even sometimes charming Mommie/Mom personality in her. But, also, there is the male-voiced demon, whose entity manifests as "Mother." He is the violent, domineering evil spirit residing within her as well. It's prudent to always be "on guard" when talking to or being in the same room with Mom. You never know <u>who</u> is responding or when there might be a switch from one personage to the other. Relating to Mom is tense and stressful.

As children trying to survive a dangerous environment, the role of peacemaker was developed in me *(Matt. 5:9)*. My sisters would urge me to "go see" if it was safe to approach Mom, before they'd venture out. More able to sense when our Mommie "wasn't herself," assisted all of us in averting or defusing potentially threatening situations. Thus, the gift of "discerning of spirits" *(Ezek. 44:23)* started to be molded within me as a youngster. No doubt, it was better for one of us to chance upon an encounter with "Mother," than for all of us children to get exposed to his wrath. Reflecting back, it is apparent that the demon inside Mom feeds on and gets excited over being able to terrorize those who are defenseless. Yes, a real bully that one!

Normally, when making an effort to visit family members, I would not have stayed alone at Mom's place. In earlier years, I'd spend the night at one of my friends or with a sister. Mom would believe that we just wanted "gabby girl" time alone. After John and I were married, we'd stay at a hotel nearby, letting Mom guess we preferred the extra privacy.

Although we'd tried to speak about it to her, Mom has never been open to even consider the possibility that she is demonized. Of course, "Mother" enjoys keeping Mom blindfolded. It has been heart-wrenching to see how often Mom's feelings have been hurt, because a

About Her Father's Business

former friend, husband or family member suddenly has had enough of "Mother's" cruel weirdness! Often, they just bail out of the relationship, leaving Mom bewildered as to what went wrong *(John 10:10a)*. It would devastate her that people, who once said they cared for her, would then accuse her of doing such awful things. Even the rare times any of my sister's families lived near Mom's area, they'd not take the risk of letting Grandma baby-sit their children for more than a few hours. For their own safety, they were never permitted to stay with her overnight. It makes me righteously angry that "Mother" has denied Mom several of the normal joys of motherhood and of being a grandmother. But, unless Mom sincerely chooses to submit to the Lordship of Christ, a "deliverance" session could be harmful, even dangerous for her *(Luke 11:24, 26)*. Our help is limited, until Mom is convinced that she needs being released from that evil spirit and fully wants her freedom…on God's terms!

So, trying not to "ruffle her feathers" before my arrival, I decided to stay at Mom's place. After all, it would only be for two days and three nights. Initially, when I first agreed to stay with her, my step-father was also supposed to be there. But, since then, Mom had become estranged from this 7th husband, so Pete wasn't going to be in the house with us. Without John or any sisters nearby, I had no viable excuses this time. Besides, it'd been over a decade since the last time "Mother" had slapped me across the face, supposedly for the horrendous offense of bringing her the wrong serving platter at Thanksgiving. Also, with my recent "prayer-covering" from Pastor Don, it was hoped that "Mother" would be subdued enough to be unable to "manifest" himself during my short visit. I wasn't really looking forward to visiting Mom alone, but God was sending me there and I was obligated to obey. Also, Mom was more often "herself" since the stress of having to raise kids and earn a living had been reduced.

The plan was almost successful, too. But, near the time I was to leave, my body, mind and spirit had become too tired, worn out, and "defenseless" to keep that demon restrained alone. Even my one request that Mom leave me undisturbed in the mornings, so that I could have my devotions and pray inside her Guest Room, was an annoyance to her. Yet, I enjoyed and needed my "quiet time" with my Lord, without having to be distracted by anything or anyone else. But, that request caused Mom to begin every day being irritated at me. She didn't like having to wait her turn and "Mother" didn't like me or my God at all. But, especially, the peaceful time I shared together with my Master, made the demon angry!

One of the reasons the Lord wanted me to be there was to help get Pete out of the recent manipulative mess in which "Mother" had trapped the poor fellow. You see, Pete went blind about 10 years ago, but had lots of retirement money from both a military and civilian career. More than once, when "Mother" was tired of Mom having to accommodate Pete's handicap, the demon would digress into cruel, verbal harassment: clearly voicing that the funds Mom would get when Pete died were the only reason she'd stayed with him this long. Alas, it was true, too.

About Her Father's Business

Just prior to leaving North Carolina, I got a call from an Arizona mental hospital. Pete had requested them to phone me. Probably under the influence of "Mother," my Mom had taken Pete on a drive. Then, through pretense and lies about where they were going, she dumped him in the local Mental Ward. Mom was hoping that his frightened and angry reaction would cause the doctor's to evaluate Pete as "incompetent," as was her claim. But, this was merely an attempt for Mom to have all the control over Pete's money. Later, she even boasted to her chums how her plan had almost worked! The problem was that Pete remembered encountering other such examples of malicious, odd conduct from his wife. So, he had just "kept his cool" and rationally talked through every test the doctors gave him. In three days, the hospital staff called Mom and said "Lady, you have to come back and get your husband. He's not insane, imbalanced or the least bit mentally incompetent. But, he is *very* angry at you! We have to discharge him. We have no basis for keeping him here."

So, "Mother's" plan had backfired, and now Mom was too afraid to get Pete and bring him home. Therefore, my 76-year-old, blind step-dad was stranded at the "loony bin" waiting for me to arrive in Arizona to get him released. Also, they both needed an intermediary to help oversee the matter of their "heated" decision to get legally Separated. What a lot of unpleasantness to "greet me" on my first night there!

Pete had been given numbers and addresses of a couple of private "Room and Board" homes that were willing to take him in and provide extra assistance. So, the next morning I drove over to look at both places, choose one, and then go pick up my step-dad at the mental hospital. It didn't take long to get Pete settled in, as I'd already collected the things he wanted from Mom. Just had to make sure he knew where all of his essential items were located in the new room. Next, we confirmed the hiring of a home health care nurse to check on Pete every other day, as she had to regulate his medication. Mom used to manage Pete's "meds," but I did not trust her to have anything more to do with administering his correct dosage. This way Pete was protected from Mom, and Mom was protected from any demonic urgings from "Mother" towards Pete!

The remainder of that morning, I helped Pete in the process of meeting with his lawyers to start on the Separation papers. He divided his and Mom's resources in a manner fair to both. We arranged a Power-of-Attorney to be given to Pete's nephew in Georgia. That way, should he die or ever really become incompetent, Pete's blood-relative could manage his affairs.

Once we finished at Pete's lawyer's, I took him to lunch and Mom joined us on that neutral ground. It was a tension-filled meal but, praise the Lord, they didn't get into a shouting match! Afterwards, I transported Pete back to his new place. To leave him was sad, but he was safe now. When I returned to Mom's house, it was time to leave for an appointment with her lawyers. Methodically, I went through the whole yucky, mind and emotion draining procedure again! Isn't it marvelous how well God prepares us to helping others? In recent months, I'd been forced to cram in an understanding about different wills, trusts, living

About Her Father's Business

wills, annuities, IRA's and varied legal matters. All of which, before John's death, I was totally ignorant, but had to learn. So, now I could be of some real help to Mom and Pete in their time of need.

Early that evening, Mom and I went to briefly see my older sister's son, Billy, at his night-shift job. Then, we drove to his sister's home for supper. Billy was newly engaged and his older sister, Dana, was married and expecting their first baby. Visiting with them after the meal, Dana said it showed that my faith was helping me through losing John. She doubted if what she still had, as a sometimes Mormon, would "cut it" for her, if the tables were turned *(Matt. 14:31b)*. It was difficult to talk freely with Mom there, but I told my niece to seek elsewhere to fill that true longing in her soul and to call me if she had any questions. **(She became a Christian soon after!)*

Back at Mom's house and just before I went to bed, my older sister, Jackie, called. We only got to chat for a short while and I didn't get to see or hug her. Jackie had been wandering out of state, from place to place, trying to mentally and emotionally adjust to being divorced. She had been married for twenty-five years and her self-esteem had dropped to "rock bottom" over this change. Although Jackie had lived nearby, obviously, she couldn't depend on Mom for uplifting advice or encouragement.

CHAPTER EIGHTEEN

Danger From Within

All the following day, as the new Executor of Mom's Will, I had to help her change names and/or "signature cards" on her bank accounts, stocks, Retirement Funds, and house. Also, we had to make a list describing each of her "items of value:" things like household furniture, pieces of crystal, expensive jewelry, silver place settings, and other potential "heirlooms." The Will needed this detailed account to accurately state which item she wanted given to whom, after her demise. Many times, during those long two days, it crossed my mind how strange it was being entrusted to do these tasks for Mom. Out of all of her family and friends, the one in whose company Mom felt least comfortable, was also the one person she most trusted. At least, in regards to carrying out the decrees of her Will, she had no worry that I'd become greedy and cheat or deal unfairly with the other beneficiaries *(Prov. 11:3a)*. Remember folks, God's integrity, practiced in *our* lives, speaks volumes to the unsaved. Even *they* consider it a valuable commodity, when they need to depend on someone's honesty. Oh if only they'd be willing to, one day, meet the Person *we* depend upon!

It was after 8 p.m. and I was exhausted. We finally had completed all the legal chores, so I showered and got into my night clothes. Entering the kitchen, to find a bite to eat before going to bed, a crisis in spiritual warfare began to build. Before I'd even put my salad together, Mom became demanding about us doing her jewelry list again. Being just too weary to deal with anymore mind-bending stuff right then, I said, "Just give me twenty minutes to eat and relax, then I'll review the list again." Well, that just wasn't a good enough answer to satisfy her and Mom began showing obvious signs of losing control *(Matt. 12:34)*.

So, I led her to the side of my bed, patted the mattress in an invitation, and gently sat her down next to me. Gently, with my arm over her shoulder and my head tenderly resting on the top of hers, I began softly talking to her. "Mom, do you remember telling me that I was to come here, 'just to rest, feel loved and mend?' Something you agreed that I'd need, after having to experience the resurgence of grief at John's Memorial and being in Durango alone? Well, instead, you've kept me busy from dawn to dusk assisting you and Pete settle tough, legal problems. I've been pleased to be of help, but both of you have wasted too much time hatefully bad-mouthing each other… even though I've begged you to stop. It harms, not heals, my spirit and emotions to hear such loveless words spoken between a marriage partners.

Noticeably, you keep switching the subject every time I mention John and you won't look at any of the photos. Is this helping me to mend? Mom, I've done every task you've asked of me and we are both weary. Therefore, can you tell me now…slow and easy, why you're getting so upset with me?"

Well, it came out that she was frustrated to even have to depend on me, of all people! Besides, Mom was irritated that I kept denying her request to take her

About Her Father's Business

along on my next three days of driving. It would fully take me that long to reach my Uncle's place in Texas by the Labor Day weekend.

Now, Mom already had a vastly discounted plane reservation to get to her brother's home. But, she wanted to use that money to see the sights and do "touristy stuff" along the way, via my car and "Kimberly the chauffeur." Yet, I needed that time alone to rest my brain and restore drained energy, before having to be among people again. This gal was eagerly looking forward to those peaceful days alone, *without* having to accommodate the schedule or chatter of anyone. Even before I arrived, Mom had been "needling" me about this in letters and phone calls.

My answer was always the same, but she kept trying to wear me down anyway. It's funny how that made her company even LESS appealing to me. Mom's tactics, to convince me to do what she wanted, were getting less subtle or friendly.

It reminded me of the way she bullied John at our wedding, when I wasn't around. The ugly and selfish trick she connived spoiled all of our first day as newlyweds. Wanting to please his bride's parent and not used to Mom's scheming ways, she had verbally backed John into a corner. Reluctantly, he had agreed to let her "hitch at ride" with us to the next destination on our honeymoon trip. Impatiently, she had called up to our Bridal Suite the next morning, before they had even served us breakfast. Mom was in a hurry "to hit the road!" Self-centered "Mother" didn't like being made to wait or refused anything he wanted, no matter how inconvenient it was on others. To punish us as we traveled, she thought it was comical to taint our honorable union by issuing embarrassing and lewd comments from the backseat regarding our wedding night. Angered, and wishing he had better protected us, John never fell for Mom's... or "Mother's" wiles again!

So, again, I tried to kindly explain my reasons to Mom. Hoping there was still a chance of reaching through to her and keeping "Mother" at bay, I reaffirmed how it was vital for me to have those days of solitude. Most people have the ability to measure out reasonable amounts of their energy for each task and each person, yet are still able to keep a "reserve tank" in supply. On the other hand, I never seemed to develop a "stop valve" to prevent all of my energy and emotional resources from being freely siphoned out of me by others. The only method by which I can "recharge my batteries" is to be entirely away from people for awhile.

At first, John didn't believe that I truly needed times completely alone. It hurt his feelings that I wanted to be away from even his nice company for a few days, at least twice a year. But, after he saw clearly the advantages of my returned sense of humor and other pleasing benefits, he willingly began to "give me some space" occasionally. Thereafter, John trusted me to let him know when I sensed being at the threshold of feeling "unhinged," due to becoming overly drained emotionally. In his love, John encouraged and "stood guard" over my bi-annual sabbaticals alone with God.

Oops! At that last word, I immediately sensed a bad spiritual change! Even through my fingertips resting on her shoulder, the transformation from soft, pliable

About Her Father's Business

Mom into rigid, hate-filled "Mother" was palatable. She bolted off the side of the bed and a deep, male voice bellowed, "It seems to only be MY company that you don't want!" That was the only warning given before the demon in my Mom's body began to growl and lunge at me with fists and kicking feet. Swiftly, the Lord helped me to duck under a powerful swing and grasp hold of Mom from the back. But, before I could secure both arms, the demon gouged Mom's fingernails into my left shoulder and clawed three long, painful scratches down my arm! Soon enough, the Holy Spirit gave me supernatural calm and strength to confine and subdue the attack *(II Tim. 1:7)*. Even so, out of frustrated wrath, the demon kept Mom's feet trying to kick my legs and used her head to strike backwards, attempting to injure my face. Speaking "in the authority" and through the "blood of the Jesus," God began demolishing that unclean spirit's power. Together, we disarmed the "weapons" that manifesting demon was using against me, through the use of Mom's own body *(I John 4:4)*. At the same time, I was silently pleading with God to help me not lose my own temper, so as not to "return evil for evil." Knowing that, if I reacted "in the flesh," and gave into my feelings to retaliate, it would actually be Mom who would feel the discomfort. Like always, she would suffer any pain inflicted because the demon would just retreat away, leaving Mom his victim again *(Eph. 6:12)*. Suddenly, there was a noticeable lessening of resistance. Mom just slumped forward, mouth slackened and drooling. With the demon's power temporarily shriveled, I led Mom's vacant, lethargic form back to her room.

Carefully, helping her to lie down on the bed, I covered her with warm blankets. Sadly, I left her to sleep off the semi-unconscious state, knowing full-well that she'd remember little, if any, of the incident when she awoke.

For a long while I just sat on the edge of the Guest bed, frightened, weeping and utterly disappointed. At about 11 o'clock, it dawned on me that instead of just crying out for God's protection, He wanted me to take some action *(Ex. 14:15b)*! I was not to even consider sleeping under Mom's roof that night. After all, there was no guarantee that "Mother" wouldn't re-emerge while I was sleeping. Most definitely, he would show no mercy! So, very quietly, I packed all of my things. During trips back and forth to the garage loading my car, I stayed in continual prayer for God to keep Mom asleep until I got safely away. God knew that it would've been beyond my present endurance, to encounter any other attacks that night. Before leaving, I wrote Mom a note saying something like "Seems we are unable to be compatible for this many days running, so I've gone to a motel. Have a good flight and see you at Uncle Bert's."

There was an open motel nearby, so I checked in, but was too rattled to unpack or undress. Apprehensive at still being so close to Mom's, my spirit felt uneasy. If she did reawaken before morning, it sure wouldn't take much effort to call around and find me again. So, without ever sleeping, I left the motel around 4 a.m., with daylight barely detectable in the sky.

(To research more on this topic, see references below and at the ends of Chapters # 7 & # 23.)

<u>*The Bondage Breaker*</u>*, by Neil Anderson (also;* <u>*Victory Over Darkness*</u>*)*

<u>*Liberating Ministries for Christ*</u>*, Int'l, Inc. – Issue # 11*

<u>*The Weapons of Your Warfare*</u>*, by Larry Lea*

<u>*Deliverance and Demonology*</u>*, by Derek Prince Publications*

<u>*Pray in the Spirit*</u>*, by Arthur Wallis*

<u>*Beyond the Darkness*</u>*, by Cynthia and Dr. James Mallory*

<u>*Warfare Prayer*</u>*, by Victor M. Matthews*

<u>*Is There Really a Devil?*</u> *by Loren Seibold – October 2001*

<u>*The Handbook of Spiritual Warfare*</u>*, by Dr. Ed Murphy*

CHAPTER NINETEEN

Covered in Prayer

Driving on for many miles, I often pulled off the road to just sit and cry. After a few hours, I began to wonder if I was truly so upset, just overly tired, or being afflicted by a "spirit of depression" attaching itself to me because of the ordeal *(Psalms 42:5)*. At about ten-thirty in the morning, I still couldn't stop my eyes from filling up with tears. Sensing I could actually be a danger to myself or others, the Spirit led me to pull off the road into the vacant parking lot of a mall. I must have crossed a time-zone because the stores were all still closed.

God prompted me to "call the cavalry" by phoning, Jeanette, a strong "sister-in-the-faith" who had promised to pray for me every day the journey. She was home with her three sons in Mississippi. But, she had to almost *guess* who had called, as I'd broken into sobs as soon as I heard her voice. Jeanette let me express all my feelings of remorse about the incident at Mom's place. Then she prayed for me to regain the "peace of God" and a renewed sense of His protection.

Jeanette realized that I'd not yet taken time for my own morning devotions, advising that I do so before driving any further. Her calm spirit and sound mind was very effective. Soon, I was laughing at what Mom's neighbors might have thought, had they seen me "sneaking" out of her house in the wee hours of the morning. Jeanette and I hung up after she pledged to call our shared Ohio friends, Anita and Charlie, as well as call one of my North Carolina co-pastor's to ask my church family to cover me in a "hedge of protection" and comfort that day *(Job 1:10a)*.

Afterwards, I remained in the parking lot, praying and reading scripture. Soon, I was amazed at the lightness of my spirit again *(Psalms 3:3)*! It is important for each of us "soldiers" to be ready to use our own battle shields, in order to also cover and protect an injured companion. I praised God for His help during the attack and for the support of His other saints! Yet, I did wonder why He had me face these scary experiences. Drawn to Psalm 112:7, I recalled how we Christians are not to be surprised by evil trials in our lives. Yet, if we are easily devastated by them, how are we any different from the unsaved that don't have the confidence in God to go to? We have already proven His faithfulness by prior victorious experiences. It is no wonder that the unredeemed are overcome with fear, but we have God's Spirit to guide and rescue us. If we become habitually distressed like them, how will they see the value of the grace and help from above, that we profess to receive. We gain peace and calm assurance from scriptures like John 14:27. After all, as it says in Psalm 126:3, we have MUCH to be glad about!

As Christians, we are not to go around looking on the gloomy side of everything. Nor to dwell more on what we have endured, than on how God has brought us *through* those things we've had to face. We should not be so eager to talk about all our woes instead of boastfully exclaiming about the mercy and help God

About Her Father's Business

has given us! A grateful and healthy spirit is one that is eager to speak of things that direct honor back towards God, instead of focusing the attention of others onto ourselves. It is true that we do have numerous trials and tests *(John 16:33)*. But, it is equally true that we've always been delivered safely through them. The deeper our troubles, the louder should be our thanks... not just our *complaints,* to God who preserves us until the end!

In the November issue of a David Wilkerson message, it read, "We *waste* our afflictions when we face new ones, without remembering our deliverances from past ones. We have a sad tendency to easily forget every good thing God has ever done for us! We waste our afflictions when we refuse to see God bring us through them, *in order* to help and teach others by sharing our victorious experiences to prove to them God's faithfulness. We must remember also that in whatsoever the hardship we are currently going through, it shall eventually pass and be over with."

As I sat in my car now composed, calm, and dry-eyed, I asked the Lord to remain "closer to me than even my next heartbeat" throughout the rest of this trip. My human strength was at very low ebb and in my weakness, I needed to depend on His strength all the more! As I began driving again, the sky's cloud cover lifted and I was delighted to be able to see off into the distances for miles and miles. Jesus helped me to enjoy the scenery, as well as being grateful for the long, flat stretches of easy desert roads. My eyes watered a few times, but it had a sort of cleansing effect, sort of like getting the last of some toxic residue out of my system so I could feel light and free again. About 2:30 p.m., I stopped for gas and bought some lunch. Ah, it tasted so-o-o good! It had been a stress filled 24-hours since my body had last been given anything to eat. Why, shame on me! In apology, I treated it to an ice cream cone and went off down the road grinning as I ate the sweet, yummy stuff!

* * * * * * * * * * * *

Arriving in El Paso that night, I went straight to bed. Waking up rather late, it dawned on me that I missed a whole night of sleep. But, praise to God, He had kept me awake and safe all those 10-hours of driving the day before!

Heading out the next morning, I stopped by Fort Bliss Hospital to deliver a surprise package for Mom. You see, she was to go there for minor surgery after her visit in Texas. Knowing this earlier, I began collecting unique, humorous, or classy Hallmark cards to give her. Mom was a little nervous about this hospital because she had never seen it before and didn't know its doctors or quality of care. So, I decided to secretly "check it out" for her on my way towards Texas; it was fine. While there, I left my bundle of cards at the desk. Each had a special note written in it from me and was numbered for Mom's arrival later *(Matt. 5:44)*. That way, the nurse could give Mom a card for each day she was recuperating in their hospital.

CHAPTER TWENTY

Gently Humbled

The end of that Saturday's drive brought me to Sonora, Texas. From my room in a motel, I called Uncle Bert. I wanted to make sure Mom's flight had arrived there safely and to inform him that I would not make it to his house late Sunday night, as planned. It would be easier on me, if I got there by 10 o'clock on Labor Day morning, instead. That way, I'd still be there a couple of hours before more of the relatives were scheduled to arrive.

Actually, I did remain on schedule and drove all the way to Uncle Bert's part of Texas the next evening. But, after another long day on the road, I knew this gal would need to be alone that night. Just didn't think it would be wise for me to have to deal with my Mom again, plus several family members, at the end of another exhausting day. Therefore, after a good night's sleep, I arrived at my uncle's home the next morning. Mom greeted me with civil words, yet cold, suspicious eyes.

As Uncle Bert helped unload my car, he revealed that when I'd called two days earlier, Mom assumed that I'd blabbed all about her to him. So, she had jumped right in to tell him her version of the story. How she had been so stressed and I'd just "huffed off" to a motel after she'd lost her temper a bit. When Mom's brother told her that I'd not even mentioned the event, but had only inquired after her safe arrival, she looked uncomfortable and didn't say anything more. With a little humor, I wondered if she had felt a touch of those "burning coals" *(Prov. 25:22)* of kindness "heaped upon her head."

Uncle Bert asked which town I'd stopped in the night before. So, I admitted to staying only a few blocks away from his house, confessing that, "I'd just had my fill of Mom for awhile." Chuckling that he could sure relate, he remarked, "Your Mom's only been here one night and I'm glad she's leaving this afternoon." After settling into the room I was to use and admiring their fancy home, I got acquainted with Uncle Bert's new third wife, Connie. His spacey-acting step-daughter, Kate, was in her early twenties, between jobs, and also living with them, yet mostly avoided all of us. So, I helped Connie set the lunch things before the other guests arrived.

The relatives that soon joined us at Uncle Bert's were my grandmother's sister, Great Aunt Cathy, along with her husband and two generations of their family. After lunch and fellowship, they were going to take Mom home with them for a couple of days. During the pleasant time of visiting among all of the kinfolk, John's awards and our photos were conversed about and passed around. While Mom was looking slowly and quietly at several pages, I silently prayed that the Lord was prodding her heart *more than* Satan was riding it with accusations.

You see, I knew she still felt guilty over not coming to be with me during the ordeal of John's death and funeral. Returning from the morgue, I'd delayed calling Mom until being able to reach Johns parents. I felt

About Her Father's Business

they were due the respect of my telling them first and personally about their son's accident, before they heard the bad news from anyone else. When Mom learned that she'd not been called immediately, she got angry and hung up on me. Before she did, I tried explaining that it would have been risking a cruel shock of having anyone else call to "offer their condolences" to John's parents, before I'd had the chance to yet inform them of his death.

Hoping that Mom would be off her "high horse," I called back the next day. My step-dad, Pete, had answered the phone and told me that Mom wasn't home. She had gotten a "bee in her bonnet" yesterday and had hopped on a plane to Las Vegas with a girlfriend. He didn't know where they were staying, but she told him not to expect her home until the following Thursday. It was obvious that Mom hadn't told Pete about John's accident. I guess I had offended "Mother's" pride by not phoning Mom first, before anyone else, about our sad news *(Prov. 16:18)*. So, the demon was trying to dole out punishment, by forcing me to handle the crushing ordeal without any support from my side of the family. Poor bewildered Pete would have been unable to come and help, so I decided not to yet inform him about John's accident. Although, I did let him know that Mom probably left because she was angry at *me*, not him.

There he was, an elderly blind man left alone to make due for over a week, until his weird wife decided to return. If Mom did happen to call Pete from Vegas, I asked him to give me the phone number, so I could also talk to her. She didn't; thus; I couldn't.

Over a week later, I was able to catch Mom the evening she returned home. Apparently, she was genuinely unaware that I'd even told her about John's death. She regretted having been away and not giving Pete a number where he could've reached her. Mom said she would have flown right down to "help me bear" the crisis. But, then she asked when the funeral was to be held. I had to tell Mom that it had already occurred almost five days ago. Well, that made "Mother" real mad again, insulted that we'd not "kept the body on ice" and waited to do the funeral until *he* could arrive! Trying to reconnect with Mom, I explained that it would've been heartless to have kept John's parents and friends "on hold" until his widow's parent decided to resurface. It had been emotionally hard enough, waiting even four days to do the service, in order to give John's parents enough time to arrive from Colorado. Mom thought I had shown bad manners and embarrassed her in front of John's parents. But, she guessed she'd not have to see them again anyway… and off she went talking about unrelated and trivial matters. Yes, at times, it's a *strange* experience talking with my Mom.

Thus, I suppose, is why she hadn't liked me bringing up the mention of John at her place in Arizona. Yet, at my uncle's home, Mom had no right to stop anyone else from speaking about the subject or asking many interesting questions.

CHAPTER TWENTY-ONE

Distressed Daughter

After my great aunt's family left, taking Mom with them, I was able to really visit my Uncle Bert and his gals. He was a non-practicing "Jack-Mormon," yet Connie was a Christian. But, she had compromised her convictions and mellowed her stand for Christ when she dated and married my uncle. Even so, Connie was still a dear, sweet lady and it was entirely obvious that Uncle Bert adored her. Because John's life of faith had been discussed by relatives earlier, my uncle now felt comfortable asking, "How do I become more like my wife and you? Why does being 'born again' make you ladies so loving, compared to regular folks or even to most Mormons? Is it the difference in your beliefs about God and Jesus? Aren't they really about the same as what the L.D.S. church teaches?" So, once again, I started explaining some of the larger doctrinal differences between orthodox Christian theology and the Mormon cult. Uncle Bert was very receptive and I suspected that Connie had spent much time in prayer over him.

Beginning, I explained that I'd first suspected that "something was wrong in Denmark" when our Ward's Bishop became angry at not being able to give me a logical answer to my earnest questions. Things such as, what heaven would be like for my older sister, who had recently married an Episcopalian? Also, what would happen to our parents, now that they weren't married to each other "in this life" anymore? Yet, supposedly they'd been "sealed for time and all eternity" in the temple. And, since all of their children were to be "sealed" with them, where would we now end up? Furthermore, we had a sweet, younger half-sister, who didn't have the same father, plus three smaller half-siblings who had a different mother, so WHAT would happen to all of them? These were honest inquiries, because I was confused about the different "levels of worthiness" in the Mormon's concept of heaven. Having been a recent, teenage "Youth Missionary," which had accompanied a pair of lady missionaries on some of their home-visits, I sincerely thought reasonable answers were available for my questions. I just figured I wasn't learned or wise enough to understand them on my own yet, so I'd asked my Bishop. Therefore, it was a surprise and really hurt to have him accuse me of being a "trouble-maker!" Yet, his unexpected reaction was actually sobering and helped to raise my first doubts about the validity of what my church was teaching me to believe. Looking back, I'm certain that God used that disappointing encounter to inspire me to search deeper into other known Mormon oddities. *(For more scholarly account of facts about this topic, refer to the pamphlet called, "A Closer Look at the Mormon Concept of God," by Home Mission Board, SBC.)

In the discussion with my uncle's family, I got to an ugly part in the Mormon's false teachings: Their doctrines proudly state that their god came down from heaven, took on a physical body and had actual incestuous relations with the Virgin Mary! That same

About Her Father's Business

maiden, they promote, was his own daughter, born to one of his wives in heaven, as a spirit-child reared to young adulthood. Mary had obtained her own physical "temple" (body) when she was birthed again on earth (They also say that the process of stuffing a grown spirit-body into a newborn earth-body is painful, which is why *they* claim that infants cry at birth). Thus, to the shocked amazement of most Christians, documents from the L.D.S. church teach a horribly perverted belief on how Jesus was conceived. They explain that when Mary was "overshadowed," their god sired Jesus by having her submit to sex with him! *(Experts also report, that Mormons proclaim that Jesus had "many wives" and sired children before he died.) Whereas, in Isaiah 7:14, true Christians believe in the "miraculous conception." Christ did not come from the "seed of a man" (or a false god), but by the creative power of the Holy Spirit. Jesus was born without any taint or stain from the first Adam's original sin nature. After all, when before or since did angels sing a glorious midnight song or God Almighty hang a new star in the sky, except for the birth of His pure Son Jesus, our blessed Messiah! *(For verification on this shameful doctrine, read the chapter, 'Conception and Marriages of Christ' in the book, The Mormon Mirage.)*

While talking about this subject, I realized that my uncle's grown step-daughter was getting very agitated. Kate couldn't sit still, but nor did she to get up and leave. It was easy to perceive that she was being tormented by an evil spirit, probably due to having experienced some degree of sexual molestation in her background. So, keeping one eye on Kate, I continued to tell Uncle Bert and Connie how, in Utah, there is almost no legal penalty for molestation or incest within a family. Think about it: how could Mormons pass a harsh law against something they claim their own god, by his very example, has shown his approval? It is a historical fact that Mormon-dominated states have a substantially larger percentage of such indecencies than does our national average. Also, it is surmised that many cases never even get reported, much less processed. Often, no one will take seriously the young girl's embarrassing accounts regarding such "respectable men."

Right then, Kate jumped up out of her seat saying, "Well I can surely believe that! It happened to me. But, everyone thought I was just a creep for lying, when I told my family that Dad kept touching me in places he shouldn't! Even after he and Mom divorced, no one would believe a twelve-year-old girl."

In the midst of sputtering denials from my uncle's shocked wife, I stood and fully turned to face her daughter. Looking at the young woman straight in her eyes, I told Kate, "I believe you and I know you are speaking the truth!"

"How do you know?" she cried.

"Well dear, I've known other girls who have had similar experiences."

"No one could have suffered the way I have," she said. "I'm a mental wreck and have to be on medication all the time. I'll never again be well."

"Is that so?" I continued. "Well, sit down and let me tell you about other girls who have weathered as much as you have. Yet, they still found wholeness, emotional health and happiness in their lives. Kate, there is *still* hope for you! Just determine to find someway to turn every unpleasant experience in life, into something that is positive and productive. Listen to these examples; let them begin to renew hope in your heart and in your life."

To my depths, I dreaded the challenge God had just set before me. But, I knew that wounded Kate needed to be ready for deliverance, more than I needed to remain comfortable. Purposefully, I turned my back on Uncle Bert and Connie. I wanted to give them the clear message that they could stay or leave, but *don't* interfere! Bringing a footstool over to Kate's chair, I began to tell her of several cases of evil trials… that were turned into victories, by the gentle love of Jesus Christ *(I Cor. 15:57)*!

(For more resources about Mormon's differing beliefs, see bottom of Chapters # 7 & # 23.)

CHAPTER TWENTY-TWO

And, yet…God!

- (A) -

The child I first recalled had been enduring tortures from her perverted step-father whenever she'd resist his molesting touches at the tender age of 3 ½ years old. Although there was never actual penetration, she was eventually forced to look at and touch parts of his body that she did *NOT* want to. When her mother went to a weekly hair appointment, he'd bring the scared, little girl into her parent's bedroom. Slowly and methodically, he'd close each blind and curtain against the daylight *(John 3:20)*. It only took one ugly experience inside that darkened room for the child to dread with nauseous fear, the closing of those blinds.

The step-dad smoked and he liked to play toss with his sharp army knife. Whenever the small girl tried to struggle out of his grasp or run to the door for escape, he'd easily catch her. As punishment, he would firmly hold one of her ankles, then cruelly burn round cigarette holes in the spaces between her little, pink toes. Or, with the point of his knife, he'd carve shallow slices on the arches of her tender feet. Frozen with terror from his threats "if she ever told" anyone, she learned to tolerate most anything he'd do to her, except for the one time he tried to force his slippery tip into her tiny mouth. At that intrusion, the child gagged and vomited wholeheartedly! Even though he slapped her face and bloodied her nose for it, he never tried *that* move again.

To this day, that gal cannot walk barefooted in comfort. She has spent all of these years with scarred soles that become painful whenever her feet swell. Even in adult life, she is unable to tolerate the sensation of any slimy texture in her mouth, not even Jell-O. It doesn't matter how pleasant might actually be the taste or flavor of the food.

And, yet…God used those prior bad exposures to sexual interplay, to keep her more upright and moral than were many of her teenage friends *(Prov. 13:6a)*. She'd not indulge in casual flirting, heated kissing or heavy petting and necking. She discouraged all inappropriate sexual touches attempted by "the guys." Also, on more than a few occasions, she'd had the awkward, yet privileged opportunity of being God's vessel, one which was able to warn and help other young girls to avoid the "unseemly advances" of older men, before things got out of control for the girls.

* * * * * * * * * * * *

- (B) -

Some gals, I told Kate, had to live through other kinds of abuses. There was the young girl who was often worried about her playmates safety. She was almost a teenager before realizing that, when friends remarked, "I'd better get home before I get beat," their definition of the term was vastly less violent than were the facts

About Her Father's Business

in her home. Early, she acknowledged the presence of evil sometimes overlapping the facial expressions and actions of her parents. As a youngster, each of her shoulders had been yanked out of their sockets, the right one so many times she'd even lost count. Once, while trying to run out of harms way, she was caught and tackled to the floor. It resulted in a wrenching dislocation of her right hip and a torn knee cap. Because of such excruciating jars, when her parents threatened to "pull her leg off and beat her with the bloody stump of it," the girl feared that they were serious. She didn't understand it was only a cruel jest, a joke. What she *did* comprehend is that the punishment and accompanying pain of running away from unavoidable trouble, was far worse than just squarely facing the briefer moment of discomfort. That lesson to face, not run away from, conflicts in life helped her to ride out many future trials without falling apart. But, the rest of her life, that girl had to be careful about how she stretched her arms, especially the right one, and to not overly pivot her hips outwards. Such movements could cause those joint sockets to slip painfully out of place again. Yet, due to years of experience, she became very adept at "popping" them back in by herself.

And, yet...God's redeeming ways helped that youngster to grow-up with a deep sense of compassion and protection towards other physically abused children. For a few years, she even allowed the use of her own home to receive emergency cases. Why? Because that gal was thrilled over being rescued herself from the fear of violent oppression and of being a victim in Satan's hands, through his use of others. She is better able to relate to and be patient with the infirm or people who have physical weakness. She "rejoices with gladness" over the day she discovered that God was good, kind, and just *(Ps. 106:5a)*. But, to her, the best of His attributes are that Jesus is far stronger than evil! God is more powerful than any of the demons she'd experienced through the cruelty of her parent. The Lord even granted her a deep pity for adults who do harm to their own children. She had learned that, once the anger was spent, most of those parents really did feel awful about their behavior. The decent ones were open to attending classes that focused on helping them learn how to react more kindly toward their little ones.

* * * * * * * * * * * *

- (C.) -

There was also the little four-year-old girl who almost died from a sexual abuse, which turned into a horrible, physical onslaught. This small fighter refused to stop struggling against the grown-man's attempt at incest. He became so frustratingly enraged, that he grabbed a knife and yelled, "If you won't stay still and open up for my peter, then I'll open you up myself!" And, with that, he angrily plunge the blade deep into that young child's private parts.

It was the blood spurting on the floor, not her terrified screams, which brought the crazed man to his senses. At least, enough to realize that he might be

About Her Father's Business

in real trouble now. Worried about his own skin, he ordered the child to go to the bathroom, clean up and get dressed. Trembling too hard to stand, she began crawling towards the hall, trailing blood all the way. The mess on the floor alarmed the now dressed man. Hollering at the girl, his boots clomped loudly on the floor boards after her. Fearing he would kick her, the child tried to crawl away faster, incensing the guy even more. To stop her from moving, he stomped his heavy work boot down on her fragile ankle; which crushed several of its tiny bones. Picking her up around the waist, he dumped her on the floor in the bathroom.

Dazed and whimpering in pain, the girl limped around cleaning the floor and herself, where it so burned. With a heavy sense of foreboding, she went to lie down on her bed. But, she hobbled painfully to the bathroom a couple more times, to stuff great wads of toilet paper inside her ruffled little panties, trying to soak up the continual flow of blood. She knew nothing about the possibility of bleeding to death. She only knew she had to avoid getting her "daddy" mad at her again. In about an hour, the child's mother came home and the man gave her a false tale about the girl's misbehavior. Thus, he made excuses to explain why the child had been sent to her room and now walked funny. Soon called for supper, the girl could only nibble at her food; she throbbed, ached… and so felt *very* sleepy. She must have looked pale because her mother touched her forehead to check for a fever, and then gave her child permission to go to bed. It was only after the girl emitted a scream, when stepping onto her swollen ankle and collapsing onto the floor, that her mother first noticed the blood on the bottom of her child's britches. Aghast, the mother then saw the smeared blood left on the wooden seat of her daughter's chair. The girl was only conscious for a few more minutes before passing out. But, she did remember her mother scooping her up, rushing to the car, and driving fast down the street.

Ten days after the attack the girl was surprised to wake up in a hospital. Years later, she suspected that her body could have awoken sooner. But, guessed that the hospital staff had kindly kept her sedated on purpose, until the internal and external wounds had been repaired and the stitches had already been removed. It was supposed that they wanted to spare her most of the pain of healing. As well as, to prevent further trauma over the terror of having her genital area touched and probed by yet another grown man....even if he was the doctor.

In the crisis of the moment, the girl's swollen ankle was only thought to be badly sprained. It was wrapped accordingly, but therefore, never properly set. Months later, when it still hurt to walk on that right foot, x-rays revealed the wrongly healed broken bones in her ankle. They were now beyond repair. That ankle would always be weaker than the left one, and sorely ache in cold weather or if overly used.

Her step-father confessed and was in jail. Yet, because of the incident, the child's mother lost temporary custody of all of her children. After the girl was released from the hospital, a foster lady took her to join her other siblings. The stitches from brutal knifing resulted in very uncomfortable ridges of scar tissue inside the child's little vagina. Also, the long blade punctured all the way *through* the back wall of her little, immature womb. Due to the shock to her female organs, the child began her woman's cycle at barely 9-years-old. The monthly process was always a misery of uterine cramps. The internal tissue, around the scars on the outside of her womb swiftly produced increasingly painful endometriosis. She had repeated infections that caused damage to her fallopian tubes, and the need for surgery on them by age twenty. Later, the growth of abnormal tumors, originating in her scarred area, caused her to miscarry. Eventually, it cost the complete removal of her womb, along with the last of hope to having a baby of her own.

And, yet…God endeared this girl, as an adult, with a heart softened towards handicapped people that so often lacked the love of a close family. She understood well the limitations of a damaged or malformed body and loved easily those whom most others would consider unlovely *(Psalms 36:10)*. Having a weakened achy limb herself, she never overly pushed others (from children to the elderly) to continue walking or standing once they became tired. Destined to be childless, her quiver always empty, she saw where God had given her a multitude of other sweet blessings instead. A large part of His mercy included a husband, who had the self-discipline and control to make love to her gently, so she would never feel violated again.

One of the richest blessings in her life was the joy of being able to fully, completely forgive the man who had harmed her as a child. While he had been in jail, he'd become a strong believer in Jesus. The last years of his life, before he died of cancer, the two of them thrived and mended in a wholesome, healing relationship. His absolute change of character was one of the main reasons that she longed to know more about the Lord. That man was her first vivid example of the old nature becoming "a new creature" in Christ *(II Cor. 5:17).*

* * * * * * * * * * * * *

- (D) -

Speaking of a profound impact to Jesus and his loving sacrificial gift reminds me another example. There was a girl who had an unusual encounter that bonded her heart to His Lordship deeply. This gal had an older, blonde-haired, light-eyed sister and a toddling, younger brother of the same coloring. But, she was born with the similar features of her mother, with dark hair and eyes. Alas, this was also a physically abusive household. The mother was on her third marriage, not counting the so called "uncle" this or that of her temporary live-in boyfriends. The current husband resented the mother's kids, as they represented other previous men in his wife's life. He was unkind to all of them and very severe in discipline. But, his temper and strength was especially dangerous to the little brother.

One day, after a minor misbehavior the girl doesn't even recall, her step-dad forced her into the dryer and turned it on. Spinning backwards and bouncing hard inside that dark, damp interior was bad enough. But, as the five-year-old tried to wedge her body against the top and bottom of the drum to lessen her rolling, the dryer's heating element warmed up and her hands and knees were getting burned. She was already afraid to be left in the dark, because of an unkind method of discipline by her parents. They'd repeatedly locked her in a small under-the-stairs closet and told her that it was "full of black widows" that would crawl on her and "bite her to death." That rattling form of punishment made her nerves raw, but the dryer was making her draw close to losing her sanity completely. She had gotten so dizzy in there, she threw up and it made her hold slippery. At that, she began screaming and wailing, no longer caring if she got a harsh spanking, if only they'd let her out! Soon, neighbors were banging on the door, demanding to know what was being done to that poor, frightened child *(Matt. 26:40b)*. They stopped the dryer and the girl fell out the opened door, babbling in shock.

Even to this day, spinning easily upsets her stomach, especially if she has to travel backwards. The police took her siblings to an orphanage-foster home and, after being checked by a doctor for physical injuries, she was released to the same foster home. The doctor instructed the care-giver to let the child sleep as much as she needed. It was a couple of days before she spoke or even recognized her older sister. Together, later that week, the sisters ventured through the confusing hallways, to find the room where her brother and the rest of the babies in cribs were kept. From then on, after each meal, the sisters would take the long trek to the nursery to visit and play with him.

But, one morning their brother wasn't in his crib. Thinking he was being bathed or fed elsewhere, they decided to try back after lunch. But, when he still wasn't in the nursery, this same girl mustered up the courage to ask a black cleaning-lady if *she* knew where their little brother had been moved. The dear woman's eyes teared up as she gently took the young girl by the hand. That robust woman marched right into the administrator's office and demanded, "Tell des child about da baby!" That is how the sisters found out that their mother had allowed her 18-month-old son to be adopted by another family. Ever after, that young girl felt insecure about whether or not she'd be the next to be given away to strangers! Satan convinced the child that she was always at risk and that, one day, she might be too naughty or too much trouble; then her mother would also get rid of her. So, under that bondage of fear, the girl never complained of the gross mistreatment still to come her way.

You see, the girl's step-father had convinced her mother and the judge that it was only the little boy that caused him to feel jealous and do mean things, because the lad still carried the name of his wife's former husband. He'd be willing to even adopt his wife's two daughters, if she'd agree to let the boy go to someone else. *(After all, he wheeled, he had money and security for her and the girls.) The mother agreed and the courts decided to give them both another chance to prove they could be "fit parents." A few days after her small son was "out of the family picture," the judge gave custody of her two daughters back to the mother.

About Her Father's Business

It was a big mistake, because now the husband felt really powerful about the financial leverage he held over his wife. Satan was soon in full control of this man's lower, cruel instincts. Anytime his wife displeased him, he'd not take his spite out on her because then she'd turn cold in bed. No, he began using her dark-haired, "look-alike" daughter as a scapegoat to vent his anger. With a snap, off would slither his thin leather belt, then the girl was commanded to strip to the waist and lean over the edge of her bed. He'd then whip that almost five-year-olds' back, until many of the welts oozed *(Micah 3:2)*. For months, that child often had to wear one of two stained T-shirts beneath her clothing. She'd even wear one at night, so her pajamas wouldn't stick to the scabs. In the morning, she'd run a few inches of warm water in the tub and lay in it with back her submerged. This softened the scabs enough for her older sister to gently peel off the wet T-shirt. Once bare, the girl could dab the moisture off her skin, put on the dry T-shirt, and get dressed. The girl learned quickly that, if she did anything to remind her stepfather of a recent beating, it risked incurring his further wrath. So, most days, she'd hand wash, rinse, and squeeze the water out of the soiled T-shirt. Then the young child would hang it on the lower bar of her own bed's headboard, to hide it out of sight.

A "good week" was if <u>both</u> T-shirts were hanging dry on the headboard. That meant enough time has elapsed between whippings, to let her seeping back heal. A "bad week" was if the belt landed repeatedly on top of recent scabs, cutting bleeding welts into her back until deep, criss-cross scars were formed. And, if both girls were about to "get the belt," this younger sister would volunteer to go first. She knew that, after her turn, the force of the strap would be less severe on her sister. The tactic was used hoping that the older girls' back would not form ugly scars, but remain pretty; like the younger girl wished hers still was. Going to kindergarten was the highlight and safest part of that child's day. From then on, school and its homework became a haven out of reach of the cruelties at home.

After nearly three years, her mother divorced that man. As the damage to the girl's skin healed she would carry bluish-purple, then reddish-pink, and finally white lines on her back, which caused her to "tan like a zebra" even decades later. As a teenager, a potential boyfriend happened to feel the scars under her light blouse and quickly terminated the relationship. He told the girl that the ridges "turned his stomach." His tactless comment was just a sample of the many things that caused that girl to feel that her body was physically unattractive and undesirable. During her late teens, the hurtful words spoken by some girls in the gym's locker room only magnified that girl's low self-esteem and unrealistic perception about her looks.

And, yet...God helped that girl, through her own experiences, to choose never to verbally "wound" others by similar, cruel teasing. And, in *her* presence, peers soon learned she'd not tolerate them "making fun" of others. She understood, too well, the pathetic self-image caused by real or imagined body flaws. In later years, she took young girls under her wing, encouraging them to override their fears and self-consciousness

About Her Father's Business

about being attractive. Amazingly, the Lord used her own prior experiences of sometimes being whipped until her back bled, to bring her to Himself. When she learned how Jesus willingly endured a severe flogging, as part of His sacrifice to "stand in our place" (paying the price of our sins and allowing us to receive God's undeserved mercy), she instantly wept in empathy and appreciation *(II Cor. 5:15)*. Jesus also granted her a further blessing, its fruits not to be seen until years later, but which had begun when she was only eight-years-old.

Her mother told the two sisters that she was not going to write any more letters to their brother. A safety deposit box had been reserved, via the adoption lawyer, so that after the boy reached 21, he could read why his family had given him away. The girl's mother gave her two daughters the attorneys' long address, saying one of them could use it if they wanted to begin writing their lost brother. But, that *she* didn't want the sisters to ever mention their brother to her again! The younger sister had been worrying that, if she was being treated so poorly within a family that actually contained one "real" parent, might her baby brother be faring even worse? So, she decided to become his one way "Pen-pal"…for nearly fifteen years. But, she wanted her brother to know, when the contents of the box would be opened, that at least one member of his blood-family had not forgotten him.

Then came the wonderful day many years later, when a young man called the phone number left inside that bulging safety deposit box. Finally, he got to hear the voice of his own "letter-writing" sister. Thus began, "the return of the years the locust had eaten" *(Joel 2:25a)*! Eventually, that brother would feel ready to meet his other sister, and even birth mother. A show on TV had learned of their story and "footed the bill" for their first family reunion. The girl even has a video tape of that recorded program to keep and cherish!

* * * * * * * * * * * *

- (E) -

Connie's daughter had been listening to the examples and was being calmed by their affect. She asked me if I knew of any more girls who had survived such ordeals. Thus, I told her of a girl who lived in a physically abusive environment with two frequently squabbling sisters. If the other sisters' fussing got too noisy, it would annoy the girl's mother, who would then "come in swinging" at whoever happened to be nearest. One day, during the mother's lunch hour at home, the older sister was teasing the younger one over the use of a hairbrush. The smaller girl then began to whine loudly. Attempting to keep the peace, the middle sister took the brush out of her bigger sister's hand and was just handing it over to the younger one when their mother came storming in the room! As was common, the woman didn't ask what was happening or who was at fault, she just exploded in anger. Snatching the hairbrush from the innocent girl, the mother began brutally hitting her all over with its handle, until the woman's rage was spent.

About Her Father's Business

That was "the last straw" for that 6 1/2 year old girl *(Eph. 6:4)*. She determined to "run away from home," for just a few days. She was hoping to obtain leverage from the scare, to negotiate "fairer treatment" in the future. So, after the mother went back to work, the middle sister packed an old, battered suitcase and calmly exited the house. To protect her sisters, she did not reveal to them where she intended to go. In fact, her plan was to walk back to the neighbor of their prior residence in the next town. It was an eleven mile trek along the railroad ties. It took the girl until almost dusk to reach the correct household. They were very surprised to see her, but after being refreshed with a sliced apple, the older "lady of the house" told the wandering young girl that her mother had phoned them about an hour earlier.

Fishing around for places her daughter may have gone, the mother had told these people to call, if they spotted the girl. This kind family had no legal right to keep the youngster and had to inform her mother that she had arrived on their doorstep. Hopes dashed and so tired, the girl dreaded having to talk to her mom on the phone. The hollering and threats were even worse than she'd expected. The daughter had not reckoned on how inflamed her mother would be over the embarrassment of having her parental authority challenged. In the end, the girl was given an ultimatum: "Either be ready to be picked up in twenty minutes and receive the worst spanking of your life when I get you home! Or, choose to never come back at all," she sneered, "and I'll give you away to strangers, making certain that you'll never see your sisters again." No words of regretful apology, entreating, or love, just threats of harm! Eyes wild and body trembling, the girl was near frozen in panicked indecision. Yet, she realized that she was more afraid of losing contact with her sisters, than she was of enduring another parental hitting spree. So, when her mother barked for an answer or she'd "just hang up," the girl submissively agreed to be waiting for her mother's car. Everyone in that household had tears in their eyes and worried expressions on their faces, but said not a word. The young girl lifted her unopened suitcase again and quietly stepped out of their door and of their lives. She waited on the street curb, trying to steel her nerves for what lay ahead. But there was no way that child could've prepared herself for the evil about to be unleashed upon her!

After the hate-filled, silent ride home, the girl was told to stand in front of her mother's current, "boyfriend." *(Her sisters had been ordered to remain out of sight, and were fearfully hiding in their shared bedroom.) The guy seethed out his promise that he'd "give her something permanent" to remind the girl that she'd better never humiliate her mother again or "step outside of her rules." Then he asked her which foot had she used to first walk out of the house? After the girl's meek reply, the man jerked that foot up so hard that the child fell backwards on the floor. Before she could even comprehend his intent, he'd grabbed a kitchen knife and plunged the blade deeply into the side of her left foot's arch! Since he had planned to do this before the girl had even arrived home, her mother's "friend" also had a towel ready to wrap around the bleeding foot. Then the man instructed the youngster that when

About Her Father's Business

they stitched up her foot at the hospital, she was to agree with her mother's lie that she had accidentally stepped on a broken coke bottle. If not, he'd "slap her up one side and down the other" when she got back. While being driven to the emergency room, the girl's mother never said a word, just glared at her with suppressed rage. At the hospital, the mother told the young doctor to, "Skip the pain-killer. I'll hold her foot still for you." Then, as the child screamed and twisted in repeated pain, that demented mother's face grinned at her daughter's suffering with glittering, cold eyes.

It was late night when the girl was brought back home with a bandaged foot. She'd only been given a sliced apple since breakfast. Yet now, her mother's wrath unfurled in a vengeance *(Matt. 12:35b)*! The girl endured the worst beating she'd ever experienced in her life. It lasted until, and perhaps even after, the child lost consciousness. The assault was severe enough that the child actually blocked most of its memory from her conscious mind for decades. Instead, she guessed that she must have fainted on the way home from the hospital. For a young child to be so horribly battered by her own mother was just too much for her tender mind to comprehend and accept! Her own brain's mental protectiveness suppressed the shock of it for many years. Its bad memory rushed into clarity, twenty years later, after being triggered by remarks from her older sister. The girl was told that after the beating she got for "running away" and wasn't able to wake up "for so long," her older sister had fearfully thought, "Mom had killed you for sure that time."

It was more than a week before the girl's foot and bruises were healed enough for her to go back to school. At least, the wounds were mended where they could be seen by human eyes. But, after that experience, the daughter never doubted that there was a hidden part inside her mother, which hated her. One that actually enjoyed dishing out pain to her own child. That night's episode severed the natural bonds of loving trust from a daughter's heart towards her mother, which most children enjoy all of their lives. To this day, although that girl *chooses* to love her mother, it is purely an effort of her will and doesn't come naturally.

And, yet...God used that experience to teach that girl to depend and trust in Him alone *(Ps. 40:4)*. She learned that "no company was better than bad company" and, in some cases, loneliness was a far safer risk. Many times, that motto served her well through her teen and young adult years. Unsuccessfully, peers tried to entice her into the drug scene and other unwholesome behaviors.

Also, she determined in her heart to never purposely strike, paddle or cause pain to a child with her bare hands. If discipline was needed, she'd deliver it justly and with the use of some humane object. She didn't want her future children to, instinctively, flinch away from her touch, like she'd done with her own mother. The girl wanted her hands to only connote the message of love and safety to the children around her. Later, God used her developed sense of protectiveness and patience to teach little handicapped pre-school youngsters.

About Her Father's Business

* * * * * * * * * * *

- (F) -

There were a couple of other examples of abuse and betrayal of teenage girls described to my uncle's stepdaughter. But, this last tale is what seemed to finally trigger a valid response in Kate. There was a girl, I expounded, which had a step-dad whose interest in her was far less than noble. Recently, the preteen who had begun "budding," had just arrived home with her mother from buying and wearing her first "training-bra." After lunch, she went outside with her siblings to play tag with some neighborhood friends. Before long, the mother bellowed for her to come back inside the house - NOW! From that tone of voice, the girl knew she was in "big trouble!" She had guessed, though, that it was over the slimy okra she'd left uneaten on her plate. The likely punishment she was expecting was to be "grounded" from playing outside anymore that day. *(Oh dear, ignorance *is* bliss…until reality slaps you in the face!)

Actually, the problem was that her step-father had seen her bending over to dodge a tag and had caught a glimpse of her new, barely-needed bra. He'd gotten jealous and accused her of "flaunting" her chest to the boys! *(Even though, two days earlier, she'd worn that same blouse with just her skin under it, so his claim made no sense to her.) Right in front of the step-dad, her mother demanded the girl to take off every stitch of her clothes. Then the woman, with use of a sapling, viciously "switched" the girl all over her body. When the mother was vented and tired, she told her daughter to go to the step-father. "See if he has anything more to say!" she remarked. The embarrassed and nude girl, dressed only in the lattice design of stings from the sapling, did as she was ordered. Immediately, he unlaced his belt, grabbed the girl by the waist, bent her over his lap, and gave her backside a thorough "tanning."

Instinctively, even while these discipline measures were being meted out, the girl knew that their degree was out of proportion to the supposed misdeed *(Prov. 29:27a)*. Since she was innocent of any intentional wrongdoing, the treatment was totally unfair! Also, she was very humiliated because, through the screen door any kids outside could look in and see she was getting spanked in the "buff." So, although she couldn't help crying, her rebellious thought must have shown as defiance in her eyes to the stepfather.

His evil face contorting, he vowed that he'd teach her a lesson to keep her from ever wanting to play "the hussy" again! With that, he instructed the mother to get behind the girl and hold on to her daughter's arms. He then proceeded to make eleven shallow lines down the girl's tender chest, right to her budding tips. He slowly sliced her skin with a razor-sharp carpet knife, giving her one line for every year of her age. He claimed they were to remind her to heed his warning to never "show herself" to the guys again. If she did, he vowed to cut her off her breasts completely! The girl didn't know if such a thing was possible, she just tried to hardly move or breathe; not wanting to risk causing his hand to cut even more deeply. That girl still bears most of the thin white scars from that day. A few of them widened to almost 1/4", due to the growth of expansion in her young chest, before the wounds were completely healed.

And, yet...God allowed "good to come from evil" *(Gen. 50:20a)* through that encounter, by causing the girl to become an exceptionally modest person. She would often sew on an extra closure, if she felt a neckline was a tad too low. Ones that couldn't be adjusted high enough were filled in by a "modesty scarf" or lace panel. Being self-conscious about her lined chest did make the girl far less inclined to be promiscuous. Other girls, who also hungered for male attention due to a poor father-image in their early lives, often fell into that trap. It became her acquired behavior to always conduct herself "like a lady." Eventually, such attributes led a fine Christian man to fall in love and marry her. To her amazement, under her husband's tender persuasion, she finally began to feel like a lovely and desirable person.

(For research references on this topic, see bottom of Chapters # 7, # 18 and # 23.)

CHAPTER TWENTY-THREE

Freedom and Forgiveness

At this point my uncle's step-daughter argued that, "Those stories can't be true!" Half-crying, Kate said, "No one could remain sane through stuff like that, much less find happiness. I don't believe you know any of those girls!" she accused.

Very quietly I said, "Oh, yes I do, dear, quite well in fact! You see they were all...me." Sensing Kate's yearning to believe in my Lord of mercy and healed wounds, God gave me the courage to offer to "prove" His goodness. To do so, I'd have to show that troubled young woman several of my body's hidden scars. Things like the reminders of cuts and burns on my feet, my crackling ankle bones, floating and easily displaced knee cap, loose-jointed shoulders, grinding hip socket, obvious lines on my chest, and even my stripped-patterned back *(Prov. 20:30)*. All of my life, besides doctors, it was something I'd only been willing to show to John before. In the bathroom where the lights were the brightest, I took my arms out of my long-sleeved dress. But, as I prepared to let Kate view the residual marks, she gawked at the newer scratches on my left arm. In talking about past abuse, I'd totally forgotten about Mom's recent outburst three days earlier. So, briefly, I explained how those fresh lines were received.

Before I was redressed enough to go back to Uncle Bert's living room, his step-daughter was already telling him and her mama about my recent trouble in Arizona. Kate was proclaiming that all the other things I'd said must be true as well. Still, she didn't know how to "get over" her own ordeal to ever trust another man or father-figure. Dear Lord, she was so open and so needy!

In front of her parents, Jesus helped me walk that young woman through the steps to believing in Him *(Ps. 13:5)*. He enabled Kate to understand and discover the true, dependable Father-heart of God *(Ezek. 18:31)*. How kind and patient is our long-suffering Savior. He does not give up on any of us, even after years of rebellion against Him and of resistance to the Holy Spirit's wooing. It's wonderful that He keeps extending His loving mercy, drawing us in small and large ways to be reconciled to Him.

Worriedly, Kate confessed some of her own previous, wanton lifestyle. In reassurance, she was reminded that, in the Bible, there were hardened criminals, all kinds of foolish sinners and even harlots for pay welcomed to drink from the Living Water and quench their thirst for a new chance at life (John 7:37b-38). We don't have to *first* be perfect for Jesus to want us to belong to Him. It is only *in* Christ that we are made truly perfect and righteous (Col. 1:28). In God's sight, through the atonement of His Son, we are already accepted and beloved. Kate was encouraged to let Jesus take every sad or dark experience in her life… and make it clean and whole again. He is able to make everything within you completely beautiful. In the next few minutes, with extra help from Connie,

About Her Father's Business

both Kate <u>and</u> Uncle Bert asked the "true" Jesus into their hearts!

Knowing she still had a battle ahead to get rid of any demonic oppression, Kate needed her life's slate completely cleaned. So, the first big challenge to her faith had to be confronted. In appreciation to God for forgiving her own sins, Kate was told it was now time for her to freely forgive her mother. Yes, it'd hurt badly when Connie did not believe her preteen daughter. Yet, after all, such an accusation was almost unthinkable for a devoted wife to accept about her kind and seemingly decent husband. Back then, Kate's mother had no clue that what her child had confided was valid and true. The two ladies wept in relief over forgiven grudges and renewed bonding. The walls of disbelief and mistrust crumbled in the power of Jesus' love!

Now, though, it was time to inform Kate that the Lord expected her to also choose to forgive her father *(Mark 11:25)*. She needed to put away the lingering resentment and bitterness his memory brought to her mind and stop wallowing in her own destructive self-pity. "But he doesn't deserve it!" she complained. "True, but neither did any of us deserve God's forgiveness for our wrongs," I reminded her. Besides, your father may not even think about the harm he did to you as a youngster. Yet, because you have chosen to keep picking at the wound, it's continued to fester and pollute your life all these years since then. If nothing else, decide to forgive out of obedience and for *your* own mental and emotional health. Why allow the wrong he did in the past, to keep crippling your life now and into the future? Your father does *not* deserve to be "let off the hook," but allow the God of justice to apply the appropriate and due punishment. Kate, you *are* entitled to be freed from the harmful effects of holding onto such hate. It is so true that your "brightest future will always be based on a forgotten past; you can't go forward in life until you let go of your past failures and heartaches." Choose with your *will* to do so and God will help your "feelings" to line up with your mind's choice. Submissively, Connie's daughter did so. Next, I encouraged her to repeatedly yield her bitterness up to Christ every time she felt those old feelings return, to keep choosing to forgive, until the work was completely done inside. One day, there will not even be an inkling of the former hurt and resentment lurking within her heart.

With all the smiles and warmth abounding, it was unpleasant to have to bring up the next big challenge to Kate's new faith. Still sitting on the footstool near her chair, I placed my hand gently on her knee and said, "Part of what's been happening in your life is not only from human interference." You see, in any profound crisis or willful act to hold resentment towards another, it creates an "open door" of opportunity for one or more evil spirits to attach and harass that person *(Gen. 4:7b)*. Those unclean "tormentors" can influence your thinking and actions.

Explaining briefly about the spirit realms, I told Kate that she probably had a spirit of molestation or incest hindering her life. It needed to be denounced and gotten rid of in order for her to fully, ultimately forgive the offender and be freed from those past wounds. Also, due to her years of being on tranquilizers, she

About Her Father's Business

most likely had a drug-related demon increasing her cravings for mental escape. Kate might have the "old folks" buffaloed into thinking she only goes outside to smoke a cigarette, but the smell of marijuana was obviously upon her. Smoking pot, I told her, was not her only non-prescription drug use, either! Kate's mouth dropped open exclaiming, "How did you know?" Some demons, I said, travel in "groups" relating to the beginning sin. It was a logical conclusion, from past spiritual warfare, about what other things might be involved. So, Kate confessed her prolonged dabbling in different types of drugs, often done right under the very noses of her parents and asked for their forgiveness *(Deut. 18:10-11)*. Then we spent a long while fighting to free and deliver Kate from the holds of those and other demonic influences in her life. *(Necromancy in the Old Testament = pharmaceutical, i.e. – "mind-altering drugs.") All three of them were getting an eye-opening, crash course in battling spiritual forces. They were also instructed on how to remain free of demonic tormentors in the future. It is our acknowledged inheritance in Christ, of being covered by His purified blood and under His own authority that empowers Christians to "cast out" or expel demons. The victim must believe in Jesus and be willing to submit to the deliverance process, which is not always an easy or pleasant experience. Born-again, Spirit-filled believers can also be afflicted. They are not "possessed" by an evil spirit, because their spirit and soul belongs only to God. But, until any unclean spirits are denounced, Christians might be hindered or powerfully tempted by oppressive, evil spirits.

By Kate's invitation, we watched her retrieve and "flush away" every type of hidden drug she had stashed around the house. By then, it was very late at night. So, we all enjoy a quick snack of lunch "left-overs," before happily going off to bed!

* * * * * * * * * *

Just before I left the next morning, Uncle Bert joked nervously about how his older sister would not be a "pleased puppy" when she found out that he wasn't a Mormon anymore, but had become a real Christian. Then he asked, "Why do you keep trying to stay in contact with your Mom? After everything she has done, why still be nice to her, make efforts to call, write and occasionally go visit her?" he wondered. "She is such a difficult person to be around for long; why do you even bother," he asked? So, I told my uncle that when I begged God to help me to forgive my Mom of past wrongs, I also requested that He confirm in my heart that the job was fully done. How did He honor that plea? Christ gave me the ability to feel unconditional love and compassion for her. Much of what I currently feel toward Mom is sympathy for her plight, not anger. It saddens me to know she is practically friendless and none of her relatives actually enjoy her company. It hurts knowing she is often lonely, bewildered as to why everyone seems to abandon her. Suppose I didn't keep showing her the "love of Jesus," then who else would *(John 15:13)?* Christ has delivered me from that bondage of evil, but Mom is still trapped in it *(Romans 8:35).* Perhaps someday, she will accept God's boundless love *if* she can see a small reflection of it, through just one person who remains in her life, one who stays in contact no matter how ugly Mom behaves or how hateful the demon within her retaliates. After all, in stressful circumstances, the test of a Christian's walk is not just how we act…but how we react!

(For related information, see references below and those at the end of Chapters # 7 & # 18.)
<u>How to Conduct Spiritual Warfare</u>, by Mary Garrison
<u>The Battle</u>, by Thomas E. Trask & Wayde I. Goodall
<u>Beyond the Darkness (Sexual Abuse)</u>, by Cynthia A. Kubetin & James Mallory, M.D.
<u>They Shall Expell Demons</u>, by Derek Prince
<u>Lord, Is This Warfare?</u>, by Kay Arthur
<u>Forgive and Forget: Putting the Past Behind You</u>, by Lewis B. Smedes
<u>The Three Battlegrounds</u>, by Francis Frangipane
<u>True & False Prophets</u>, by Don Basham
<u>Know What & Why We Believe</u>, by Paul Little
<u>Blessing or Curse</u>, by Derek Prince
<u>Children Today, Warriors Tomorrow</u>, by Dale Rumble

CHAPTER TWENTY-FOUR

A Loving Sister

The next place to visit was a brief one hour drive to Pasadena, just east of Houston. Happily, it was time to go visit Gail and her family. She was the middle of my three half-siblings from our father's second marriage. Adventurous and daring Kaye was the oldest and "outdoorsman" Lee, whose blond hair was always sun-belched, was the youngest. Since Gail's family wouldn't be home from work or school for about five hours, I went to a nearby library's parking lot. Tilting my car's seat back in the reclining position, I just gave Jesus a thankful prayer and allowed myself a long relaxed nap *(Matt. 11:28)*. Operating on low energy again, I knew time alone was needed to let the Holy Spirit sort of "fuel up my tank." This was most certainly a "working" vacation! By this time, I'd given up on the idea that, "Oh the next stop should be an easy one." Some *were* easier, but all of them took their toll.

Gail had two sons, Lester and Garrett, from her own previous, teenage marriage. She had renewed her commitment to the Lord *and* met her current husband at the AA meetings, enjoying her strength over alcohol's lure. His addiction was more about drugs and, upon my arrival I was told that she and her husband were recently separated, due to his return to cocaine. They'd had five good years of marriage, so an uncontested divorce was in process and he no longer resided there.

Gail and her elementary-age boys were doing okay financially and even emotionally, but it was still a sad and yucky situation for all concerned.

That evening we four went out to supper with Lester and Garrett's birth-dad, his new wife, and her young son. All pleasant folks really, but the blood-line and family-ties sure get mighty complicated. The new youngster asked if he could also call me "Aunt Kimmy." Thinking it was as nearly appropriate as the lineage could be figured, I said, "Why not?" Actually, I was *his* new step-dad's *real* son's half-aunt, as I was *their* mother's half-sister. Due to Gail's and my shared father, that sort of made me the new lad's "half-step-aunt." What confusion split-families cause to the identity of each child involved. As we waited for our meal to be brought, I pulled out the Word-picture flash-cards to entertain all three boys *(Prov. 12:22a)*. The grown-ups also did the fun guessing game. I hoped our table wasn't getting overly noisy. If so, the other smiling patrons seemed to be forgiving us.

The next day, while her sons were at school, Gail and I had some quality time to share deeply with each other. She was a cute, pixie-faced lass with a big, warm smile. We had both inherited the darker hair and eyes from our Dad, as well as similar personalities. We conversed about the different, yet disheartening ways both of us had recently "lost" our husbands and shared our hopes and dreams relating to our futures. Then Gail took me on a tour of her workplace and let me see her own, upscale office. It was fun just being sisters and enjoying each other's company! Gail felt enough concern to lovingly reprimand me for still opening myself up to Mom and permitting her to occasionally make me her "victim." My half-sister had gained much inner-strength through AA, so I understood how my own behavior, in dealing with Mom, could appear weak and cowardly. Gail was just worried... and it touched me *(Prov. 16:24).*

Our shared father had died about five years earlier, from a heart attack. It had occurred a few months before John's and my prior visit to Texas. During that earlier vacation, we girls talked warmly about our Dad. Finally, I revealed to Gail how rough some of my childhood and teenage years had been. I really cared about and admired my birth-father and his second family. I always looked forward to the part in any year that it was time to go visit or live with them. It was only their hot Texas humidity that caused me such grief and misery! Gail said that hearing about my "other life" helped solve some mysteries she'd wondered about. "Things like how you'd always emerge from your bedroom fully dressed. You'd never casually sit around in P.J.'s with the rest of the family. Your room was tidy and would get "spiffed-up" on Saturday mornings, before you'd go to stay with your Mom's parents each weekend. *(That's the "agreement" which permitted me to live at my Dad's during the week.)

Now, though, Gail understood my embarrassment about the scars and my habit of not "leaving any messes" as punishment was fast and harsh at my Mom's home for such offenses. My "sis" asked why I hadn't told them sooner about how awful we kids had been treated. But, I'd known that the revelation would've crushed our Dad's feelings. It had been better that he'd never found out. His heart would have been sorely wounded to have learned that, without his type of kind protection all those years, family-life had turned out to be a very scary place for his first set of children.

Mom had made certain that our birth-father retained no custody rights on any of us. It was many years before he had even discovered that she had given away the son of his name-sake to strangers. We two sisters guessed that, had our Dad but known about his first-born son being made available for adoption, he and his second wife would've gladly taken the boy themselves. We knew that Gail's own Mama, Beth, would have loved the boy like her own. But, since I saw no way Dad could help or change things for us, it seemed best to remain silent and hope to escape the lingering weirdness when I became of age. Being a teenager didn't help me to fully reason things out well. By the time I'd met his second family, at age thirteen, I thought it would've been cruel of me to tell Dad about the mess we'd endured. Besides, I felt ashamed and didn't want to become a "taint" in the lives of his wholesome, second family (Ps. 69:19a).

From early-to-mid teens, it was GREAT each time I was allowed to visit or stay with them. It was nice to observe and feel included within a real and "normal" family for part of most years. And, I would not be surprised to someday learn that Beth was the first Christian who ever prayed for Jackie and me. Seeing the love of Christ shown in their family was a good object lesson to recall later. Hoping to model my own, future home-life after their example, I observed the warm, fun-loving interactions between them closely *(Eccl. 2:24)*. Also, after Jackie got married, when I got to stay at Dad's home, it was neat being "the oldest" and very enjoyable to feel connected to the lives of my three loving, younger half-siblings.

Gail shared that it had hurt their feelings, when I went back my "other family." Dad and Beth had offered to convince Mom to allow me to always live in Texas with them. At first, I'd been so excited that maybe it could really happen! The possibility was very tempting, even though, for the first time in my life, I'd had to struggle through unreasonable piles of nightly homework just to retain passable grades. *(This was due to my joining classes' half-way into the year, having not yet learned some of the material to their more advanced curriculum.) Still, getting to remain with my Dad's family made it all worth it! Then, not long afterwards, I seemed to have changed my mind. Back then, my returning to Mom had saddened and confused Gail.

So many wasted years later, I was finally able to explain to her about our strange, unsafe home-life with Mom. As well as, how my smallest half-sister, Rose, (Mom's youngest daughter) had begun pleading with me to "please come back" and help her! She was worried about not being able to keep fending-off the current step-father's molesting touches. Also, Rose never had a reliable sense of discerning when Mom just "wasn't herself." So, without me there to guide and protect her, young Rose was suddenly getting yelled at and slapped a lot. She confessed to experimenting with drugs, just to have to excuse to "crash" at different party-houses, instead of having to return to her own creepy home. Rose just couldn't take anymore of her ugly life and begged that if I didn't return soon, she was going to run away for good! Trying to convince her that being "on the streets" would be even worse became hopeless, as 12 ½-year-old Rose was just too desperate to listen. Honestly, it was tempting to just stay in Texas, but I knew that if Rose was later dealt serious harm, I'd always feel undeserving of any forgiveness.

Back then, Gail had mistakenly believed that I had not really cared enough for my Texas family after all. Later, she felt relieved when it was revealed that I had, indeed, MUCH preferred to live at her home. But, Rose was losing the fight to stay emotionally afloat and, if I did not return soon, she was going under! Having been close to that brink myself, more than once, there was no doubt that Rose needed my help back there in the "snake's pit" *(Ps. 40:2)*. Those final weeks of living with my Dad's family made me feel sad at having to leave all of them, as well as fearful over having to soon bear the awful situation back at Mom's. Those last weeks together, steeling my resolve for what lay ahead, caused me to be more quiet and distant with my Texas clan. Also, becoming a disappointment to *them* made me feel just awful!

Gail remembered Beth trying to help her children feel less disappointed about me leaving them. Commenting how she felt certain that I really didn't want to go back, but for some reason they didn't understand, I seemed to believe that I just *had* to return. Beth was a very discerning lady. Yet, it was over twenty years before she ever knew why this gal declined their wonderful

About Her Father's Business

offer to remain with them. I hadn't loved Rose more; she just *needed* me so much more!

Gail said that after she'd told Beth about our terrible home life, her Mama claimed that, had she and my Dad just have *known*, they would have been willing to take in both Rose *and* me. Within the warmth of my Texas family, we girls would've been given shelter and protection for the rest of our teen years.

CHAPTER TWENTY-FIVE

Poor Life Choices

Oh, how different our desperate lives may have been, had such a kindness really been granted early enough. Jackie, our oldest sister, escaped Mom's clutches at nineteen *(Job 19:20)*. She married a weak, spoiled young man, whose behavior never matured past adolescence. "Babied" by his parents, Jackie had to raise him along with their two children. But, at least, *they* grew up! Rose, searching to replace a father-figure, dated, got pregnant and married a man almost twice her age the day after her 18th birthday. She would have gotten married several weeks sooner, before her condition began to show, but Mom wanted Rose to get an abortion. Because she did not, Mom wouldn't give her underage daughter legal permission to marry. As Rose got nearer to eighteen, Mom would not help us to plan the wedding or contribute more than $50 towards the expenses. Even so, the rented gown looked pretty on Rose and the other decorations we pulled together made the Rec.-Room very festive! Jackie was the Matron-of-Honor, her small daughter was the Flower Girl and I was her only Bridesmaid. Mom did, at least, attend.

Soon afterwards, though, Mom did finally convince Rose to abort her baby. It was something from which the young bride never recovered. Perhaps, if Rose would have been blessed with a more supportive set of parents, she might not have latched onto the first grown man who flattered her with his ignoble attentions. Also, if Mom had been less mean and sarcastic, Rose probably would have heeded our "warnings" to not keep dating that man. It was no surprise to us that he turned out to be a vulgar bum, who rarely ever worked. Yet, lack of paid bills or decent food did not stop him from making dear, young Rose pregnant four more times, in quick succession.

Each birth further depleted her health and, in such a few years, caused Rose to be susceptible to, and then develop the same lymph-cancer that had killed her birth-father. Sick, weary, and slowly dying, Rose refused anymore radiation treatments. Yet, being the only worker bringing home money to feed her children, Rose continued at her waitress job. On her way home from a night-shift, blond, blue-eyed Rose was struck and killed by a drunk driver. Thankfully, only two weeks earlier, knowing her death from cancer was near, Rose had decided to give her heart to Jesus! Yet, my cute "baby sister" had enjoyed so little happiness in her short, hard life. *(I feel extremely, richly blessed in comparison, even considering my own trials and heartaches along the way.) After Rose was gone and her children were not being well tended, the Lord provided her husbands' two, older, middle-aged sisters to finish rearing and nurturing her four small children. The aunts divided up Rose's two boys and two girls, ages 2, 4, 6, and 8. The children had to only live a few blocks apart and were able to attend the same schools. Life was not easy for them, but *they* became the real "survivors"!

About Her Father's Business

Also, I wondered if I had been able to remain with my Texas family, how different would my own earlier life have been? Eager to be away from Mom's hatefulness, I gladly left her home early. Yet, desiring a life companion, I married in my late teens. He was a supervisor from work and ten years my senior. I thought he'd provide safety and a secure environment to begin to rear a family of our own. But, I was still too naive to be a good judge of character. A non-drinker by choice, I noticed that he drank a lot of beer. Yet, it wasn't straight whiskey sipped out of the bottle like my Grandpa indulged in, or strong mixed drinks that caused my parents to sometimes stumble around drunk. So, I did not realize, back then, that a person who only drinks beer could still be an alcoholic *(Ob. 16b)*. Less than a month after the wedding, I was pregnant. But, after learning the news, I did *not* tell anyone. Why? The fact was that a second DUI, since our marriage, had caused a federal warrant to surface for the arrest of my new groom! He'd just been jailed and transported back to the state of his crime. He was being sent to prison on a seven-year sentence, for jumping bail on the charge of manslaughter. He had shot his best friend, while both were in a drug-induced argument. It had occurred two years before we'd met, so he thought he was safe.

Driving to the Mid-West to stay with my brand new father-in-law, we both worked hard at dealing with attorneys to lessen the charges, because his only son had "been clean" and out of trouble since the incident. Within a couple of days, though, my father-in-law knew that I must be pregnant. Morning sickness is rather hard to hide, especially when one is sick most of the day! After first being hand-body-searched by a guard for hidden weapons or drugs, I visited his son and told him about our baby. To my surprise and horror, he pointedly told me "to get rid of it," as he needed me to use any money earned to get him out of jail...not to look after a baby.

As expected, my mother and then several others argued with me to end the pregnancy too. Yet, I was determined to keep safe the life of my unborn baby *(Jer. 2:34a)*! Lastly, even my kindly father-in-law agreed that I should end the life of his first grandchild. But, his vote was wrought from worry about my present safety, not just the convenience to my future. Only he could see how rapidly my health was deteriorating and how frequently I was experiencing abdominal pains. He did not know about my slight bleeding and fever, though.

A few days later, his son's first wife called. He'd told me he'd been married before, but failed to inform me that he also had two children. Nor that he'd never bothered to complete the divorce's legal proceedings *before* deserting all of them when he jumped bail. When the attorney heard those facts, his advice to me was to go back home and get an annulment before the courts find out this guy is also a bigamist, and end that pregnancy! So, with a defeated spirit, I faltered in my resolve. That Friday, I allowed my father-in-law to make the consultation appointment at the clinic, for the following Monday. Of all the forgiving Jesus had me do, forgiving my own self for even seriously considering the option of aborting my own baby has

About Her Father's Business

been the most difficult. Although, I know God forgives and can renew all things *(Ex. 34:6-7a)*, I feel sorry for the girls who actually get pressured into going ahead with such a decision.

Yet, God's mercy intervened on my behalf, because by 3 a.m. on Saturday, awful pains and copious bleeding got so bad that my father-in-law rushed me to the Emergency Room. My body was *trying* to miscarry. But, my scared cervix would not dilate my deformed womb effectively enough for the contractions to dispel my unborn baby. The doctors recognized the sickly odor of decayed tissue and took me right into surgery. It was found that my baby's life had ceased almost two weeks before and the tiny body and placenta were decomposing within me. The walls of my uterus were inflamed and filled with a horrid-smelling mucous. No wonder I'd felt so sickly!

Months later, when chemotherapy alone could not abate the abnormal cells, it would take surgery to remove most of my repeatedly infected fallopian tubes. Several weeks after that, I finally regained full health. Yet, by then I had been rendered 85-90% medically sterile. "Barren" ...is such an utterly lifeless word and an ugly label to endure the rest of one's life *(Gen. 30:1)*.

The doctor theorized that the infection began from abnormal cells growing around my old uterine scars, as well as to the chemical changes in my body associated with pregnancy. Thus, both together, had caused the death of my unborn child. But, since my body was unable to release my dead, unnamed child, my own life had been threatened as well. Never even knowing the gender of my baby, I left two days later and soon reacquired my maiden name. But, I was certainly a "maiden" no more. Instead, I was a sadly experienced ex-bride, and an "almost Mommie." One which felt betrayed and who had no one with which to share her grief, not over the loss of her baby, or the loss of her dreams of a good marriage.

As an example, when I first got back into town, I'd stopped at Mom's and her fifth husband's place, to let them know I'd made it back safely. Mom was just leaving for a birthday party, so thus hustled me out the door with her remarking that, "I needed to be around people and cheer up." That was correct; her choice of parties was *not*! Instead, it turned out to be a belated baby shower for the newborn son of her friend's daughter. As we got in the door Mom unthinkingly (or was it "Mother") scooped up the tiny baby and plopped him in my arms, gushing on about how much I always loved babies. Then, she turned to deliver her party food to the kitchen. At first rigid, I then sunk into a nearby chair and, as silent tears coursed down my face, I delicately studied all of the miniature details of that infant's face and hands. In a few minutes, the baby's unwed mother came into the room. She looked at me oddly, then without speaking, she firmly took her infant out of my arms. Rising, I walked out the door to my car and drove home alone.

Even though Mom called later, to apologize for "being such a dunce," I would never feel open to sharing the pain of my loss with her. Since both of my sisters were living out-of-state, I knew of no one else to lean on during that time either. But, I did wonder if

About Her Father's Business

unborn babies got to go to heaven. The loss caused me to be more determined than ever to find a merciful God on which to believe. Even though it would still take many years, He was faithful to keep calling out to this very discouraged sheep!

After Lester and Garrett arrived home from school, we drove to Houston to share dinner with the rest of my "Texas clan!" So I enjoyed visiting with Beth, my dear step-mother, as well as seeing and hugging on pretty, light-haired Kaye, my other half-sister. Young Lee wasn't in town, but knew which night I was expected to be at his Mama's place. So, he called to say "howdy" and chat with me for awhile. Catching up on each other's lives, via phone or over supper, was a real treat. Then after the meal, the boys and I talked their Mom, their grandmother and their other aunt into doing a silly, but fun "ditty" called "My Aunt Came Back" *(Gal. 2:9b)*. They were good sports to join us in "clowning around" and the photos of those antics are priceless!

CHAPTER TWENTY-SIX

Of Worthy Stature

The next morning, I drove a couple of hours north of Houston, to visit John's younger Christian brother, Jim, and his family of beautiful, little girls. It was satisfying to be in their company and to look at Jim's already developed photos of John's Memorial Service. Unlike in Denver, here we got to enjoy sharing "below the surface" about God, without the strain of having their other non-believing family members around.

Jim and his wife are relatively young Christians, not long "freed" from the clutches of The Way International cult. So, they asked some questions that launched off more instructions and discussions. They inquired, "Should I mention Christ to my folks in letters?" and "I'm so new at this; what if I say something wrong?" Also, "How can it be that we feel closer to and safer with our Christian-family than with our blood-families?" and "Will things get easier?"

So, we began by talking about Galatians 3:26 and how all Christians are God's children, of which He is very proud. A lifelong Christian is not one bit more God's child than is a newborn in the Lord. Peter, Paul, and all the early Believers are of the "family of God" and so are we. The young-in-Christ are as much a beloved child of God, as is the more mature and long-serving Christian. All of our names are in the same "family register," the Book of Life! Still many Christians remain stunted in their spiritual walk.

They exist in Christ, but they do not choose to willfully "grow up unto Him in all things" (Eph 4:15). We ought not to remain content as a green blade, but mature into the blossom stage, then onward to the nourishing fruit stage to be enjoyed by and used for others as well. If we want to ripen in grace, we need to live near to Jesus. Don't feel inadequate because you are still young "babes in Christ" (I Cor. 3:1), I told them, for you have much to count as your own and be grateful for.

In some things you are equal to the greatest and most full grown Christians that ever lived! You are as much bought with the blood of Jesus as they are. You are as much an adopted child of God as any other of His Believers. You are completely justified, because it does not come in degrees, according to a saints' spiritual maturity or growth. Only in our individual sanctification do we need to progress "from glory to glory." Your true faith, however feeble, has given you the right to be completely made clean. Your equal claim to the Lord's mercies lies not in *your* growth or merit, but in the precious New Covenant itself.

Jim and his wife wanted to know, "What strengthens faith, so we won't be afraid of telling others about Jesus...or of failing Him ourselves?" We need, I informed them, to regularly "feed" our spirits just like we must nourish our physical bodies. Listen to Christian songs of praises and exhortation, read the Bible and pray often as well as, lean more on deeper Truths by paying attention to valid sermons and absorb wise instruction from other reliable Believers. Continually put forth the effort to do our part in "growing our faith." Yet, expect the Lord to aid us in

About Her Father's Business

"maturing." He usually allows it to happen in a slow, progressive manner. But, sometimes, God permits an encounter to occur in our lives, whose end result causes a permanent "leap of faith" within us. "As an example, you know I'd had a massive, tumor surgery four years ago. Well, let me explain the unexpected spiritual gain that occurred through it."

For many years, a concern of mine I'd voiced was that my faith might not be strong enough. That if I came under a trial of physical torture, which would cease if I denied Christ, would I eventually denounce my Lord, in order to acquire mercy from the pain? Even though God would know, in my heart, I fully believed in my Savior? Would I remain steadfast enough to bravely endure the inflicted evil *without* dishonoring my King *(Matt. 10:33)?* Back then, I didn't know that Satan and his unclean spirits can't read our minds. But, they can *hear* our words and observe our behavior in different situations; which gives them very accurate "clues" about our fears and weaknesses. Since then, I've learned to rarely verbalize aloud, even while praying alone, any information I don't want the enemy to have a chance to use against me later.

Well, the needed surgery was tedious and taking much longer than had been expected. Suddenly, my body began lapsing into tremors indicative of toxic shock! Whether its cause was from the combination of medicines or of their added duration in my system, the doctors were never decisively sure. But, they hurriedly closed the gaping wound, uncertain if all of the tumor cells had been fully removed.* It became essential that they get my body warmed and my mind awakened to help them fight for my survival. Forcing a person to wake up immediately after surgery was done only in a life-threatening crisis. They knew I'd have a slightly better chance to survive the toxic effects *if* I was made aware of the current, real danger. It was a calculated risk, which proved to be a wise decision. As my foggy, medicated brain cleared, I understood the alarming situation. Spasms began to rage through my torso. I remember the pain of harsh shaking, jerking muscles and wondering if the fresh incision would burst wide open!

Unable yet to verbalize, I began to silently pray for God's help. Immediately, with vision through "spiritual eyes," I saw three small, ugly demons mocking and harassing me around the gurney. One would punch me in the abdomen, the other would pull the warmed blanket off of my cold, shaking body, and another would yank on great wads of my hair; forcing my head to jerk backwards It was easy to see that the medical staff working to save me, were unaware of those unclean spirits perched along my body. They taunted me that *if* I said that Jesus was NOT my Lord, then they would stop tormenting me. Even if this just turned out to be a drug-induced hallucination, I was not taking any chances! Therefore, I decided to scripturally resist and stand against these demons that were inflicting so much pain. They wanted me to become discouraged and just let myself die. Yet, expecting that I would soon pass from this life anyway, I was not going to begin eternity having to feel ashamed before my Master. The issue in my mind became loyalty to Him…over life for me!

Before long, I was exhausted and the doctors could not stabilize my vital signs. My skin had taken on an ashen, grayish pallor and the medical team did not expect me to live. Thus, after the staff had done all that they could, they wheeled me into a private room....and away from the other post-op patients. John, so worried that my surgery had now taken three more hours than had been estimated, saw me on the gurney being moved out of ICU and into room that wasn't mine. He rushed over, very alarmed at my strange coloring, and the nurse tried to keep John from going into the room with me. But, then she relented, deciding to let him stay with me thinking, "Perhaps his voice might still encourage her to fight through this reaction." Now, though my body was raked with increasing waves of intense convulsions. John was told that within the next 20-minutes, I'd "pull through" or he would be saying his "good-byes."

While the staff was transferring me onto the hospital bed, John phoned one of our co-pastors to plead for our church family to pray for me... right NOW! Perplexingly mute, yet clear-minded, I knew that John was praying and crying at my bedside. Whenever one of the massive spasms began, he'd lean over my form and wrap his long arms around me, to help protect my head and new incision from injury. It wounded *him* deeply to watch me in such misery and knowing that the medical staff dared NOT give me any thing for the seizure-like contractions. Able to nod "yes/no," allowed John to know when I needed more chips of crushed ice to relieve my thirst. He reassured me that many of the church folks were praying for me. Yet, I was unable to explain to him about the satanic assault.

Fifteen minutes went by, and I began to detect a lessening in the force and frequency of the spasms. Opening my physical eyes, yet "seeing" with my spiritual ones, I realized that I was in the same hospital bed…yet, it was encircled within a ring of soft-glowing light. Its source was gently beaming down on me from above. Just at the edge of the circle were large, strong angels, standing side-by-side in battle stance. Looking beyond their tall shoulders, I saw those three demons angrily glaring over at me, as they dodged sword points and spit out vulgar insults at God's army. Without a shadow of doubt, I *knew* that the barrier of angels were assigned to guard and defend me, as a result of the "hedge of protection" set in place by the urgent prayers of fellow Christians *(Job 1:10a)*.

Twenty…thirty…forty minutes went by! Not only was I still alive, but my normal skin color was returning. I was even able to doze-off for a few precious minutes! Only twice more did harsh convulsions rake my body. Each time I saw it coming because one of the angels had lost strength and had to kneel in weakness. Then, a demon would leap over that lower spot in their ranks, land hard on my raw wound, before hurriedly scampering out of reach of other nearby swords. It dawned upon me that a few Believers had stopped praying for me, causing the "hedge" to develop weak spots. Therefore, feeling encouraged now, I renewed my own prayers to help fortify the angels with increased power. Gratefully, the demons soon departed and I was able to rest and a kindly nurse checked my vital signs,

About Her Father's Business

inspected my incision, and washed the sweat of fear from my body. To everyone's amazement, the crisis was over and I'd survived! Even in my exhaustion, and drifting off to sleep, I felt so *pleased* knowing that I'd **not** cowardly denounced my Jesus, just to save myself *(Matt. 10:28)*. Never again would that issue concern me!

It was about 90-minutes later, before I was finally able to verbalize to John what had actually been taking place in the spiritual realm. We rejoiced together and he told a few others of the encounter, so they could praise and glorify Jesus also! Up until then, I'd thought of myself as spiritually inferior to John. His faith was always so steadfast and his strength in Christ sure. When we had married, I was relatively young-in-the Lord and had so admired John's unflinching shoulder-to-the-grindstone "walk." He did much to motivate me to mature onto the "meatier" things of the gospel. But, after that very personal and God-sent victory, I knew that my faith was solid in its own right. I continued to value all of John's prayers and insights, but thereafter I stopped leaning on *his* faith and worked at growing and exercising my own more. *(Little did I know then how valuable those lessons would later be to me as John's widow.) The "toxic shock" encounter was my "leap of faith." It caused an increase of confidence in my own prayers, but the sense of being "worthy in God's eyes," on my own merit, was a gift more precious than life!

"Jim," I continued, "It is hard to see any reason, in ourselves, why the good Lord should take pleasure in us...but He does! God actually rejoices over us (Jer. 32:41). No where in scripture does it state that God the Father delights in snow-capped mountains, the angels, or the multitude of sparkling stars. But, it *does* say that He delights in us, even with singing (Zeph. 3:17). It says in Ephesians 1:6, the term 'acceptance' in the Greek means 'objects of divine delight.' We are accepted even when we don't particularly <u>feel</u> spiritually minded. Why? Because our acceptance rests in Christ, who never changes, is ever loved by God, and is without spot or wrinkle."

Jim wondered if their life, now that they were "real" Christians, would become smoother and happier. So, I explained that, yes, there will be a much expanded sense of "holy joy" in their lives, but that all of God's people still have to endure trials (Acts 14:22). We are reminded that it was never designed by the Master to be His people's "fairy-godfather." Certain tribulations and challenges are allotted to each one of us. Christ Jesus has ordained their season, their place, their intensity, and their duration for the ultimate and best effect they will have upon us. None who are partakers of God's mercy, will completely escape all fires of affliction. But, God's children have the comfort of His presence being supportively near to always strengthen us. The Lord's example of victory teaches us how to overcome, even with praises to His name! When we reach Glory, it will more than make amends for the hard times we had to endure. A quote by Randy Acorn compares a home-baked cake to God's ways. As I recall, he remarked that God "takes all the undesirable stresses in our lives, mixes them together, puts them under the heat of crisis, and produces a perfect result."

About Her Father's Business

Untried faith may be true, but it is sure to remain small without trials. Stubbornly, faith always grows best when things are against her (I Pet. 1:6-7). Faith is more precious to us *after* it has been proven triumphant in times of adversity. Also, its strength increases the more regularly it is exercised. Rough seas may still be ahead, but our Father is at the helm and He will never let you, me, or any of His children drown! So, yes, it is very normal to feel more closely bonded to like-minded Believers in Jesus, than to even most of our non-Christian family members. And, yes again, go ahead and add a few words about Jesus in each of your letters home to your folks. Remember, our job is to take the gospel that never changes, to a world that will never stay the same. Who knows, if nothing else, (hee-hee) maybe it will help to lessen their complaints about your not writing them often enough!

(There **were a few abnormal cells left in the tumor's scar tissue. Such resulted in a much larger tumor, about five years later. Extensive surgery and oral chemotherapy restored my health.)*

CHAPTER TWENTY-SEVEN

Tidbits About Life

The next morning, after leaving their home under a "covering of prayer," I drove about 45 minutes further north to visit my Mormon grandmother in a nursing home. Arrangements had been made for Rose's youngest three children to join me there to visit their great-grandmother. Their older, traditionally-churched aunts, who had been raising these teens, kindly drove them down south to help me in this "Grandparents Day" surprise!

While in Arizona, I'd expressed a desire of mine to Mom about this event. I was yearning that, after seeing Grandma for a couple of hours, the aunts would "gift" me a private visit with my nieces and nephew. I had not seen them for years and I wanted to *really* find out how they were doing. Yet, Mom hated to be left out of anything and, without telling me, had stubbornly shown up at the same time to "horn in" on the gathering as well. Unaware that my surprise was already planned, Uncle Bert agreed to Mom's request to drive her to the nursing home to visit their mother. Thus, he and Connie were also there enlarging the group. Accepting the reality of the situation, I graciously conceded that my hoped-for time alone with Roses' children was *not* going to happen. Who knows? Perhaps Mom was afraid now to leave me alone with any more of her Mormon or non-committed family members.

Anyway, my alert Grandma now had three generations of family coming to see her all at the same time. Though a bit disappointed at how large the group had become, I also knew that my elderly grandmother would be the applauded "talk of the nursing home" for weeks! And, that thought did give me a big tickle.

Actually, we all had a very pleasant time together. Intermixed with looking at the old family photos I'd brought of Rose for my nieces and nephew to see, they and Grandma also asked questions about John's death and our life together while viewing his photos. Then, to lighten the mood, we began "cutting up" over the Word-picture Flash cards. Soon everyone added some humorous story, about one incident or another, in our jointly-mixed family backgrounds. After a lunch was brought in of "fast-food," we acted out my "silly ditty" and then the nieces "hammed it up" with a short mime skit that was a huge success with the older folks! Now that people were feeling more comfortable with each other, a number of interesting questions surfaced.

Worriedly, my grandmother wondered aloud, "Wouldn't John be angered that you let him be burned?" and "How awful that strangers are now walking around with some parts of your dead husband in them." So, for her benefit, came the explanation of the Bible's promise of resurrected, glorified, bodies *(Phil. 3:21)* as well as how organ donations occur and the benefits of new vision for two people, due to John's corneas, and others whose health were restored or life even saved because of receiving his strong heart, pure kidneys, and revitalizing bone marrow. Also, a volume of helpful medical research was done on John's damaged

About Her Father's Business

tissue, because he'd been in such perfect health and without any food or drug addictions. The doctor said it was very rare, indeed, to have such a prime candidate for receptive organ donations. It made me wonder if that was why God had so convicted John's heart, for so many years, to be very strict about what he ate or drank. After all, the Master knew people would be in need of that son's healthier tissue, when it was time to bring John home.

The hospital, I told them, wasn't ready to release John's body to the funeral home within the usual couple of hours. Instead, the Director received word about 10:30 that night that they could now pick up John's remains. There had just been so much "harvesting" to do that it had taken the hospital staff a lengthy time to finish their tasks. Afterwards, it also took a long time to "reconstruct" John's form back to its previous size, so that it would fit his clothes I had brought to the funeral home.

Although I didn't tell Grandma this, so much of John's lower section had been "donated" to others, that neither the hospital nor funeral home attempted to "repair" that part. That's why I insisted that John's casket have a securely attached drape folded down over the bottom half. It needed to entirely cover John's lower section in order to spare others, especially his parents, from any further shock *(James 5:11b)*. I did not wish them to notice that, after John's belt... his pants and their legs were completely empty.

Rhonda, my youngest niece, asked my opinion about teens and dating. The thirteen-year-old probably got more information than she wanted, poor lass! But,

I sensed more that her older siblings needed to hear how John and I courted and what the Bible said on the topic.

Grandma had experienced a long and troubling marriage to Grandpa. He had died about twenty years ago, when his liver gave out due to prolonged alcoholism. Therefore, she listened intently when one of the older aunts asked, "What made your and John's marriage so happy?" What followed was a brief conversation about how any married couple would fare if they made Jesus their focus and truly devoted their hearts to continually serve Him better. Their love of that very Savior, poured out as the oil of Gilead, is what beautifully coats each individual marriage and that couple's joined lives together. God pays heed to those whose hearts yearn to please Him (Psalm 33:18). Perhaps no figure of speech represents the Almighty King in more tender, gracious light than when He is spoken of as willingly "stooping" from His throne to identify with the problems and burdens of mankind. He became as one of us, to help all of us! The Lord that John and I honored in our marriage, is the same One who'd even bend His ear from highest glory, to put it close to the whispering, repentant lips of a dying sinner.

Raymond, my high school sophomore nephew asked, "How do we know which classes to take to best prepare us for the jobs and careers ahead; does God even care for those kinds of details?" I told him, "Yes, He sure does!" The Father heart of God longs for His children's good. When we are fretful or weep, God is very aware of it and has pity for our

About Her Father's Business

pain and our confusion (Psalm 103:13). Jesus does not just sit uncaringly "on high" without any concern or compassion for our decisions and worries here below (II Chronicles 16:9). We must learn to pray, then listen to His promptings, direction, and peace in any needed situations. God knows what best will satisfy you in your future, so trust Him with it!

The older aunts had faithfully taken all four children to a fundamental church over the years. This included the oldest boy, who at eighteen, was unable to join us since he'd married six months earlier and was now living in Mississippi. So, I knew that my nieces and nephews had been exposed to the gospel. Yet, there didn't seem to be a deep knowledge or commitment showing. Except, that is, in the oldest girl: 16 ½-year-old Rene.

CHAPTER TWENTY-EIGHT

Childlike Faith

Rene got an early start trying to learn about Jesus and I well remember the story of her conversion. It was after the funeral of their mother, when the Rene was only six. My youngest half-sister, Rose had begun walking her children to a nearby Baptist church, as she knew the cancer would take her life fairly soon. She wanted to "get her life in order" and try being a good example to her children. She'd not been a strong Mormon for years and had been the most receptive of my kinfolk to let me share about the "true" Jesus.

Having recently moved to a new area, she decided to go to a local, non-Mormon church to see what they preached. Soon, she had invited the pastor of that church over to ask him some deep questions. The Lord's Spirit moved to satisfy Rose's longing heart. Before that pastor left, he had helped lead her to the one true God and to ask Jesus to save her. Never being a diligent letter writer, Rose was working on a note to me when she'd gotten interrupted. It was still unfinished when the fatal car accident happened two weeks later. In that letter, Rose had written that she wanted her missionary sister to know that she wasn't wearing the dresses I had sewn for her to the Mormon church anymore. No, she'd found "a real church" nearby and... That was all she had put down on paper. But, by the time I'd been sent a copy of the handwritten letter, I'd already known the best "good news" she was about to tell me!

As, then, stateside missionaries, John and I didn't have the extra money to fly to Rose's funeral. Also, we first thought it would be a Mormon-conducted service. So, the night we learned of her death, we told her husband's family that we would not be able to attend. Yet, the next day, Rose's husband called to inform us that she had recently left the L.D.S. church and had indeed been saved. I so hoped it was true! Then, I was more eager to go, but we still didn't have the money. The following day, Philip Z., a brother-in-Christ, offered to loan us the extra funds needed *(Ps. 41:1).* Yet, by then, I could not get a seat on any plane, which made the necessary connections, for me to arrive at the funeral in time. Instead, I got the name of the Baptist church that Rose had newly been attending and called the day after her burial. The pastor confirmed that my blonde half-sister would, indeed, wear a crown of the King on her pretty head!

He was also the one who related the precious story of how my six-year-old niece, Rene, had approached him after her mother's funeral service. She had asked him these few questions: "Pastor, my Mommie isn't coming home to be with us anymore, is she?...That mean ole man squished her dead, didn't he?... "Is my Mama up in heaven with her new friend, Jesus?...Well, Pastor, would you int'duce me to my Mommy's Friend, too?...Then, someday, I could go to heaven and see her, huh?" So, with childlike faith, Rene trusted in her own mother's example. The pastor was given the privilege of explaining, then escorting, that small, innocent lamb into the Kingdom of Light.

About Her Father's Business

So now, nearing 17-years-old, Rene assuredly proclaimed, "I know that your John and my Mom will be together. I'm so glad too, that you were able to get a headstone for your husband." That sweet comment was from Rene recalling how sad her brothers had felt (Rhonda was only two) over the cheap "name-plate" their father had bought for their Mama's gravesite, after that fatal Easter weekend. John and I knew the children were planning to go back to visit Rose's burial place on Mother's Day. Also, we understood how awful her children felt that only their mother's grave didn't have a nice headstone. Therefore, John and I felt prompted by God to make a hard sacrifice. To bring comfort to Rose's small children, we decide to pay for a modest headstone and have it put in place.

Where did the funds come from? Well, in Colorado, we had our wedding rings custom-made by a jeweler and brother-in-the-Lord. Each was a chevron design with a 1/4 carat diamond at its base. John's had a cross sticking up above the small diamond and my engagement ring had a larger cross with a 2-carat diamond at its base. The larger stone didn't cost us anything, as it had been a gift to me from Rose's birth-father. Originally, it had been in his gold tie-tack. He had willed it to me at his death because, after forgiving him, he said our friendship had been the "jewel" of his latter years. More than ten years later, John had allowed me to use the large diamond in my wedding set. To utilize the entire memento, I had the tie-tack reset with John's own birthstone.

But, now the grandchildren of that deceased step-father were in need. *(Rose had been his only child.) So, John and I had a local jeweler remove all three diamonds from our wedding set, melt down our fancy gold bands and reform them into wide, simple, matching ones; without any stones. The jeweler kept our two smaller diamonds, as payment for his work, and then gave us a fair price for the perfect, 2-carat one. We used that money to pay for my Rose's engraved headstone. Also, it gave me a chance to appropriately pass onto Rose's children her own father's legacy. I still admire John for agreeing and helping me to "gift" that special blessing. After all these years, Rene might have been remembering the joy and pride that she felt when they arrived at their Mama's gravesite and found her new, inscribed headstone on that Mother's Day long ago.

We talked about other general things again, and then the older of the aunts tasked, "Do people have to belong to just one church to please God?" No, I reassured her, there are several Bible-believing, God-honoring churches in which one may enjoy fellowship. Yet, often within, many people spend too much time, energy and tempers fussing and fuming over minor doctrinal differences, things not even pertaining to one's salvation (Titus 3:9). Our days would be far better spent in doing good and encouraging others than in disputing over matters that are of no "major" gospel importance. Sadly, there are some church people who have suffered from petty, in-house wars over absurd points and foolish unimportant questions. Often, when the "smoke" cleared neither party was wiser or had been won over to the other's rigid opinion. Little valuable knowledge had been exchanged and the

About Her Father's Business

episode certainly did *not* promote an increase in love between the opposing sides. We should avoid, or at least not overly focus upon, things where Scripture is silent or vague. If more saints would strive harder to be peacemakers, instead of trying to hammer their point of view into others, those in "the world" might be *far* more attracted to loving the gospel Jesus.

Before departing from the nursing home, I was able to give a few personal and semi-valuable items of mine to Rose's children. For, Rose, I wanted them to have a heritage from their mother's side of the family. A few of the things had been passed on down to me from women relatives of prior generations. The older aunts will keep safe those items, until each child marries or graduates. Except for a few girlhood photos of their Mama, those material things were all I had to give them of Rose's childhood, Hopefully, the legacy-in-the-Lord will one day be what each of them values most from their Mama …and me *(Luke 4:18-19)*!

CHAPTER TWENTY-NINE

A Vow Challenged

Leaving Grandma's nursing home close to four in the afternoon, I drove to a motel on the Arkansas-Texas border and spent the night. The next mid-day, I arrived at the home of another couple John knew when he had worked in Gunnison, Colorado. Back then, John had encouraged the "fence-sitting" husband and his sweet, but unsaved wife, to get serious with God. But, in the years since, Matthew had further backslidden and cultivated a hardened heart. After looking at John's photos and awards with their two young sons present, Matthew whined, "Why does a good guy like John have to be taken?" and "Why do nice people have to suffer loss?" So, I gave him all the possible formerly stated reasons that I felt peace about it. Also, I reminded him that if only "bad" people died young, then they'd have lost needed time and opportunities to mend their ways and bend their knee in submission to Jesus *(Rom. 14:11)*. God may well give some of those folks more years to live, as He waits patiently to have them respond to His wooing. The Lord Jesus does not desire that anyone would be cast into hell. We Christians have no right to complain about what God permits to pass our way, because we believe all of it will ultimately turn out for our best. There are some hidden strengths within us that we'd never discover on our own, but which show up in times of trouble. Sad afflictions are often the backdrops that God uses to let shine the jewels of His children's graces. How can we know the depth of our faith, unless it is tested? The "Lord of the army" rarely trains His valued soldiers in tents of luxury. Instead, our Master 'sergeant' must sometimes put us through hard work, so that we can grow stronger and be able to endure future difficult tasks... with relative ease. God is not being unkind or "contending against" us *(Job 10:2a)*. No, Jesus is only allowing life's harsher experiences teach us to deepen our trust and devotion towards Him.

At that point, Matthew voiced a frequent complaint and excuse remarking that, "Most people who say they are Christians are just phony hypocrites!" I agreed that <u>too</u> often such can be true. But, I also, convinced Matthew to concede that, "Yes, there probably are *more* sincere and godly believers in churches as well." Then I reminded him that the two types will often dwell together for a season *(Matt. 13:25, 30)*. But, under adversity, a hypocrite's so called "devotion to Jesus" will dry up and wither away. It is spongy and hollow like the marshy rush plant that needs constant and easy watering *(Job 8:11)*. Their faith is like a desert's shallow-rooted tumbleweed that gets blown away in the first windy storm. It then aimlessly rolls around, until it's shattered to bits by the impact of a hard and real trial. But, one who really loves and chooses to remain faithful to the Lord will not lose their integrity during a crisis. They are not focused on, dependant upon or seeking after "the world's" favor. Faithful servants of the Most High conduct their lives, in church and out of it, striving to be progressively conformed to His image. We are all prone to be a tad grumpy, now and then, but

About Her Father's Business

honesty and kindness should be increasingly displayed within our conduct.

By then, Matthew was softening towards the possibility that some people truly do live a noble, Christ-honoring life. Yet, still he resisted, stubbornly challenging, "Except for pastors, who get paid to know such things, I've never heard of a Christian who was able to repeat the books of the Bible. I swore, years ago, that I'd fully come back to Jesus, *if* He'd show me even one church person who cared enough to know His Word... that they'd take the trouble to learn it's books." he boasted. With a delighted chortle, I told Matthew to prepare to get *re*acquainted with his Maker! Our God sent fire from heaven, to prove His power at the challenge given on Mt. Carmel, so his brash "dare" was an easy feat, indeed, for our mighty Lord!

I explained to Matthew and his family that over two years ago, simply to please John, *this* gal had learned the names-in-order of the books of the Bible. But, even after she'd memorized them for her husband, God kept her practicing them twice a week during her morning devotions. Until He revealed it to me right now, I did not understand why the Lord would not let me rest, from the urgency to keep refreshing my memory of them all this time! "Matthew, God Almighty began answering your bold challenge soon after you'd made it. But, it has taken all this time, combining these connecting events, to bring this one vessel to you" *(Prov. 15:26b)*!

"Now remember, you *promised* in front of your wife and sons, to wholeheartedly come back to God if a 'non-paid' Christian would recite the books of the Bible to you. So, I'm praying you are a man of your word, because God is about to cancel out your last remaining excuse for not serving Him!" At that, I began... "There's 39 books in the Old Testament, each one's a special part. So, I learned this rhyme and it took no time, till I knew them all by heart...those 39 books by heart. Genesis, Exodus, Leviticus, Numbers, Deuteronomy... Joshua, Judges, Ruth, 1st Samuel, 2nd Samuel. First & 2nd Kings, 1st & 2nd Chronicles... Ezra, Nehemiah, Esther, Job, Psalms, Proverbs, Ecclesiastes. Song of Solomon, Isaiah, Jeremiah... Lamentations, Ezekiel, Daniel, Hosea. Joel, Amos, Obadiah... Jonah, Micah, Nahum. Habakkuk, Zephaniah, Haggai... Zechariah, Malachi.

There's 27 books in the New Testament, each one's a special part. So, I learned this rhyme and it took no time, till I knew them all by heart...those 27 books by heart. Matthew, Mark, Luke, John, Acts... and Romans. Then, guess who, it's 1 & 2 Corinthians. Then we find Galatians, followed by Ephesians... Philippians, Colossians and 1st & 2nd Thessalonians. We're almost through, now 1 & 2 for Timothy. Titus, Philemon, Hebrews, James, are next you see. First & 2 Peter, no time for hesitation. It's... 1st John, 2nd John, 3rd John, Jude and finally Revelation! There's 66 books in the whole Bible, each one's a special part. If *you'd* learn this rhyme, it'd take no time, till *you'd* know them all by heart... those 66 books by heart!"

Laughing, the boys and wife good-naturedly teased a humbled Matthew. Then, far more seriously he asked, "How can I come back to Jesus after drifting belligerently so far away?" The Lord brought to mind

About Her Father's Business

the story of Hosea and his repeatedly unfaithful wife. God told him a great truth, in Hosea 14:4, about His freely given love and restoration to all who turn their hearts of affection back to seeking after the Father's face! Matthew, true to his word, then prayed for God to forgive his years of wandering and giving lame excuses, and to please, accept him back as His own. Matthew's wife had been listening intently and, right before her eyes, saw the subdued change in her husband. That was enough to convince her to want to pray to this Jesus herself! Afterwards, though, she wondered if she could be "good enough." I shared that she ought not to consider the "saints of old," or even so-called renowned saints of today, as more special than a brand new child of God.

All of the King's children are called by His grace and cleansed by His Spirit. It's just that the nearer a person abides in Christ, the more likely he is to grieve over the evil in his own heart. Yet, as the Master gives us honorable service to do, the more the enemy and our carnal flesh will tempt us to stumble. If she had ever been able to observe the Apostle Paul, she'd probably find him remarkably like the rest of God's chosen, but imperfect family. All of us have some trials to endure and some weaknesses to overcome, but we also have the same grace and help available to us as he did! Paul, and others like him, just grew to be more like Jesus because they constantly strove to live in a manner that honored Him. We can, also, do the same. A new believer is just as highly regarded as an old saint. They are both as equally justified and precious in the sight of God.

In truth, many older believers need to guard their hearts and minds against a "prideful attitude." Presumably, one which boasts that they are more loved or privileged in the eyes of their Master, and they ought to merit more of *His* gratefulness, due to their years of service. No, no way, Jose`! They are merely the King's bond-slaves, doing their required duties and should not expect additional praise just because they have served Him longer *(Luke 17:10)*. Instead, they should only be pleased that they have had more time to acquire the skills to delight His heart more easily. *That* should be reward enough, without seeking after the acclaim from mankind as well. Remember, in God's sight, the spirits of newly "saved" saints are dressed in as pure a white now as all the rest of His children. After Paul died, old in his service to God, he was not more cleansed or more justified to enter heaven than was the thief on the cross who submitted to Jesus with no "service" at all to his credit. Yes, one had a larger, more jeweled crown to lie before his King than did the other, but each was pardoned and accepted equally. While we still live, let us spend our energies in service to our sweet Lord Jesus. He is well pleased with any of our efforts and we ought to let the warmth of His smile be reward enough for our toils.

I spent a few more minutes explaining what the Lord expected from a true child of God. Then, with his parent's permission, Matthew's youngest son knelt at their sofa and let kind Jesus also welcome him into His eternal embrace! All of us slept well in such a happy home that night.

CHAPTER THIRTY

Rededicated Hearts

Leaving Matthew and his Arkansas family the next morning, I headed across the state border to Jackson, Tennessee. There was a family, from my home church, which had recently transferred to that area. Arriving about mid-day, I called the husband at work to get their new home number. I made connections with his energetic wife, Peggy, and got directions to their upscale apartment. I had a little trouble locating their correct unit, until I noticed a parked vehicle that bore North Carolina license plates! I parked next to it and Peggy came out to greet, then escort me into their blissfully air-conditioned dwelling! We gals had a "gabby good time," just talking at lightning speed to catch up on news about several things. The added cost of going only a few miles and a couple of hours out of my way, was well worth it. As a representative from our church family, I so enjoyed being the Lord's blessing to Peggy. Now, I could report back that she and her family were adjusting well to their new environment. They had just found a new home church, a friend for their 13-year-old daughter, and had already put a house to buy under contract. Each of these "news flashes" was an answer to prayers from North Carolina friends *(I Col. 1:9)*.

As I left a few hours later, so Peggy could take her sons to swim practice, she happened to notice the long, pinkish scratches on my arm. After quickly explaining where they came from, I asked her family to keep in prayer the touchy situation with my Mom. How I so longed to see that demented lady outside of Satan's camp... and standing safely on the side of God's Kingdom!

* * * * * * * * * * * * *

In order to get back home, in time to begin my special education re-certification classes, I had to catch up one more day in my schedule. So, I opted not to drive the extra miles to visit and have supper with a family in Georgia. Instead, about mid-day, I called them long distance from my motel room in a small town not far from Nashville, Tennessee. By then, I was just getting too "saddle-sore" to remain in the driver's seat any longer that day. They forgave my altered plans and, as will soon become apparent, we had a very productive, God-anointed conversation. But, oh what that call did to my total phone bill was nearly shameful... yet worth every dollar!

The husband, Professor Billings, was John's and my former college professor back in Colorado. We took different classes from him, but he liked us both. Professor Billings knew that John was interested in me, long before I picked up on my fella's subtle flirting. It tickled this college professor to watch our relationship slowly blossom into a courtship. After the professor and his family had transferred to Georgia, John and I had gotten married, but we had each kept in touch by newsletters around Christmas.

Being intellectuals, I knew these people were Christians, but doubted if they were truly devoted to

About Her Father's Business

the things that really pleased God's heart. Therefore, when the likable Professor Billings asked a couple of general and socially polite questions, Jesus gave me the boldness to respond with very direct and non-superficial answers endorsing the value of God's ways. With his wife, Helen, listening in on the other line, the professor asked, "Now that John's gone, what is most important to you?" and "What are your goals for the future?" I told him that what was important to me before John died, living for Jesus, is what is still most important to me now. That being a good servant to my Master was my continued main goal, as it had always been. I am no longer able to strive towards being a good wife to John, but I can now have more time to better work at becoming a good daughter to my Heavenly Father, and a helpful, encouraging sister to the rest of His children. Then, I informed the professor about the work being done on our house to create an "Elijah Room." The separate, upstairs quarters for Christians needing a safe place to get away from other people and just draw near to God for awhile without a costly motel bill.

A bit rebuffed, professor Billings now let Helen speak to me for several minutes, while he just listened. Since they had adopted two young siblings just before John and I got to know them in Colorado, they were aware of our own longing for children and of our attempt to qualify as adoptive parents. But, our modest finances and, especially, my own mother's track record, had long kept us waiting for a child of our own to love *(Ps. 113:9)*. Their own daughter was now grown, moved out, working and newly engaged. Their son was living on campus and doing well in college. Neither offspring believed in Jesus, and each had put their good parents through some turbulent teen years. Helen remarked, "This world is a scary place for singles, even with a caring family nearby for moral support, so how can you be so confident and unafraid being all alone out there? Don't you want to move back "home" to be near your own relatives now?" she inquired. I told Helen that I had no longings to move away. Where else could I go to feel more "at home" than by staying right where John and I had lived for over a decade? In the "house" that the Lord allowed us to labor with Him, to build a safe place for our own family unit. It wasn't in vain.

Continuing, I reminded Helen that, at 4-years-old, I lived in Alaska for eleven months, as our Army step-dad was stationed there. Our family moved often! Until I married John, that icy abode was the longest time I'd lived any place! Of those several months in Alaska, I acquired more memories of landscapes, our compound area, shops, houses, school friends and teachers' faces... than the accumulation of the following dozen years. We had simply remained in that spot long enough for a child to gather such memories. Things like the afternoon that a big moose wandered into the Kindergarten playground. It was attracted to the uncovered grass that showed through the trodden down snow, where we kids had been playing. It was near noon dismissal, but you could only know that by looking at the clock, since it was always dusk-looking about 6 months of the year. My older sister always came across the yard from the elementary school grounds to pick me up and walk me home at lunch time. I could see her waiting outside the fence, but our teacher wouldn't let us leave the safety of the building, fearing the wild moose might charge at one of us. Actually, it was rather fun watching the big animal's jaw move slowly and lazily as it munched on blades of grass. The older kids and teachers were all "a tether" over the beast's intrusion into our yard. Eventually, the moose had its fill, and so ambled on off to the far fields. We youngsters all arrived home safely, but did scare many parents with "the moose story" and chattered about the exciting event at school for days afterwards.

In spite of all the snow and cold, I'd have rather remained there than to have kept moving all around so much. Alas, I never did have even one drop of "gypsy blood" in my veins. Being a contented "homebody" was bliss enough for me! Even after buying and living on a 32-ft. Cabin Cruiser for several months, at age 20, I only traveled out to open sea once. It was too massive and powerful for my taste! Besides, the boat's purpose was to let me scuba dive, *without* having to battle shoreline "breakers" in full diving gear. Such could be accomplished by keeping my craft relatively close to land, so why take the risk? To Helen's tease, I admitted that, "Yes, I'm also a very 'moderate' road driver!"

More seriously, I explained to the Georgia couple that I was unafraid about the future, as my security did not rest only on John being with me. The Lord solidified my confidence in *His* faithfulness during the battle for my life after the surgery to remove large, growing tumors four years ago *(Prov. 3:26)*. Also, He taught me the extreme value, and tremendous angelic strength released when "brothers and sisters-in-Christ" grant a "prayer covering" to another who is in dire need. Since John's death, I have asked for and adequately, continually received such a covering. There have been a few diligent, Christian friends who have been willing to protect and keep me in their lives as a co-sibling in Jesus.

The Spirit nudged me to realize that this dear, but intellectual couple didn't put much "stock" in prayer themselves. So, I just elaborated on the subject some more. After all it was my quarter! In Lamentations 3:41, it reminds us that praying helps to keep us humble, something most of us proud humans need more. It covers God's earthly warriors with *His* armor and sends them forth into battle triumphantly. Rarely, does a Christian emerge from their own prayer closet without a lightened and rejoicing heart! Prayer overrides human weakness, to impart Divine strength. It redirects foolish thoughts, into heaven's wisdom, and gives troubled souls the real peace of God (Acts 9:15-16). Our prayers, even silent ones, are instantly noted in the heavenly realm. No matter how weak or trembling, ever is a prayer unrewarded by our God Most High. His open heart loves to hear us communicate with Him! Our great Father puts our prayers, like fresh rose petals, between the pages of His "Book of Remembrance." When the volume is open at our reunion in Glory, there will be a precious, pleasing fragrance springing up from it.

Even King David asked for God's help and protection time and again (2 Samuel 5:23a). He learned early that it was not by his might alone, but by the strength of the

About Her Father's Business

Lord, that David's many battles were won. We, also, need to ask…then WAIT for God's directing answer to lead us before heading off into any new venture (Psalm 32:8). God promises to instruct and teach us, but we must be willing to ask, listen, and *obey* His Word. Children of God, who truly depend on His care, are wise to never begin the day's activities without *first* spending time to inquire of the Lord about any special tasks or opportunities (Rev. 5:5). Without the Lionheart of God to impart to us His courage, believers are often like easily frightened sheep. We panic and will take to our heels and flee whenever we see a "wolf of affliction" coming our way! It is one thing to promise faithfulness to the Lord and quite another to exhibit it during a stormy attack. Yet, where else could the followers of Christ be safer than to snuggle closely to our Good Shepherd's side, the One Who could have easily called for 12,000 legions of angelic protection? Without a prayerful "abiding in Christ," we can stray from our true "safety zone," falling prey to temptations offered by "the world," which try to make us depart or, at least, distance ourselves from our Creator God. Each time a Believer shamefully forsakes the Lord, it must pain Him like being crucified afresh. Instead, let our cowardly hearts *faithfully* proclaim His great mercies!

As the Holy Counselor convicted their hearts, both Professor Billings and Helen chose to recommit their lives and stand for Jesus. They promised to work at living more closely to His ways, finally becoming a solid witness of God's loving power to their grown, yet unsaved children. Those two rededicated hearts were more than worth the added charge to my phone bill. Besides, I had no doubt that my Master would provide the extra funds needed, since the expense was incurred as His daughter was "about her Father's business" *(Luke 2:49).*

CHAPTER THIRTY-ONE

Unavoidable Changes

The next morning, I drove through and briefly stopped at Pigeon Forge, then continued on to Newport, Tennessee to see Linda-Sue and her husband. They were the final people on my list of travels, before I headed back to North Carolina. It was so refreshing to be going to a true Christian home again. No matter what trial any of them might presently be undergoing, brothers and sisters-in-Christ are like a deep well of "Living Water" in a parched, dry land *(Ps. 107:33).*

Being allowed to stay at this couple's place was like coming home, where I could actually begin to unwind a bit and even be partly ministered *to...* not only giving out. After these weeks of poor sleep and many energy-draining encounters at stops along the way, I was now feeling rather fumble-brained. Even so, my Lord upheld me with added stamina to enjoy an evening and morning of quality fellowship with my Tennessee friends. Linda-Sue felt close to me enough to risk being indelicate by asking a few of the meatier questions about my new status. She inquired, "Do people still reach out and hug you?" and "Are your church friends and neighbors still giving you help in chores or minor repairs around the house and yard?" also, Are you worried about paying bills now?" Because her concern was genuine, her words were not considered the least bit rude, nosey, or offensive *(Prov. 17:17).*

Except for getting to hold the handicapped toddlers from work, I've had to remind friends nearby that I continue to need the affectionate touch from other human beings. Yet, woundedly, and to Linda-Sue's shock, there have also been a few people who've expressed doubts that I even really loved John! They were just unable to comprehend the depth of my affections and caring for him *because* I seemed to be functioning with a curiously unrattled behavior. So, I had to more openly confess to them that when death unexpectedly claimed *my* special loved one, it hurt...BAD! It still hurts when I wake up alone without John...then remember I always will. It hurts at different "trigger" moments anytime throughout the day. Things like hearing John's favorite songs, picking up the repaired boots that he'd first bought for our wedding, having his last roll of developed film arrive in the mail at our home, seeing our dance costumes hanging on the back of our bedroom door, and occasionally still finding one of his auburn-red whiskers on bathroom surfaces when I cleaned. The pain of his loss intensifies and recedes in alternating, unpredictable waves. It is to be expected that, from time to time, my heart will feel cut and bruised to the core from the injury of losing him. Yet, in sympathy, I said it is understandable that I am not the ONLY one who feels the ache of losing John. Each person, who held a special place of real affection in their hearts for him, is also suffering to some degree. But, we must allow for individual, non-judgmental expressions of grief by all.

Most of the help that was first offered after the accident, I told my friend, has dwindled away. Except

About Her Father's Business

for an occasional sprinkling of folks who, like my neighbor Mr. Daniels, have continued to show a willingness to haul away my weekly trash, once raked my fallen leaves, or who've kept a watchful eye on the house while I've been gone. But, most of the rest of the chores or projects still being completed have had to be done by myself or paid for out of my meager funds. But, since I owe no debts, I'm not particularly anxious about paying normal bills.

With irregular, but hopefully ample income from donations generated from Guests soon able to come to the Elijah Room and paychecks from my own part-time hours, I have enough income. Being used to living on a frugal budget, I'm certain that God will provide me with "the basics." After all, it is said that "people in life who are the happiest don't *have* everything ...they just make the best of everything they do have!" As an example, even with the unexpected cost of needing to replace my house furnace, the Lord more than balanced out that unpleasant surprise by showing me grace and mercy from the contractor who did the major house renovations and installed the spiral staircase upstairs. That Brother Hackman, from church, gave me a reduced bill and has offered to wait for his pay until the auto insurance settlement funds arrive. Once again, as always, God proves His faithfulness to provide for the needs of His tithing saints! Also, it seemed about time now for me to stop depending so much on certain people. God gave me John, and then He allowed a part of that "vacancy" to be filled in by others and their kindnesses and to help me those first several months. But, the fact, which I need to accept, is that I am no longer on anyone's "top priority" list. People have their own families with which to share their time and rightful sacrifices of their labor.

Yet, although my existence may be of little value to any one person on earth, I am still of insurmountable value to my King in heaven *(Dan. 10:19)*. If I died today, no one's life would be particularly altered by it, but while I live, God is interested and cares about every intricate part of my day and thoughts. I am not proclaiming that my life is better now, without John, but I've certainly never felt abandoned by my Lord. Being without a mate, after having been married for years, is more difficult in some ways than in my former, unmarried days. And yet, in a sense, it is easier to be alone now, than it was before being wed. At least, now, I have had the experience of knowing (not just fretfully hoping), that I was capable of being a good wife to a godly man. The Lord helped to "retrain" me from my prior home life's examples and allowed me to be part of a successful, loving marriage. That fact still helps me to feel contented.

Even so, I shared with her, although the struggle for a sense of equilibrium hasn't been as monumental as I'd expected, neither has it been the least bit fun and rarely easy. Being a new, sudden widow turned my self-image upside down for awhile. It made me feel sort of dizzy and off-centered, without clear direction, all on top of the grief and immediate changes to be made. My mental compass needed to be reset, but at times, I could hardly remember which way was up. Time was needed to make this "big adjustment," but

About Her Father's Business

I wasn't given such a gift... and, at first, didn't even know where to start.

"Linda-Sue, widowhood is a role no one is ever taught at home or at school and we've had no practice in playing. There were given no 'cues' about my expected part, how to behave, what to wear to which place, and what to say to whom. At first, I really didn't want to leave the house, because I felt it might show to others how much I was hurting inside. Even while experiencing God's multitude of gentle, soothing comfort, I felt so ill at ease. Everyone treated me so odd and uncomfortably different; as if I had suddenly gone 'strange.' Well, perhaps it was true, because I sure didn't feel like my familiar old self. Also, I soon found that I no longer 'fit in' with any group of people socially. Still feeling like John's widow, not just an unmarried person, so there is no real connection for me with the "singles" yet. Yet, I could no longer identify with the still-married couples, because of not actually being anyone's wife anymore. This has, indeed, been an odd "limbo" stage to endure, and I know not when or if it will end. It concerns me that I'm still the cause of other people's discomfort, too. I have tried to lessen the strain of awkwardness to those around me, but the reminder of a recent death makes everyone still feel a bit awkward. The abrupt transition from being a happy wife to becoming a solitary widow is very real, painful, and personally complex. The trauma of trying to adjust to an indefinable role, while besieged by a multitude of prying questions and urgent decisions to be made, seemed nearly overwhelming at times. Having such little preparation for what I'd be going through, and no background from my own family experiences to be a helpful guide in such a difficult ordeal, it occasionally seemed that the agony of loss and rebuilding would never end. But, rest assured, that it does... that it is... that it will. It's best for me to keep remembering that, 'Life is not measured by the number of breaths we take, but by what takes our breath away!' God is not yet finished using me for His purposes here, and I don't believe His goodness and mercy would force me to endure the rest of my life without some happy moments in my future."

Then, I shared with Linda-Sue, and later in my own North Carolina church, part of this recent, encouraging devotional from "Morning by Morning," by C. H. Spurgeon:

"Casting all your cares upon Him; for He careth for you." (I Peter 5:7)

It is a happy way of soothing sorrow when we can feel..."He careth for me." Christian, do not dishonor your Savior by always wearing a brow of care. Cast your burden upon the Lord. You are staggering beneath a weight that Your Father would not feel. Oh, child of suffering, be patient. God has not passed you over in His providence. He who is the feeder of sparrows will also furnish you with what you need. The blackest gloom will give place to the morning. He will bind up your wounds and heal your broken heart. Do not doubt His grace because of your tribulation, but believe that He loves you as much in seasons of trouble as in times of happiness. Can you trust Him for your soul, and not for your body? Each of us has our trials and struggles whether financial, emotional, physical, etc. Be encouraged to keep in your minds' eye God's "eternal vision" of the situation.

CHAPTER THIRTY-TWO

Finishing the Journey

(A.)

After Linda-Sue and I spent part of the next morning in mutual prayer for one another, I left to make the final drive back to North Carolina and pulled into my driveway by early evening. Being on the road for so long, walking into the house felt like just another impersonal motel room. It made me feel sad that "our" house no longer permeated the familiar sense of "coming home." Thus, I began to quickly empty out my suitcases to give it a more lived-in, personal touch. That helped, so I burrowed in for a long, overdue rest. I slept for over 10 hours, then got up and ate a bite. Yet, I was still so groggy and just went back to bed. To my surprise, I slept all the rest of that afternoon and through the night again. I had not comprehended just how rundown I'd become! It actually took three to four weeks, before I finally started perking up with enough stamina and energy to last for more than just a half or 2/3 of the day *(Isa. 40:29)*.

The first Sunday back at my own church, I gave (in comparison to *this* "report") a brief account of my trip and of the births of the new "babes-in-Christ." About a week later, one of our co-elders, Clay, and his wife, invited me over for supper and to share more of the details of this "pilgrimage." Those poor dears endured an almost 3-hour discourse, telling them most of what

I've said *(written)* here. Near the end, Clay asked me, "What do you think the Lord may have in store for you now?" The Master for a season, I sensed, wanted me to "minister to the bereaved" and be more available in helping others become "freed," by engaging in "Spiritual Warfare" as God led me. I explained that my John was often embarrassed by what could possibly happen or be said during a demonic manifestation. Also, he was concerned for my own welfare because participating in such encounters was tremendously draining on me and could get ugly. Thus, John rarely gave his approval for me to assist in "deliverance" sessions. *(Refer to Chapters # 17, 18, 22, and 23 for more information about this topic.)* Whenever I discerned a demonic influence upon someone, which was about to manifest its presence, John would allow me to quietly usher that person away to a more private area, removing them from the influence of whatever was causing the evil spirit to be so agitated. Usually, it was hearing the word of God spoken at church or by others.

Either at Clay and Teresa's home, or in conversation afterwards, I also remarked that "out west" people from all races intermingled in churches and socially far more regularly than here. So, I was hoping the Lords' desire would be for me to start, or just be included within, a small group of multi-racial friends. In "the east," I so missed having warm companions from different nationalities and race backgrounds, as I had been blessed to enjoy in my California and Colorado days. *(Later, through a Winfield Committee, which lead to my joining a Christian Women's Luncheon, I was able to do this.)* Clay mentioned that having people from different races and denominations mix/interact comfortably had been one of the burdens of his heart for years as well. We both also wanted to see more unified acceptance of people with different intellectual or financial backgrounds, into our own area churches. Many of the adult handicapped people I know have no fellowship to welcome their presence; thus, they become spiritually "homeless."

In John 21:12, the "come and dine" gives us the idea of close fellowship with Jesus and with other saints as well. Christians differ in a variety of ways, but we all have the same spiritual hunger. Even if we can't all be alike, we can still feed on the same "Bread of Life" together, as our common ground. When we get closer to Jesus, we become closer to one another and more accepting of our temporal differences.

Clay gave me his blessing to pursue the road God seemed to be encouraging me to travel. Also, along the way, I could use him and the other co-pastors as counter-checks and sounding boards. As I wrote in a note to them awhile later, I wanted to learn to walk so closely behind and in step with Jesus that... my foot lands in His still warm footprint.

* * * * * * * * * * *

(B.)

For over three, long weeks, I have worked on this audio tape version of my journal notes. But now, about mid-December 1996, it is finally getting finished. *(The final "book version" was completed from July 2004 to February 2005.)* Your forgiveness, for any misquotes or credit not fully given in anything I've said, is most humbly requested. Once a Truth is "absorbed" as part of me, where it was originally heard or read is often forgotten. Even so, I have truly made efforts to be precise about those kinds of details.

Also, I apologize to the folks that I visited, for not being able to elaborate more on their varied countryside's beauty. Yet, alas, sight-seeing was not part of the Lord's goal for me on this journey. I do recall *lots* of flat desert in lower Arizona and New Mexico, plus one full day of it through west Texas. I was surprised by the lowland, swampy areas in Arkansas, but most of the other states and their mountains, or fields of corn, soy beans, cotton, wheat, and such all just sort of blended into a blur of road miles in my mind. No offense or disloyalty intended to each of your beloved hometowns. My brain just couldn't absorb or retain anymore data.

This audio "report" will be shared with a few trusted, Christian friends. Also, a copy will be given to my church pastors/elders for them to filter it down to those people whose hearts and maturity levels are ready to handle it. This gal wishes to extend her thanks to everyone who has allowed her to go below the norm of "surface niceties" in expressing her inner-thoughts. As well as, to openly expose the sometimes embarrassing facts and humbling steps our Lord caused her to walk through on this beneficial "journey of ministry to others" which He loves.

About Her Father's Business

John, my noble husband, used to be the only person in whom I'd usually confide this "deeper stuff." His attentive, understanding ear was enough to fill the need to verbalize my core-level thoughts. It will always generate a flood of gratefulness in my heart, that Jesus gave me the treasured privilege to *finally* have had one main, caring person in my life, one who listened to how I felt about what God was teaching me, as I mused over Holy Scripture or the inspired wisdom of other saints. Before this crash course in "opening up to others," that Christ pushed me through during my trip out West, I'd rarely felt inclined to share with others about some of life's unpleasant experiences. Unless, that is, Christ Jesus put someone in need directly across my path, for the Kingdom's sake. Especially, if it was a wounded person who longed to know that she wasn't the "only one" who had to survive similar treatment and betrayals. So, this is "new ground" for me, to let others peer transparently into the prior hidden chambers of my soul.

It is my hope and prayer that, at least, *some* aspect of this taped "report" will be a blessing or a vehicle of growth for you *(Num. 4:47b)*. Yet, in return, would you please extend a kindness towards me? Be tactfully disciplined enough to not bring up some of my past innocent, yet shame-filled life in casual conversation or just out of curiosity for more details. Instead, treat me as you normally would. In your minds, try not to unfairly label your now quite vulnerable sister as "strange" or an inferior specimen. But, if you have a real need to talk about a similar, hurtful past, do feel welcome to discretely arrange a time with me to pray together. May anything meant for evil be turned into something good, for us and to the honor Almighty God *(Gen. 50:20a)*!

Last, but not least, allow me express my sincere gratitude to all of those who prayed and sent cards to me during my first time of having to go through our anniversary weekend alone. The Master was merciful to this daughter and enduring the Thanksgiving holiday was not as difficult as had been anticipated, plus some healing was accomplished through it. The Lord has aided me in accepting John's departure and taken "the sting" out of losing his companionship. Yet, although the intensity of missing my dear husband has greatly eased, the mandate that I not yet seek to remarry has not lessened.

Feeling better prepared and fortified to now face the Christmas season, I can only praise my King for the uplifted outlook. As it says in I Samuel 7:12, "the Lord has helped me" and the word "hitherto" points to His rescue from our past *and* His promise to be there beside us in our times of need in the future. Whether we encounter poverty, cruelty, sickness, grief, or any kinds of disappointments or harsh trials, God will be there to help us. We have only to ask and then *obey* His promptings. We should make a conscious effort to recall His past deeds of mercy, loving-kindness, and faithfulness. That way, our confidence will remain strong in Him and we will be thrilled at the joy of those memories. So, "be of good cheer" *(John 16:33c)* believers, He who has helped us "hitherto" will be there to always help us on our journey... all the way through to the gates of glory! Dear ones, as you obey the Spirit's promptings, continue to abide in Jesus Christ and walk in the love of Father God. May His richest blessings be yours, now and always.

And, all God's people said, "Amen!"

EPILOGUE

The following are a few of the remarks or letters resulting from the sharing of my "journey" with others. It is hoped that you may find them of interest. Each of these shortened "excerpts" is presented in chronological order.

September 18, 1996

(From: Kim's Co-Pastor)

Dear Kimberly,

We enjoyed having you for supper on Sunday and getting to hear the exciting account of your trip of ministry. After absorbing its, news these past days, Teresa and I thought you'd like to hear our reflections and suggestions... a.) In Ohio, you missed the preferred "timing" of God's call, but it teaches us that He is a God of second chances! b.) Proved, many times, the benefits of a healthy prayer life! c.) Showed that you were being sensitive to be <u>used</u> by the Holy Spirit. d.) Demonstrated how we should all allow God to bring victories out of prior defeats!

As you share this account with others, we sense that preserving its continuity is what will most loudly proclaim God's "going before you" in each situation. Recording the events onto audio tapes will more easily enable others to listen to it. But, consider this, the Lord may want you to also put it all down in a book, so that it could minister to even more people. –Clay S.

September 27, 1996

(Kim's friend, Jill C., posted this notice at her own church, resulting in wonderful help!)

...Just two hours out of your busy life to help someone in need. What a neat way to do some mission work right here in your own community. Together, we can make a difference in someone's life. Won't you help?

Kim Thomas is an incredible woman. Despite the tragedy that could have made someone else bitter and resentful, she continues to witness and be an example to me of what (being a) *real Christian is all about. Kim has maintained their home...However, there are some tasks she simply cannot do on her own and needs our help for a few hours. We will meet at...*

October 11, 1996

Dear Ones All,

As these weeks apart from you have passed (while I was gone on my long trip), it is hoped that accomplishments or milestones in your lives have caused you to appreciate God more and long to be nearer to His Presence. Even trials can be remembered with contentment, as you observe the Lord's prevailing grace covering you in it.

There has been much reading material, about grief and widowhood, recommended or given to me since John's accident. All were helpful and a few were quiet excellent. But, if I had to choose only one source, to likewise suggest to another who is having to deal with *the heart and life "vacancy" of a missing loved one, it would be **Roses in December** by M. W. Heavilin. She mostly writes to parents who have lost a child, but her idea of "storing up memories" (i.e.: "Roses" to brighten and warm the chill that settles in aching, grieving hearts) is a healthy one. It reminded me of the numerous cards and notes many people wrote last January and February. They were a tremendous blessing and, often, helped give me extra courage to face the coming "unknowns." This includes the ones just ahead, of enduring my first Thanksgiving and Christmas season without John being a part of them.*

After John died, I felt compelled to hurry up and get back into some kind of "regular" routine again. As if repeating my "normal" patterns would help me to <u>feel</u> normal again. Such activity was a stabilizing force at first, but now that I have returned from the long trip out West, all of my "regulars" are different. *(Such as, my new job which means different duties, plus still getting used to the vast rearrangement of up/down household furniture, which makes everything look and feel so different from when John was here.) So, it is getting close to the time for me to begin learning a "new" kind of "normal", one that can no longer include any special routines with John. Alas, not everything we <u>should</u> do...is enjoyable to do! Thus, I am allowing myself these final weeks to admit that missing John still hurts, but that I am healing and will try to bring a noble "closure" to this uncomfortable year of "firsts" without him.

I ask your forgiveness if the way I've dealt with the unpleasantness of this ordeal of mourning seems odd to you. If you, someday, discover that you can manage the grief process better...good for you! I would be truly blessed if such an encounter dealt you a kinder blow. But, really, when our heart aches, it is a very solitary experience and we all hurt and heal differently. The important thing is to keep mending and looking forward!

The Master will help this life to become enjoyable again... even without John. But, I want to bring comfort to others, by sharing insights gained through this year of my own personal sorrow. I have accepted that, for me, life will never be the same again. Yet, I trust that Jesus will again direct it to be a good one...different, but still good. John's love for me would have wanted that!

In the Father's Love, ---Kimberly

November 27, 1996

(Note in Thanksgiving card from Kim's missionary friend to China.)

Dear Kimmy,

I haven't enough words to sufficiently say "thank you" for your hugs, prayers, encouragement, for letting me bask in your care, for allowing the Holy Spirit to flow through you (to others), *for making the effort in your drive* (to Denver) *to see me, by being a woman of courage, and a minister of the Most High God.*

I'm praying for you... Love, Dinae H.

October 4, 1996

(Note from Kim's older sister.)
Dear Kimberly,
I hope you had a wonderful finish to your trip. Thanks for taking care of all the legal things of Mom's. I know it wasn't pleasant for you.
*   –Thinking of you,   Jackie*

December 18, 1996

(Note from wife of man who used to work with John.)
Dear Kimmy,
These tapes are such a blessing! Thank you for recording them. Our Lord has used you in many ways. You are our "sister" and we hold you in our prayers before the throne of our gracious and merciful God.
*   ----All my Love,   Melanie H.*

December 23, 1996

Dear Kim,
Being allowed to listen to your tapes has been our best Christmas "gift" this season. Here are some things that had an impact on us. Tape #1 - Indiana family: the affect of physical contact and expressing caring for others,... - Where you talked about courtship with John and dating relationships (father was a backslider) and spending time with the Lord. Tape # 2- Talking with Aunt Kathy and her conversion. Tape # 3 -Time at mall after incident with your mother, where you talked

about not dwelling on the bad things that happened. Jimmy suggested that possibly you could cut down on the details of your childhood. However, your <u>whole</u> "story" could be very important for some people to hear.

We think your whole testimony should be put onto <u>one</u> tape that could be beneficial for many to hear! Very encouraging for those who've been through tough times as well. ---Lori P.

End of Year "Update" *(December 31, 1996)*

Hello, Dear Ones!

During the potentially difficult Thanksgiving weekend, the Lord helped arrange for me to be in Pennsylvania, instead of here alone. Was able to stay Wednesday night enjoying a refreshing visit with Dave and Sherree's family and share the "Turkey" meal at their table the next day. *(To my delight, Sherree is the kind and lovely Christian wife the Master gave to Dave and his two children after the loss of his first wife, Rita. Dave and Rita had clung to their faith in Jesus through the sudden auto deaths of their first three youngsters, as well as through the long, painful time of Rita's cancer. Near the end, Rita stated, "So, what am I going to do? Well, in the physical, I'm going to keep taking vitamin therapy... In the spiritual, I will read God's Word, bathe myself in worship tapes and just let God be God. I believe He can, with His very breath, bring health back into my body; whether on this side of the "veil" or on the next matters little anymore. But, whatever happens, He is in control... and I like it that way. Romans 14:6 says, 'Whether we die, we die unto the Lord. Whether we live or die, we are the Lord's!' That's pretty plain, isn't it?") *Next, I drove on to York and joined with Leland and his wife to spend the rest of the weekend at a fun seminar.*

After getting back home, I began the laborious task of recording the journal of my trip-West onto audio tapes. Plans for Christmas with others fell through, due to a flu bug. Occurring impromptu, it turned out fine to only have Jesus as my holiday "family" that morning. After all, it was <u>His</u> birthday being celebrated, so who could have been any better company? So, as my gift to the Christ Child, I volunteered at a church in town to help serve their holiday luncheon to the needy folks in our community, those who had no family around and/or whose funds were too low for such a bountiful fare. The experiences and people encountered were so uplifting that I've already volunteered to help serve the meal next year as well. *(Try it, you might like it!)

This past week, I went up to the Elijah Room on a fasting sabbatical. It was a much needed, undisturbed time to be away from other people. Like a small wilderness animal, this gal feels most comfortable "retreating away" for awhile, when needing to heal from life's deeper wounds. During these recent days of only being with God, our gentle Shepherd led this lamb through "reliving" last years' events and memories. It was painful, but good. In respectful memory of John, I've already made a silk "Roses in January" floral arrangement to be displayed at church on the Sunday closest to the 16th. Also, a cross "marker" is being *made, with Johns' nameplate attached, to be placed on the side of the road near the accident site, to warn other motorists to be extra careful this winter! Charlie R., the husband of a good friend, gave me the nice wooden, cedar pieces and is putting them together for me. Omega, a formerly widowed friend among my black "sisters," will come with me for emotional support when I set the "marker" in place. Lastly, apricot-colored roses are being sent to help comfort John's parents, on this first anniversary of his death. Could think of nothing more to still do <u>for</u> John, so am at peace over what is or will be done in his memory.*

There is a good, eternal reason for every "season" (Ecc. 3:1) the Lord allows to be brought our way. How we respond to each one is what really matters. This past year, the Master has helped me to progress over many difficult paths. But, one who is forgiven and <u>rescued</u> from much, appreciates VERY MUCH the One who helped her to endure it all (Luke 12:48b).

It is normal for the love felt for a lost "dearly departed" to remain in a deep part of the heart. My love for John did not die when he did. My Beloved was gone, but the affectionate ties to our relationship still lived on. We had made a substantial emotional investment into our marriage and those feelings survived long after his funeral was over! God continued to use the presence of our shared love to sustain me through the "stages" of grieving John's absence. Now, the clarity of his face, voice, and touch is beginning to fade away from me. It makes me feel sad, but I realize that it is normal and must be so.

Therefore, as this first year of widowhood ends, this daughter has been sensing her Lord's gentle nudging to do what has proven to be a very emotional hurtle. He has shown me that I was to remove my wedding band! Recently, I've twice awakened crying, with such a feeling of heaviness over the stark realization that I did not "belong" to anyone ...not even to John anymore. So, in kind affection, the Master reminded me that it has <u>not</u> been John's gold band on my finger that has protected and guided me this past year. No, it has been the Good Shepherd, along with His extended flock, who have been looking out for me. Thus, last week, with much internal reluctance, I tenderly placed my wedding ring next to John's in our jewelry box...and gently closed the lid. I can no longer strive to hold on to a husband I'm not allowed to keep. I have become John's widow, and am not his wife anymore. Although, I still look forward to seeing him in heaven, as it says in Luke 20:34 and 35, we will not be a married couple up there. Our bonding will continue to be special in glory, but it will have to be of a different and holier kind. After all, John never did <u>really</u> belong to me. His rightful Owner just kindly permitted me to borrow John, on loan, for a delightful season. Now though, in order for me to maintain a healthy emotional and mental balance, I have to let John "go." It is a sad and tender process, one that can't be "hurried up" in me by others. Yet, over these past months, God has slowly worked in me a calm acceptance and gentle sense of separation from John. The Master has filled the new emptiness with even more of Himself instead. The "sting of death" (I Cor.15:55) is gone from his *'going home'. The Lord is helping me to release those feelings of being "in love" with John to, instead, just recalling those "loving memories" of our past and blessed time together.*

For this coming year, I sense the Lord's instruction for me to <u>not</u> pursue another relationship yet. Instead, God wants me to devote more time, energy, attention, strength, and affection to drawing closer to Himself. As well as, being available to minister to people He brings my way. Like another 'sister' wrote, "If John could see from the other side, he would rejoice in the work God has granted you." *(We know he can't, but it's a nice thought anyway.) Still, John and I were so closely united that, with his passing, a part of my own being was torn away, severed, and it may always be missing. Unless Jesus one day restores that portion, like the re-knitting of a splintered bone, it would be unfair to give some other kind man so much less of me. So, if later, it <u>is</u> God's will for me to remarry, He will have to install a large amount of "want to" in me first! Even so, for those who the Master has enabled to "love again," I applaud and rejoice in your happy union! For most definitely, if Christ has ordained it, second marriages are NOT "second-rate!" Fully identifying, I agree with the proclamation by Becky Smith-Greer, in her excellent book, <u>Keepsakes for the Heart</u>. "I have come a long way since the accident. I have learned a lot about life and loving, death and dying, grief and giving. I have grown in ways I never dreamed possible. Without a moments' hesitation (to love and marry, even if the ending heartache is still there), *I would go back* *and do it all over again, exactly the same way. I have no regrets."*

To further help all of us to bring a closure to this past year of loss and mending, I have included some excerpts from Tim Hansel's book titled, <u>Through the Wilderness of Loneliness</u>. Also, a few others are added in hopes that they will assist you in understanding what people must struggle through when death strikes our homes and hearts. – If I were not permitted to cry, hollow would be the sound of my laughter – Loneliness is something God teaches me, which I can learn no other way. Nobody else can experience for me, nor can I, if I keep pushing it away. – Being lonely for a close relationship is <u>not</u> unspiritual, weak, or sinful. - Just tell others the truth, as you know it at that stage in the (grief) process. It is the (main) thing that will set you free (from grief's vicious cycle). And, the truth is that the pain (of loss) has sometimes almost broken me to pieces. – Loneliness is the pain of simply being alive... but left an empty shell. – Perhaps God might nudge each of us into a wilderness experience of some kind, so that we will learn to depend on Him in new, deeper ways (Elisabeth Elliot). – Loneliness is not a time of abandonment...it just <u>feels</u> that way. It's actually an encounter with the only One who can fill that sore, empty place in our hearts. – Bereaved persons feel cut off, not only from their past, but from the future as well. - (Kim says - A widow often looses close fellowship with ones who knew her spouse, because those associations become awkward on both sides. But, she also lacks measurable bonding connections to new acquaintances because they never knew John *and their shared history, which is still a real part of her total-sum being.) – I knew that God really loved me, but in my sadness, I just forgot for awhile (Martha, age 41). – God made us human beings in His image with the need for His fellowship. At the same time, He created us with the need for other people. Thus, loneliness may be reflecting a deficiency in either or both areas. – Christ often asked people to do difficult things. His love is not wimpy; it is "hard-nosed" agape! – A broken heart can best mend by expansion, to allow it to have even more room to love others than before. – We must find peace in the midst of our loneliness. We can not wait for all the scars to go away first. (Remember, says Kim, Christ still has His!) – I said I found peace; I didn't say that I was not lonely (Elisabeth Elliot). – It has been said that no growth can occur until blaming ceases. *(Blaming others, ourselves, <u>or</u> God, proclaims Kim!) – Take time for solitude. It doesn't transform things, but it invites the inner Presence of God who can!*

Lastly, on this topic of grief, permit me to share a condensed version of a July publication. It spoke truth beyond measure in my case! Comments within parentheses are mine to aid in clarification. <u>Being Alone</u> *- "Reactions to death may cover a wide and confusing range of emotions. Grief does not proceed in an orderly fashion...anymore than life does. Your immediate response following a death is probably shock, numbness, and a sense of disbelief. You may (emotionally) feel like you're wrapped in a cocoon or blanket (and may not even realize it until weeks/months later). From the outside, you may look to others as if* *you're holding up well. In fact, the (full) reality of the death has not yet penetrated your (deepest) awareness. This gives you (to others) the appearance that you are quite accepting of your loss. In the months after the funeral, however, this numbness turns into intense feelings of separation, pain, and yearning (for the one you love). In some ways, you are searching for your lost mate. You may have dreams in which your loved one is still alive. You may think you see him on the street or hear his foot-steps down the hall." *(May I remind you hurting ones to cling very near to God's Word during this stage. Beware of the "deceiver" who may cleverly lure you away into harmful mysticism or demonic spirits, which could imitate and masquerade as a lost loved one.)*

In tears last year, I asked the Lord to reveal how the giving up of our shared dreams for the future could be for my best. He has done so by the evident expanding of this daughter's sphere of ministry to others. As Loren Cunningham remarked, "Put your dreams on the alter. They will be resurrected into something even grander." *(<u>Is That Really You God?</u> -about how hearing and obeying God's direction is what brought Y-WAM into productive existence.) *Also, I've come to believe that it is good to appraise what we have gone through, so that we can be better prepared for, and even look forward to, our tomorrows. As wise Abraham Lincoln said, "It is indispensable to have a habit of observation and reflection." No longer having John, my earthly "best friend" here to share my inner-self with anymore, I have been entirely "transparent" with a few of you instead.*

Thanks to each of you again for your prayers, kindness and assistance this past year. Our good Master directs us to thrive in the present and rejoice in the future to come (Ps. 107:42a)...by not overly clinging to the past (whether good or bad). When I now remember John, I mostly feel gratefulness, not sadness. How very thankful am I for the healing touch of Jesus...and YOUR part in it! In a large measure, this gal is doing so well now <u>because</u> of the love demonstrated by those who upheld her when she was faltering, who "stood in the gap" for her during months of difficult changes and personal adjustments. May the Lord grant me the honored privilege to somehow, someday return your graciousness.

In His Love and mine, --Kimberly

*p.s. The attached "**Letter From Heaven**" is to uplift your own hearts!*

Letter From Heaven

God promises us that life on this planet is only temporary; it is NOT "the real thing." True life is resumed beyond the little time we each spend in our earthly vessels. For those who know the Lord, there is a GREAT "rest of the story" ending!

As others, such as Leon Bates, have already preached or sung about (and I've just expanded upon), when a person moves away from home, he often writes a letter back to his loved ones, to let them know how he is doing. So, if John or any departed and "promoted" Christian, COULD send a letter back to his still earthbound loved ones, this is what he might write…

* * * * * * * * * *

Dear Ones,

I had such a wonderful trip here and suddenly felt so FREE, like being released from a decayed, old cage. Huge, gentle angels escorted me right up through the Pearly Gates and there was such energy and strength coursing through every fiber of my new being! But, no earthly words could ever describe the AWE of finally meeting, face-to-face, the One who died for me; to be in the very Presence of the God of all creation and universes…our Mighty King Jesus! I saw the nail-print scars on His welcoming, outstretched hands. It was a serene privilege to bow down, worship Him, and thank my Lord for paying the price for all of my sins, plus giving me this salvation of eternal life! Then our Master reached down, pulled me up into His embrace, and proclaimed how very much he loved me and had been so looking forward to my arrival! I was filled with such powerful JOY and could just tell by His smile that He deeply meant it, too. Until that instant, I'd not fully realized just how "precious in the sight of the Lord is the death of His saints" (Ps. 116:15).

Christ told me that He had sent "special grace" to you, and my other loved ones still there, to help all of you with the bereavement of our sudden separation. It blessed me to know that. I'm just beginning to really absorb the magnitude of our Master's grace, love and caring towards His servants. He truly is "full of compassion and gracious, slow to anger and abounding in love and faithfulness" towards us (Ps. 86:15). For example, the Lord said that, among other things, the reason He took me "home" now was to mercifully spare me from the overwhelming grief, which I would NOT have been able to handle, if instead, He would have left me on earth to live, when it was time to take you. Only God knows how much heart-pain each of His children are capable to withstand, and He will never stretch our emotions or faith "beyond that which we can endure" (Job 34:23a). Jesus knew that your mettle and courage was strong enough to bear this parting.

While still at the Lord's side, I became aware of people standing around, smiling and watching us. It dawned on me that they were other "promoted" loved ones of ours, who had arrived here before me. It has been so great to talk and share hugs with each one of them. Your sister, Rose, and her Dad send you their greetings, and want you to know that they have loved taking care of baby Kimberly for us! Getting reacquainted with my Grandpa was a special delight and were we ever surprised to also welcome sweet Grandma "home" too…just a few days later. There are some other folks here, of whom I hadn't realized but, while they were still earthbound, they had changed their loyalties from the "world's ways" to God's better way! A number of these people I don't even know, but they have been eagerly waiting, on this side of the veil, to greet and thank me for my part, directly or indirectly, that helped them to see the true Light before it was too late. Talk about depthless gratitude and unbounding joy shared with one another over the saving grace of God! Now, I no longer have to believe, by faith alone, about what God's Word…the Bible, says about heaven. I'm here, and folks…it's <u>ALL</u> true!

Be assured that I'm completely satisfied here. All my needs are supplied and just wait until you see the very beauty of this heavenly realm! I'll do my best to put details into mortal terms, but actually, this lovely place is beyond description! Try to mentally combine all of the inspiring natural sights we've ever seen together on earth. Start by envisioning the majestic, snow-capped Rocky mountains as they reflect on a high-altitude lake of crystal clear water; go on to imagine the tall, regal and tremendously huge California Redwoods; the deep Arizona, rainbow-hued Grand Canyon, fall leaves with their dazzling Aspen-yellows and bright Maple-reds, mixed with bursts of other awesomely beautiful colors. Yet, such beautiful earthly realities are mere shadow-glimpses, that don't even come close to expressing the true multi-faceted gorgeousness of heavens' reality!

I'm so eager for you to see my brand new "residence." Why, it would be like a whole estate back there…but without weeds or lawnmowers. Human eyes and minds can't possibly conceive how spectacular their future dwelling place will be. This huge, magnificent crystal city is resting on twelve foundations of rainbow-colored band of gems, sparkling and glimmering with utterly fabulous prismatic affects. All of the structures, gold and costly alloys, growing things, precious stones, and living beings are gifted with enhanced loveliness and operate in tranquil harmony together. It is always daytime in Paradise, this country of the Most High. Darkness or night is never seen here, because Jesus is the eternal Light for the whole city of God! There is also a continual sweet, soft breeze caressingly covering us all with a sense of safety and wellness. It drifts over us from our Father's own warm breath of great love. Now, we are encouraged to eat from the Tree of Life, which keeps us in optimum health and vigor.

I'm so very contented here because there is no sin of any kind, in anyone. We have no need to lock our doors; there is no strife, no sorrow, or heartaches whatsoever. We are all a big "family" here, each known by his own special name from God. Why Shadrach, Meshach, and Abednego even showed me all around the Kingdom, soon after I'd arrived. We four, and all the others, have rapport through our spirits instantly, and we feel like we've already been close friends for ages. No one here feels lonely, or like they don't "fit in," and they never will again. Perfect peace reigns in this exquisite environment and we all like it that way immensely.

Oh! Let me try to explain about this realm's wondrous music. I've never heard or even imagined anything like it. With sublime adoration and glad rejoicing, the singing voices of countless millions of enormous angels and the Redeemed, echoes and reverberates from one end of Glory to the other! Even people, who before, couldn't stay on beat or carry a tune, can now sing their hearts full in perfect, sweet-sounding pitch. All the voices of heaven's residents blend together magnificently! I like to sing, too, but LOVE how well I play guitar now! Hallelujah!

Now, I much better understand how mortal ears, connected even to the most intelligent brains, still have vast restrictions. There, we could only process a tiny portion of the total frequency spectrum in the form of sounds. Not so here! We Risen-Redeemed no longer have our enjoyment stifled by those kinds of limitations. No matter what the sound, if God gave it a voice, we get to hear it! There are multiple combinations of choirs and musical arrangements here; large and small, angelic and Redeemed, plus a mixture of them all. Why even "dancing feet" David (II Sam. 6:14a) sweetly plays his harp for all of us regularly. Although the angel's voices can sing worshipful praises around God's throne beyond parallel, we Saints have a few tunes in which we also excel. The angelic hosts can't sing some of those with us, but draw closely, intently listening and smiling, as their wings quiver with delight. In our lyrics and messages of thanksgiving, we "King's Kids" like to "Gather by the River," and "Sing a New Song" to "The Lamb That Was Slain" and lift our voices in praise to several other favorites. But, all who reside here joyfully and loudly cry a melodic, "Holy, Holy, Holy" is the Lord God Almighty!

Since your own holiday season has just passed, let me expound a bit on what the virgin birth and the Christ-Child means here. God, taking on human form and going to earth was the number one, major focal point in ALL of history...there and here, too! As you know, throughout the Old Testament, our Father gave many clues telling about the coming Messiah, the Savior to all mankind. For centuries, the hosts of heaven anxiously waited for that predicted entry to occur. Then it happened, exactly as God proclaimed it would! Mary was chosen to be the Child's mother and she was a pure and righteous vessel. Joseph was chosen to be her husband, and although he was not the human sire of Jesus, he proved to be a noble and kind step-father to the Holy One. Humble shepherds heard the "good news" of Christ's birth and got to listen to a fantastic, sky lit angelic worship service. Why, I've met and even sung with some of those very hosts of heaven. They told me THAT Christmas night everyone still remaining here at the Holy City burst into a celebration of spontaneous applause and songs of praises!

Since then, the yearly Christmas rejoicing here includes the most spectacular light display ever. Even with our improved visual perception now, it is absolutely AWESOME how the Trinity "cranks up" the power on brightness, amplifying all the colors of the stars and planets until each and every universe is thoroughly dazzling! They become a visual panorama of glorious colors crying out in delightful adoration to their Creator, Jesus Christ, the very sustainer of everything!

My former mortal brain did not fully grasp all that God had prepared for us to enjoy here. It's as if our time on earth was simply a dress rehearsal, for this more wondrous life. How short-sighted of most people to focus so much on just the "rehearsal"…instead of the MAIN event! Eternal life with Jesus is real! But, too many folks get bogged down with temporal things and thoughts. Encourage them to look higher, to yearn beyond their earthly situation and focus on <u>these</u> "gates of pearl" and the rewards of being one of Christ's own.

Kimmy, I am grateful for all of the love I received and enjoyed there for almost forty-three years, especially during the nearly decade and a half that our hearts "belonged' to each other. Yet, not even those cherished memories could entice me to leave this immensely joy-filled life. So, please, encourage folks to conduct their lives in manner honoring to the Master, while they still have the chance, so they can also one day flourish here. Be sure to take time to love the people around you now. Do it so that there are no regrets later, in case the moment of "departure" arrives sooner than expected. Tell them to heed the words to the poem which goes, "The clock of life is wound but once, and no man has the power; To know just when its hands will stop, whether late or early hour; So love, work, live with zeal, don't leave them till tomorrow, for …the clock… may then… be still."

If it were permitted, I would share many other details about Glory, but had best close for now. Until we meet again, just keep on believing that everything <u>really</u> does work out for our ultimate good…for those who love the Lord. Actually, there is no need for me to write you any further "updates" because, well, everything here is gloriously always similar...today, yesterday, and tomorrow. Don't worry about me because I am well and happy. I don't hurt anywhere, anymore. Why, I've never felt better in all of my ...uh... life before! The only thing I can think of that could even possibly increase my joy would be...for all of my friends and all of my family to one day want to enjoy being here together. To be, like me, intertwined with Jesus, in His Kingdom, totally immersed in God's indescribable and very personal love. I am eagerly awaiting each of your own "homecomings" and I will keep watching for you until...the end....of time.

Sending my Love from Heaven to Earth,
John

January 5, 1997

Dear Kim,

Thank you for sharing the four tapes with me! You may have had several reasons for putting so much effort into "telling the tale." One reason I sensed in your words, "To be genuine is to be transparent." Bless you! What you are today, an adopted daughter of God, is what matters the most. Yet, your tapes seem to say that what you <u>have been</u> does matter, because it affects what you can be for Jesus. Meaning, we can use our mental and physical scars for Him, when He provides opportunities. Your trip gave you ideal openings to do so, and more importantly to talk about what He does *for all of us "scarred" folks. Whether our childhood was ideal or troubled, when we come to Jesus we can gain "the peace that the world cannot give."*

Though I believe in demonic possession in the abstract, I've never seen it in the concrete. That made me cautious to believe. But, your description of "Mother" convinced me. You were wise to not stay that night with her! Often, you seemed to be "Kim the Invincible," but I have been very moved by what I just heard and I thank God for protecting you. --David M.

January 16, 1997

Dear Kimberly,

Thanks for the privilege of listening to your tapes. Certainly, you are much beloved in Christ for all you have overcome in Him. If you feel the need to trim anything out of the tapes or write it down later, be sure to include the account of the man who said he would repent, if he ever heard a Christian recite the books of the Bible.   —In His Mercy, John H.

January 23, 1997

(Note from saintly friend who shares Kim's birthday.)

Our Precious Kimmy,

Thank you, thank you for sharing your "missionary journey." But, more than that, you shared your life – your heart – your very soul! We were reminded of *the Scripture in Isaiah 45:2a-3... Surely the Lord has given you many "treasures of darkness." In fact, He has shaped you into a many-faceted <u>jewel</u>. Then, we thought of how through the death of our dearest John, new <u>life</u> has sprung up in the hearts of new believers (Heb. 11:4 and also Prov. 10:7a).*

Also, we were reminded of II Cor. 2:14-16, as you ministered both to believers and non-believers. We were so inspired and blessed by your undaunted courage, your Godly wisdom and spiritual maturity – a vessel for the Master's use!

We want you to have this treasure-box from a ministry overseas. Perhaps, also, the angel banner would be a blessing in your 'Elijah Room!'

Our love & continued prayers for you,
Ruth, Gordon and Beverly

(A few days later, they allowed me to read aloud "Letter From Heaven," at their mission banquet.)

February 13, 1997

(From Kim's friend's husband, who has suffered with advanced M.S.)

Dear Kimberly,

Hello, my sister! Although we've never met nor spoken as yet, I feel I know you intimately through years of communications that I have been most privileged to share in through Katie. From our first Christmas letter from you and my wife's recount of her treasured memories of you and John, I have wanted to write and know you more. Your last October letter and now the Dec. epistle, released a floodgate of tears, as I sympathized with what the Lord brought you through and the extraordinary character and heart the Lord has allowed to develop within you.

Yet, those recent newsletters gave but a hint of the image I now have of you after having heard your epic tape series. What a shining light your testimony is! You are living proof of what the gospel of Jesus is all about. The scriptures that leap to mind are... "Out of the greatest darkness shines forth the greatest light" (Isa. 60: 1-2) *and "My strength is made perfect in your weakness"* (II Cor. 12:9a) *plus "Deny thyself, take up your cross and follow me"* (Matt. 16:24). *And, do you ever! There are so many more – about a whole Bible's worth.*

Kimberly, I've been praying for you since I first heard of you and will continue. I sense, in both the spirit and the natural, some of what God has already accomplished through you. I expect much more up coming and ongoing into the future. May the Lord aid you in finding another companion someday, so you won't always have to walk through life's trials alone. I sincerely hope that one day we can meet face-to-face and share what God's been doing...

Praise Him! -- Bobby G.

(<u>Katie then added</u>: *So, how'd you like my hubby's letter? He is so enthralled by what happened on that trip! Oh, Kimmy, I am so much in awe of what our dear Lord can do!)*

March 6, 1997

Dear Ones to My Heart,

There are thoughts I'd like to share with John, on this his birth-date, but decided to write them to all of you instead. It might be years before dates like this one, or our wedding day or the one of his accident will pass unnoticed for me. But, it is a bit easier each time and, after this, I will try not to keep reminding others about them.

For your own benefit, may the Lord grant you the extra leisure time needed to sit, read, and absorb this letter. Try not to feel overwhelmed by it, as I do NOT intend to compose long epistles after this one. Why? #1- Because doing so causes such an emotional draining to earnestly pour out my heart in a manner that also is uplifting and helpful to others. #2-Some folks have pointedly stated that my "raw openness" makes them feel so uncomfortable that they would rather I did not send them my letters at all. So, for those of you who do get uneasy, take heart! This is the final one you will have to endure.

Oh, by the way, since the Open House for the "Elijah Room," have had a fairly regular flow of "guests" upstairs. Also, my work hours, with my Special Needs children picked up again, right after the holidays. One "sister" asked how I managed to make ends meet with such unpredictable income. I remarked that, besides tithing, maintaining a frugal household budget, always spending less each month than what is earned, I also try to be generous to others in even more need. As Captain Levy, of Philadelphia once said, "Oh, as I shovel out, He shovels in, and the Lord has a bigger *shovel than I." God expects me to handle my finances responsibly, but for His part, He has never failed to provide for my needs. *(Besides a few of my wants!)*

These past few months, I have jotted down thoughts, experiences and short quotes of interest. It is my sincere hope that each of you will glean at least one personal blessing from the following pages. Have read a couple of books that encourage and instruct on how to seek out and become close, accountable friends, even mentors, with persons of the same gender. Why? Because the affliction of inner loneliness, even within a crowd, does <u>not</u> have to be ours! The books were called <u>Seven Promises of a Promise Keeper</u> and <u>The Friendship Connection</u>, by Timothy Jones. There's an old saying, "If we don't demonstrate our love, it doesn't do anyone any good." Hurting people need expressions of love they can see, hear, and feel. Joni Eareckson-Tada has remarked, "Often God permits what He hates (to see <u>happen</u> in our lives) *in order to accomplish what He loves"* (to see <u>produced</u> in our lives).

It has been proven that if you hear yourself or others say something about you long enough (whether good or bad) you will get to the point where you actually believe it. This can work for your good, to encourage you to strive on towards a noble endeavor; or it can work for you harm, by discouraging you from even trying. If you constantly "talk down" to yourself, or listen to others (perhaps even tormenting spirits) doing it with phases like, "I'm a loser, a useless nobody," then you <u>will</u> begin to believe what is actually VERY false!

So, I much agree that we should all heed Allen Stockdale's following prayer: "Dear Lord, look into my mouth and see what a cruel thing my tongue is. It seeks to ruin a good reputation; it lies when crowded into a corner; it boasts to satisfy vanity; it runs on and on when silence would be golden; it does not report matters correctly; it has made trouble for me and my relatives, friends, and co-workers. Dear Lord, if You can adjust my tongue to truth and gentleness, love and fairness, You will perform a miracle of compassion in the area where I live, move, and have my being."

We children of the King should only be using the noble (honoring) words and language of His court. People have a right to expect our speech (and jokes) to be purer than is the world's. In regards to a person's need for self-worth, Julien C. Hymer recites, "Don't wound his ego or he'll be, thereafter your sworn enemy. You may have meant it as a joke, to get a laugh from other folk. And, he may not have seemed to show resentment...but you may never know, how deep your words cut, nor how strong...his hate can grow from this one wrong. Though you may do it all in fun, <u>you</u> lose, when you hurt someone."

And, remember, for those of you who are holding onto an offense, "Hatred does a great deal more damage to the vessel in which it is stored, than to the object on which it is poured." A poem by Sir Walter Scott applies here, "And many a word, at random spoken, may soothe or wound a heart that's broken."

Don't forget that a person is never so empty, as when he is full of HIMSELF. When someone mistreats you, do what comes SUPERnaturally...love them, then follow God's direction to pray for them (Luke 6:27-28). We each need to better learn how to swiftly extend grace to a person, even after they have offended us. Humanly, that's one tough cookie! But, with the help of the Holy Spirit, we can transform that potential enemy into a friend...if only inside our hearts and thoughts. And, before searching for faults to correct in others, it would behoove each of us to first "look in the mirror." Such an outlook changed one Dad who then remarked, "I'm not a model father yet. But, now I want to behave in such a way, that when people tell my son that he reminds them of me, he will stick out his chest...instead of his tongue."

Contentment, I have found, has almost nothing to do with what's going on in my <u>life</u>, but everything to do with what I let go on in my <u>mind</u>. It is achievable, depending on which mental list I dwell upon, what God hasn't done...or, what God HAS done! Norman Grub once said, "Our greatest purpose on this earth is <u>not</u> to become something, but to CONTAIN Someone." How true it is that "experience is a different (kind of) teacher; it gives you the test first, and the lessons after." Consider these revised lines: "God grant me the serenity to accept the person I cannot change, to change the person I can, and the wisdom to know that I <u>am</u> THAT person."

When the Bible says that the "poor (meek) in spirit will be blessed" (Matt. 5:5), it is talking about those people who understand and recognize the divinity and power of God, then humbly admit their need of His help and guidance. We do this through prayer and obedience. We need God to show us <u>HIS</u> "Master-

plan" for our lives. As it has been said, "People don't plan to fail, they just fail to plan." So, go ahead and ask Jesus for the" inside scoop!" And, in case you didn't know, past mistakes do NOT have to mean future failures!

As I'd shared at church one morning, a main reason to pray is to give thanks back to God. We are expected to find something worth praising and thanking Him for in <u>every</u> situation (Eph. 5:20). Not necessarily FOR every challenge, but, at least, for all the good He will be produce FROM them. We should cultivate an "attitude of gratitude," as Barbara Johnson of <u>The Joyful Journey</u> quips. She adds, "You have never outlived your dream; there are always new STARTS to come." Folks, let's not ever forget the saying, "Yesterday is a cancelled check, tomorrow is just a promissory note, but today is 'cash-in-hand!' So, let's use it, not lose it. A similar piece of wisdom is, "Yesterday is in the past, (leave it there, it's only history), Tomorrow is the future (not yet ready to be grasped), but Today is the Present (that's why we call it a gift)."

Thomas Edition understood about prayer and God's protective hand as well. It is told that one day his laboratory, with all of his experiments and notes, was burned and gutted. After the blaze was over, Mr. Edison walked through the rubble and noticed a brown paper package. It was still wrapped with string and laying on the floor. Curious, he bent down, plucked it from the warm cinders, and untied what turned out to be a framed photo of himself. Its edges were slightly singed, but the picture was perfectly intact. After standing there, silently pondering over this for awhile,

Mr. Edison picked up a tiny, charred, stick. With its tip, he wrote his thanks to God across the photo and on the bottom he declared, "It didn't touch me!" That 'set-back' only motivated him further to succeed in his goals. So, when we, too, maintain a thankful heart, none of our own "fiery trials' will ever scorch us too severely or really "touch us" (Isa. 43:2b).

Remember, dears, "happiness depends on <u>happenings</u>; joy depends on JESUS." Our trust in and attitude towards God shouldn't alter, not even when life's hardships get more complicated and perplexing. For instance, consider the plight of an old English circuit preacher named Matthew Henry. One day, while he was riding his horse through a wooded area on his way from conducting one church service to the next, he was held up at gunpoint and robbed. In his journal that night, he wrote four things that he had prayerfully thanked God about regarding that frightening encounter. Pastor Henry penned, "Thank you Lord that I have never been robbed before. Thank you Lord, that although he took all I had, it was not so very much and there is a bit more back at home. Thank you Lord, that he did not take my life or my horse. And, thank you Lord, that by your grace, I was the one being robbed...I was not the robber."

You see, folks, we ought not to be only counting our blessings one-by-one, we should be counting them TON-BY-TON, and giving prayerful thanks to God all the while! Billy Graham has stated, "I have never met a person who spent time in prayer, in the study of God's Word, and who was strong in faith, that stayed discouraged for very long." Oswald Chambers believed that, "Prayer does not equip us for greater work...prayer IS the greater work." John Wesley proclaimed, "Give me one hundred preachers who fear nothing but sin, and desire nothing but God, and I care not a straw whether they be clergymen or laymen; such alone will shake the gates of hell and set up the Kingdom of heaven on earth. God does nothing, but in answer to prayer." Dietrich Benhoeffer challenges us with this statement, "The entire day receives order and discipline when it acquires unity. That unity must be sought and found in morning prayer. Temptations which accompany each workday will be conquered on the basis of your morning breakthrough to God."

Concluding this topic, allow me to share these varied comments. "We stand best, when we have first learned to kneel...in prayerful worship." It is always best to keep our prayers very detailed and specific because, "Where prayer focuses (from us to God), power (from heaven) FALLS!" To keep one's faith strong and discouragement at bay, it is often good that, when you ask for anything, for ourselves or for others, we should pray, "If what I ask will not glorify Your Name in this situation, then don't grant it. And, Father, if You don't grant it, please give me the strength to glorify Your name without it."

Lastly, for the benefit of those who have been asking, there has emerged a couple of new goals in my life, as it has progressed, to which I hope to remain faithful. #1) Be available to and discerning of God's direction in ministering to the unsaved, without letting them do harm to me. And, #2) Continue befriending and fellowshipping with a variety of Bible-believing

Christians among all races, nationalities and denominations.

It has been so enjoyable spending quality time and sharing worship services with new friends from many different churches! If we have the same basic doctrine of the Trinity, of Who Jesus really is, of salvation by grace alone, and of life everlasting, then we have PLENTY in common to use as a solid foundation to enjoy each other's company AND to worship our Mighty King together! Enjoy the springtime and summer ahead!

Love and Blessings, Kimberly

March 20, 1997

Dear Kim,

Thanks for your recent encouraging epistle... Now, to the compelling reason that stands out head and shoulders above the other reasons I have written. It has to do with what you said in the aforementioned letter. You said, "I do not intend to compose an update after this one." You stated two reasons. The first one I can accept, but the 2nd one just ticked me off!

Sister, we think you are probably one of the sweetest, most sincere, honest, pure, righteous, wise, fair, virtuous, respectful, creditable, straightforward, polite, genuine, decent, generous, kind, honorable, considerate, enjoyable, reliable, faithful, God-fearing, gentle, patient, forgiving Christians that is now walking planet earth. And, I'm sure our Father in Heaven is well pleased.

Kimmy, you just keep up your writings, say what you want, continue to send the letters. Better yet, write a whole book and let the chips fall where they want! And, you may quote me verbatim (*Which I did not, as his mood was too explosive!) *and let those rude, ignorant people know that their childish, immature criticism doesn't sit well with your friends. I wish you would give me their names, so I could personally address them.* (*Which I didn't, but it sure lifted my heart to have such a "champion!")

Sherree and I support you 100%; your words are encouraging, well thought out, sensitive, and very proper. KEEP UP THE GOOD WORK AND DON'T LET A COUPLE OF KNOT HEADS STOP YOUR WRITING! We love you and are praying for you.

Your friends in Christ, --- Dave and Sherree M.

April 2, 1997

*(The following are verbal comments from my neighbor, Geoffrey Daniels. He is the father of some great children who let me be their friend. He was the last person to recently listen to the set of tapes.)

"I had no idea and am so sorry for all you've had to go through, mostly alone. I'm humbled that you have trusted me to hear about the trip and your life. As far as the audio tapes go, I strongly suggest that you don't take out anything! To me, and I think to others, it was how the story is connected from place to place and family to family, which kept it so real. But, what

I really believe is that you should write a book about this! It could benefit so many others."

*(Years later, a few others were allowed to hear the tapes before they were made into a book.)

ADDENDUM

Dear Kim,

May you find a loving, caring person to fill the empty spot in your heart. God knows and is the only One who can help. With Him, "all things are possible" *(Matt. 19:26b)*. When the times comes, He will take care of it for you. "May the Lord ever bless and keep you," is my prayer!

    Love Always, Your sister in Christ --Omega

"Thou hast turned for my mourning into dancing; thou hast put off my sackcloth and girded me with gladness; to the end that my glory may sing praises to thee and not be silent. O Lord my God, I will give thanks unto thee forever.' *--Psalms 30:11-12*

Although it had been over four years since my last health challenge, the verdict came in the dead of winter that the cancer was back. But, the news didn't alarm me, as I half-hoped that this would be my "ticket home." I had found contentment in my singleness, yes, but also knew that not anyone's life would be significantly disrupted if I were gone. Such didn't make me sad; it was just a fact. Ministering to others still thrilled me, but not being a viable part in the life of one person, for so very long, had made me feel unproductive and, well, expendable here. It seemed logical that the timing to be "promoted upward" could be soon. Admittedly, I was a bit excited.

Dutifully, over the next few months, I "got my house in order" *(II Kings 20:1)*, both the actual abode and its yard, plus drew up a new Will and arranged for my financial papers to be readily accessible. Figuring, if I died, then it would be considerate to make the dispersing of my things easier. Yet, in case I did survive the upcoming major surgery, PLUS the long haul of oral chemotherapy treatment afterwards, then having everything clean and in full repair would be of help. From previous experience, I knew that my body would certainly be too weak to attend to such matters for awhile. Also, expecting to be fully alone during recovery, this gal spent weeks cooking and freezing small, doctor-prescribed meals to easily microwave later. And, if it did happen that I actually got well again, the thought of selling my home and moving away from the area, with its lingering stigma of being a widow, had great appeal.

And, yet God…had been orchestrating events and hearts to provide me with surprise help from good neighbors who soon would become my "new family!"

* * * * * * * *

About a year before the accident, the Daniels' family moved into the rental house next door. Happily, John and I quickly became friends with the youngsters, although our contact with the parents was infrequent. Even so, it was that dad, Geoffrey, who had picked up John's parents from the airport, to attend their son's funeral, and drove them back again for their flight home. From then on, Mr. Daniels also made sure he or his older sons always took my trash to the local dump, whenever they were going for their own household.

Then, several months after my John was gone, that father and his children went through the heartbreak of having to also learn how to get along without their mother being with her own family anymore.

Time went by, and then one day the father asked his youngest teens if they thought they were ready for him to start dating? Basically, their response was, "It's about time Dad, but we hope you pick someone more like Miss Kimmy next door." Well, as the proverbial saying goes, "Out of the mouth of babes"... *(Matt. 21:16b).* Mr. Daniels had always thought of me as belonging to John. And, I'd learn to feel very comfortable being unmarried, and had absolutely no desire to jump into the "dating scene" and was getting rather "set in my ways." To my thinking, he was always just the kid's D-A-D; I'd never looked at him as a M-A-N. So, when Mr. Daniels asked me to consider if the Lord might want us to court, with the intent of seeing whether it was His desire for us to make a future together, I was taken aback...and flattered. *(After all, this man was offering to take a risk on me with himself AND his precious children!)

Yet, because he did not know about my current medical illness, I told Mr. Daniels that, if there were other ladies he had in mind, then he'd best start with them. *(Besides him being an almost physical opposite of John and my not having any initial romantic inclinations towards him, I was very doubtful that I had ANY future to offer anyone!) Not wishing to offend or hurt his feelings, I made some excuse about having (truthfully) too many other "irons in the fire" right now, to even consider beginning a courtship until, at least, next fall. To my surprise, he said he wasn't interested in anyone else, so he'd just wait for me. In the meantime, if I found a day when I wasn't too busy, maybe we could just go have a cup of coffee and talk? *(And, people say *I* have tenacity!)

Wanting to be truthful about my health dilemma, plus being concerned that, perhaps emotionally, Mr. Daniels was not actually ready to start any new relationships, I agreed. About a week later, I made an effort to be available for visiting with him at our local hospital café. Wrong! He was very ready… and determined! Thus, in spite of my qualms about developing any attachments, we did manage to dine out a few times before my surgery. By that time, his daughter had offered to bring the mail to my door everyday, and she and her younger brother mowed my lawn, while I was sick.

Although he knew my heart had not yet been fully won, Geoffrey showed immeasurable kindness in his "fatherly" care of me over the next few months, including nightly phone calls to encourage me to eat something, take my medicine, and try to get some needed sleep. He brought over fresh fruit, made phone calls for me and was always sympathic of the daily fever, chills, nausea, and pain. He was rightfully concerned that in my weakness and misery, I was sometimes tempted to just "give up the fight" and let death take me. Often, I was discouraged and felt utterly gross! Healing from the operation got better, but as expected, the loss of my hair got worse, yet Geoffrey still seemed to find something of loveliness within me and kept proclaiming his affection and steadfastness.

After the treatments ended, and I had regained some of my strength, I went to visit friends and go on a short vacation for 2-3 weeks. It was a brief time away from Geoffrey, but enough to be able to seriously contemplate what God really did want for our future. No longer a "spring chicken," I was very unsure about courting towards remarriage. I asked John's parents, my closest friends, co-pastors and their wives, to give me their advice and express their feelings about the possibility of me remarrying, especially into a pre-made family unit. From most people, I got hearty endorsements, which was good, as Geoffrey proposed soon afterwards…and I accepted!

Now, over five years later, all of the children are "out of the nest" and on their own. We both sensed that this was the Master's timing for this book to be written. Geoffrey was concerned that, while I had to keep this idea buried and "on the back burner," in order to help him finish rearing the children, it might not ever actually resurface again. So, it is with much relief and sincerity that we both hope that it has been a blessing you!

---In the Lord's Care,
Geoffrey and Kimberly Rae Daniels

APPENDIX

Scriptures: *(Listed in the order of their appearances.)*

Acknowledgements

Isaiah 61:3b - *...that they might be called trees of righteousness planted by the Lord, that He might be glorified.*

Forward

II Peter 3:18 – *Grow in the grace and knowledge of the Lord and Savior Jesus Christ.*

Ephesians 5:14b - *...arise from the dead, and Christ shall give thee light.*

I Corinthians 13:6-7 – *Rejoiceth not in iniquity, but rejoiceth in the truth; Beareth all thins, believeth all things, hopeth all things, endureth all things.*

Hebrews 11:10 – *...he looked for a city which hath foundation, whose builder and maker is God...*

Timothy 2:19a – *...the foundation of God standeth sure...The Lord knoweth them that are his.*

I King 8:57 – *The Lord our God be with us... let him not leave us or forsake us.*

II Corinthians 12:9a - *...My grace is sufficient for thee: for my strength is made perfect in your weakness.*

I Kings 17:9-16 – *Arise...I have commanded a widow woman there to sustain thee...behold the widow was there gathering sticks; and called to her, and said, Bring me, I pray thee, a morsel of bread in thine hand. And she said...I have but a handful of meal in a barrel, and a little oil in a cruse...And Elijah said unto her, Fear not; go and do as thou hast said: but make me thereof a little cake first, and bring it unto me, and after make for thee... For thus saith the Lord God, The barrel of meal shall not waste, neither shall the cruse of oil fail... And she did according to the saying of Elijah: and...did eat for many days.*

<u>Jeremiah 29:11</u> – For I know the thoughts (plans) that I think towards you, saith the Lord, thoughts (plans) of peace, and not of evil...

Preface

<u>I Peter 2:9</u> – But ye are a chosen generation, a royal priesthood, a holy nation, a peculiar people; that you should shew forth the praises of him who hath called you out of darkness and into his marvelous light.

<u>Romans 12:18</u> – If it be possible, as much as lieth in you, live peaceably with all men.

<u>Psalms 39:12b</u> - ...for I am a stranger with thee, and a sojourner...

<u>John 16:33b</u> – In the world ye shall have tribulation: but be of good cheer; I have overcome the world.

<u>I Peter 5:8</u> – ...be vigilant; because your adversary the devil, as a roaring lion, walketh about, seeking whom he may devour.

<u>Psalms 91:15</u> – He shall call upon me, and I will answer him: I will be with him in trouble; I will deliver him and shew him the way to salvation.

Introduction

<u>Psalms 74:17b</u> – Thou hast set all the borders of the earth: thou hast made the summer and winter.

<u>Romans 12:21</u> – be not overcome with evil, but overcome evil with good.

Philippians 1:12 – ... I would ye understand, brethren, that the things which happened unto have fallen out rather unto the furtherance of the gospel.

Colossians 4:6 – Let your speech be always with grace, seasoned with salt, that ye may know how ye ought to answer every man.

Matthew 19:19-20 - ...take no thought how or what ye shall speak: for it shall be given you...For it is not ye that speak, but the Spirit of your father which speaketh in you.

Chapter One

Leviticus 19:16a – Thou shalt not go up and as a talebearer among thy people...

Proverbs 3:12 – For whom the Lord loveth he correcteth; even as a father the son in whom he delighteth.

Hebrews 13:6 - ...The Lord is my helper, and I will not fear what man shall do unto me.

II Corinthians 12:9a - ...My grace is sufficient for thee: for my strength is made perfect in your weakness.

Isaiah 55:11 – So shall my word be that goeth forth out of my mouth: it shall not return to me void, but it shall accomplish that which I please...

Psalms 119:11 – Thy word have I hid in my heart, that I might not sin against thee.

Matthew 7:9, 11 - ...what man is there of you, whom if his son asks bread, will he give him a stone? If ye then, being evil, know how to give good gifts unto your children, how much more shall your Father in heaven give good things to them that ask him?

Chapter Two

Philippians 4:13 – *I can do all things through Christ which strengthens me.*

Ephesians 6:19 - *...that utterance can be given unto me, that I may open my mouth boldly, to make known the mystery of the gospel.*

Chapter Three

Colossians 1:4 – *In whom we have redemption through his blood, even the forgiveness of sins.*

Revelation 2:4 – *Nevertheless, I have somewhat against thee, because thou hast left thy first love.*

Joel 2:25a-26- – *And I will restore to you the years that the locust hath eaten… And ye shall be satisfied, and praise the name of the Lord your God, that hath dealt wondrously with you: and my people shall never be ashamed.*

II Corinthians 6:14 – *Be ye not unequally yoked together with unbelievers: for what fellowship hath righteousness with unrighteousness? And what communion hath light with darkness?*

Mark 8:36 – *For what shall it profit a man, if he gain the whole world, and he lose his own soul?*

Romans 8:1a, 12a – *There is now no condemnation in Christ Jesus… Therefore, we are all debtors…*

II Chronicles 29:31a - *…Now ye have consecrated yourselves unto the Lord, come near and bring sacrifices and thank offerings into the house of the Lord.*

II Corinthians 6:17 - *…come ye out of them, and be ye separate, saith the Lord…and I will receive you.*

Chapter Four

Job 40:4 – *Behold, I am vile; what shall I answer thee? I will lay mine hand upon my mouth.*

Matthew 11:28 – *Come unto me, all ye that labour and are heavy laden, and I will give you rest.*

Hebrews 13:5b - *...for he hath said, I will never leave thee, not forsake thee.*

Isaiah 61:1 – *The Spirit of the Lord is upon me; because the Lord hath anointed me to preach good tidings...to bind up the brokenhearted, to proclaim liberty to the captives,... to them that are bound;*

Genesis 39:12 – *...she caught him by his garment, saying Lie with me: and he left his garment...and fled.*

Philippians 2:10 – *...at the name of Jesus every knee should bow, of things in heaven, and things in earth, and things under the earth;*

Luke 23:26 - *...as they led him away, they hold upon one named Simon...and on him they laid the cross, that he might bear it after Jesus.*

Hebrews 5:8 – *Though he were a Son, yet learned he obedience by the thing which he suffered;*

II Timothy 2:12a – *If we suffer, we shall also reign with him...*

Chapter Five

Exodus 34:14 –*For thou shalt worship no other god: for the Lord is a jealous God:*

II Corinthians 6:17 –*Wherefore come out from among them, and be ye separate, saith the Lord...and I will receive you.*

Hosea 10:5b, 6b - *... For the glory is departed...shall receive shame, and shall be ashamed of his own counsel.*

Chapter Six

Psalms 119:15 – *I will mediate on thy precepts, and have respect unto thy ways.*

Matthew 10:1b - *...he gave them power against unclean spirits, to cast them out, and to heal disease.*

Jeremiah 30:17a – *For I will restore health unto thee, and I will heal thee of thy wounds,*

I Corinthians 14:2 – *For he that speaketh in an unknown tongue speaketh not unto men, but unto God: for no man understandeth him; howbeit in the spirit he speaketh mysteries.*

I Corinthians 14:4 – *He that speaketh an unknown tongue edifieth himself; but he that prophesieth edifieth the church.*

I Corinthians 14:13 – *Wherefore let him that speaketh in an unknown tongue pray that he may interpret.*

I Corinthians 14:27 – *If any man speak in an unknown tongue,...let one interpret.*

Matthew 7:20 – *Wherefore by their fruits ye shall know them.*

Chapter Seven

Proverbs 22:6 – *Train up a child in the way he should go: and when he is old, he will not depart from it.*

II Corinthians – *For if he that cometh preacheth another Jesus, whom we have not preached, or if ye receive another spirit,... or another gospel, which ye have not accepted...*

II Timothy 3:16 – *All scripture is given by inspiration of God, and is profitable for doctrine, for reproof, for correction, for instruction in righteousness.*

II Corinthians 13:5 – *Examine yourselves, whether ye be in the faith; Know ye...how that Jesus Christ is in you, except ye be reprobates?*

John 1:1-3 – *In the beginning was the Word, and the Word was with God, and the Word was God.*

Romans 8:11a – *But if the Spirit of him that raised Jesus from the dead dwell in you, he...shall also quicken your mortal bodies by his Spirit...*

II Corinthians 3:17 – *Now the Lord is that Spirit :and where the Spirit of the Lord is, there is liberty.*

John 6:63 – *It is the spirit that quickeneth;...the words that I speak,... they are spirit, and they are life.*

Jude 1:21 – *Keep yourselves in the love of God, looking for the mercy of our Lord Jesus Christ unto eternal life.*

I Corinthians 1:3 – *Grace be unto you, and peace, from God our father, and from the Lord Jesus Christ.*

John 10:38b - *...that ye may know, and believe, that the father is in me, and I in him.*

I Peter 1:2 – *Elect according to the foreknowledge of God the father, through sanctification of the Spirit, unto obedience and sprinkling of the blood of Jesus Christ...*

Colossians 1:28 – *Whom we preach, warning every man, and teaching every man in all wisdom; that we may present every man perfect in Christ Jesus.*

Ecclesiastes 9:10 – *Whatsoever thy hand findeth to do, do it with all thy might.*

Luke 19:17 – *And he said unto him, Well, thou good servant: because thou hast been faithful in very little, have thou authority over ten cities.* _

Chapter Eight

II Corinthians 12:9a - *.. My grace is sufficient for thee:*

Colossians 1:28a - *...warning every man, and teaching every man in all wisdom;*

Job 14:12 – *So man lieth down, and riseth not: till the heavens be no more, they shall not awake' nor be raised from out of their sleep.*

Joshua 1:7a – *Only be thou strong and very courageous...*

I Corinthians 15:44 – *It is sown a natural body; it is raised a spiritual body. There is a natural body, and there is a spiritual body.*

I Kings 8:57 – *The Lord our God be with us,...let him not leave us, nor forsake us:*

Chapter Nine

Psalms 119:173 – *Let thine hand help me; for I have chosen thy percepts.*

Psalms 119:165 – *Great peace have they which love thy law: and nothing shall offend them.*

Matthew 5:7 – *Blessed are the merciful: for they shall obtain mercy.*

Romans 12:15 – *Rejoice with them that do rejoice, and weep with them that weep.*

Proverbs 10:7a – *The memory of the just is blessed:*

Chapter Ten

John 14:2 – *In my Father's house are many mansions: I go to prepare a place for you.*

I Thessalonians 4:14 – *For if ye believe that Jesus died and rose again, even so them also which sleep in Jesus will God bring with him.*

I Thessalonians 4:13 - *...concerning them which are asleep, that ye sorrow not, even as others which have no hope.*

Psalms 4:8 – *I will both lay me down in peace, and sleep: for thou, Lord, only maketh me dwell in safety.*

Numbers 12:6b – *I the Lord will make myself known unto him in a vision, and will speak unto him in a dream.*

John 14:26a – *But the Comforter, which is the Holy Ghost, whom the Father will send in my name;*

Job 14:12 – *So man lieth down, and riseth not: till the havens be no more, they shall not awake, nor be raised out of their sleep.*

Hebrews 2:14b -*...that through death he might destroy him that had the power of death, that is, the devil;*

Chapter Eleven

Ephesians 6:12 – *For we wrestle not against flesh and blood, but against...the rulers of darkness...*

John 13:23 – *Now there was leaning on Jesus' bosom one of his disciples, whom Jesus loved.*

Psalms 66:2 – *Sing forth the honour of his name: make his praise glorious.*

Matthew 5:9 – *Blessed are the peacemakers: for they shall be called the children of God.*

Matthew 19:26b – *With men this is impossible; but with God all things are possible.*

Numbers 23:10b – *Let me die the (respected) death of the righteous...*

Chapter Twelve

Ephesians 3:14-15 – *For this cause I bow my knees unto the Father of our Lord Jesus Christ' Of whom the whole family in heaven and earth is named.*

II Peter 2:1 – *But there are false prophets also among the people, even as there shall be false teachers among you, who privily shall bring in damnable heresies, even denying the Lord that bought them. And bring upon themselves swift destruction.*

II Thessalonians 2:13-14 – *But we are bound to give thanks always to God for you, brethren beloved of the Lord, because God hath from the beginning chosen you to salvation through sanctification of the Spirit and belief in the truth: Whereunto he called you, by our gospel, to the obtaining of the glory of our Lord Jesus Christ.*

Chapter Thirteen

<u>Luke 18:1b</u> - ...that men ought always to pray, and not faint;

<u>Colossians 2:10a</u> - ...for you are complete in him.

<u>Revelation 21:9b</u> - ...and talked with me, saying, Come hither, I will shew thee the bride, the Lamb's wife.

<u>I Corinthians 6:17</u>

<u>Isaiah 65:17, 19</u> – For, behold, I create new heavens and a new earth: and the former shall not be remembered, nor come to mind...And I will rejoice in the joy of my people; and the voice of weeping shall be no more heard, nor the voice of crying.

<u>John 3:3</u> – And Jesus answered and said unto him, Verily, verily, I say unto thee, Except a man be born again, he cannot see the kingdom of God.

<u>Acts 4:13</u> – Now when they saw the boldness...and perceived that they were ignorant men, they marveled; and they took knowledge of, that they had been with Jesus.

Chapter Fourteen

<u>Isaiah 58:9a</u> – Thou shalt call, and the Lord shall answer; thou shalt cry out, and he shall say, Here I am.

<u>Psalms 89:1</u> – I will sing of the mercies of the Lord forever: with my mouth will I make known thy faithfulness to all generations.

Chapter Fifteen

<u>Psalms 48:14</u> – For this is our God for ever and ever: he will be our guide...

<u>Ecclesiastes 3:4</u> – A time to weep, and a time to laugh; a time to mourn, and a time to dance.

Hebrews 13:2 – *Be not forgetful to entertain strangers: for thereby some have entertained angels unawares.*

Chapter Sixteen

Ezekiel 18:12 – *Hath oppressed the poor and needy, hath spoiled by violence, hath not restore the pledge, and hath lifted up his eyes to idols, hath committed abomination,*

Psalms 86:5 – *For thou, Lord art good, and ready to forgive; and plenteous in mercy unto all them that call upon thee.*

Proverbs 18:24b – *...and there is a friend that sticketh closer than a brother.*

Isaiah 25:4 – *For thou hast been strength...to the needy in distress, a refuge from the storm...when the blast of the terrible ones is as a storm against a wall.*

Psalms 143:4 – *Therefore is my spirit overwhelmed within me; my heart within me is desolate.*

Revelation 12:10b – *for the accuser of our brethren is cast down, which accused them before God day and night.*

I Timothy 6:12a - *Fight the good fight of faith,*

II Timothy 2:3 – *Thou therefore endure hardness, as a good soldier of Jesus Christ.*

Romans 12:19 – *Dearly beloved, avenge not yourselves... for it is written, Vengeance is mine; I will repay, saith the Lord.*

Ezekiel 18:20 – *The soul that sinneth shall die. The son shall not bear the iniquity of the father,*

Deuteronomy 6:6-7a – *And these words, which I command thee this day, shall be in thine heart: And thou shalt teach them diligently unto thy children,*

Lamentations 1:16c - *...my children are desolate, because the enemy prevailed.*

Chapter Seventeen

II Timothy 4:8 – *Henceforth thee is laid up for me a crown of righteousness, which the Lord, the righteous judge, shall give me at that day: and not me only, but unto all them also that love his appearing.*

I Timothy 6:12 – *Fight the good fight of faith, lay hold on eternal life, whereunto thou art also called, and hast professed a good profession before many witnesses.*

Matthew 25:21b - *...enter thou into the joy of the Lord.*

Philippians 1:23b - *...to be with Christ; which is far better:*

I Thessalonians 5:12-13 – *And we beseech you, brethren, to know them which labour among you, and are over you in the Lord, and admonish you; And to esteem them very highly in love for their work's sake.*

Ephesians 6:11 – *Put on the whole armour of God, that ye may be able to stand against the wiles of the devil.*

I Timothy 4:1b-2 - *...giving heed to seducing spirits, and doctrines of devils; Speaking lies in hypocrisy; having their conscience seared with a hot iron;*

Matthew 5:9 – *Blessed are the peacemakers: for they shall be called children of God.*

Ezekiel 44:23 – *And they shall teach my people the difference between the holy and profane, and cause them to discern between the unclean and the clean.*

John 10:10a – *The thief cometh not, but to steal, and to kill, and to destroy:*

Luke 11:24, 26 – *When the unclean spirit is gone out of a man, he walketh through dry places, seeking rest; and finding none, he saith, I will return unto my house whence I came out. Then goeth he, and taketh to him seven other spirits more wicked than himself; and they enter in, and dwell there: and the last state of that man is worse than the first.*

Matthew 14:31b – *O thou of little faith, wherefore didst thou doubt?*

Chapter Eighteen

Proverbs 11:3a – *The integrity of the upright shall guide them:*

Matthew 12:43 – *O generation of vipers, how can ye, being evil, speak good things? For out of the abundance of the heart the mouth speaketh.*

II Timothy 1:7 – *For God hath not given us a spirit of fear; but of power and love, and a sound mind.*

I John 4:4 – *Ye are of God, little children, and have overcome them: because greater is he that is on you, than he that is in the world.*

Ephesians 6:12 – *For we wrestle not against flesh and blood, but against principalities, against powers, against the rulers of darkness of this world, against spiritual wickedness I high places.*

Exodus 14:15b – *Wherefore criest unto me? Speak unto the children...that they go forward;*

Chapter Nineteen

Psalms 42:5 – *Why at thou cast down, O my soul? And why art thou disquieted in me? Hope thou in God: for I shall yet praise him for the help of his countenance.*

Job 1:10a – *Hast thou not made a hedge about him, and all that he hath on every side?*

Psalms 3:3 – *But thou, O Lord, art a shield for me; my glory, and the lifter of mine head.*

Psalms 112:7 – *He shall not be afraid of evil tidings: his heart is fixed, trusting in the Lord.*

John 14:27 – *Peace I leave with you, my peace I give unto you...Let not your heart be troubled, neither let it be afraid.*

Psalms 126:3 – *The Lord hath done great things for us; whereof we are glad.*

John 16:33 – *These things I have spoken unto you, that in me ye might have peace. In the world ye shall have tribulation: but be of good cheer; I have overcome the world.*

Matthew 5:44 – *But I say unto you, Love your enemies, bless them that curse you, do good to them that hate you, ad pray for them which despitefully use you, and persecute you;*

Chapter Twenty

Proverbs 25:22 – *For thou shalt heap coals of fire upon his head, and the Lord shall reward thee.*

Proverbs 16:18 o pride goeth before destruction and a haughty spirit before a fall.

Chapter Twenty-One

Isaiah 7:14 – *Therefore the Lord himself shall give you a sing; Behold, a virgin shall conceive, and bear a son, and shall call his name Immanuel.*

I Corinthians 15:57 – *but thanks be to God, which giveth us the victory through our Lord Jesus Christ.*

Chapter Twenty-Two

John 3:20 – *For every one that doeth evil hateth the light,... lest his deeds should be reproved.*

Proverbs 13:6a – *The righteousness of the upright shall deliver them: but transgressors shall be taken in their own naughtiness.*

Psalms 106:5a – *That I may see the good of thy chosen, that I may rejoice in gladness...*

Psalms 36:10 – *O continue thy lovingkindness unto them that know thee; and thy righteousness to the upright heart.*

II Corinthians 5:17 – *Therefore if any man be in Christ, he is a new creature: old things are passed away; behold, all things become new.*

Matthew 26:40b – *Inasmuch as ye have done it unto one of the least of these my brethren, ye have done it unto me.*

Micah 3:2 – *Who hate the good, and love the evil; who pluck off their skin from off them, and their flesh from off their bones.*

II Corinthians 5:15 – *And that he died for all, that they which live should not henceforth live unto themselves, but unto him which died for them, and rose again.*

Joel 2:25a – *And I will restore to you the years that the locust hath eaten…*

Ephesians 6:4 – *And, ye fathers, provoke not your children to wrath: but bring them up in the nurture and admonition of the Lord.*

Matthew 12:35b – *… and an evil man out of the evil treasure bringeth forth evil things.*

Psalms 40:4 – *Blessed is that man that maketh the Lord his trust, and respecteth not the proud, nor such as turn aside to lies.*

Proverbs 29:27a – *An unjust man is an abomination to the just:*

Genesis 50:20a – *But as for you, ye thought evil against me; but God meant it unto good,*

Chapter Twenty-Three

Proverbs 20:30 – *The blueness of a wound cleanseth away evil: so do stripes the inward parts of the belly.*

Psalms 13:5 – *But I have trusted in thy mercy; my heart shall rejoice in thy salvation.*

Ezekiel 18:31 – *Cast away from you all your transgressions... and make a new heart and a new spirit:*

John 7:37b-38 – *If any man thirst, let him come unto me, and drink. He that believeth on me, ...out of his belly shall flow rivers of living water.*

Colossians 1:28 – *Whom we preach, warning every man, and teaching every man in all wisdom; that we may present every man perfect in Christ Jesus:*

Mark 11:25 – *And when ye stand praying, forgive, if ye have ought against any: that your Father also which is in heaven may forgive you your trespasses.*

Genesis 4:7b - *...and if thou doeth not well, sin lieth at the door.*

Deuteronomy 18:10-11 – *There shall not be found among you any one that...useth divination, or an observer of times, or an enchanter, or a witch, or a charmer, or a consulter with familiar spirits, or a wizard, or a necromancer.*

John 15:13 – *Greater love hath no man than this, that a man lay down his life for his friends.*

Romans 8:35 – *Who shall separate us from the love of Christ?*

Chapter Twenty-Four

Matthew 11:28 – *Come unto me, all ye that labour and are heavy laden, and I will give you rest*

Proverbs 17:22a – *A merry heart doeth good like a medicine:*

Proverbs 16:24 – *Pleasant words are as an honeycomb, sweet to the soul, and health to the bones.*

Psalms 69:19a – *Thou hast known my reproach, and my shame, and my dishonour:*

Ecclesiastes 2:24 – *There is nothing better for a man, than that he should eat... and that he should make his soul enjoy good in his labour. This I also saw, that it was from the hand of God.*

Psalms 40:2 – *He brought me up also out of an horrible pit, out of the miry clay, and set my feet upon a rock, and established my goings.*

Chapter Twenty-Five

Job 19:20 My bone cleaveth to my skin and to my flesh, and I am escaped with the skin of my teeth.

Obadiah 16b – so shall all the heathen drink continually, yea, they shall drink, and swallow it down, and they shall be as though they had not been.

Jeremiah 2:34a – Also in thy skirts is found the blood of the souls of the poor innocents:

Exodus 34:6-7a – And the Lord passed by before him, and proclaimed... The Lord God, merciful and gracious, longsuffering, and abundant in goodness and truth; Keeping mercy for thousands, forgiving iniquity and transgression and sin,

Genesis 30:1 – ... when Rachel saw that she bore...no children...said..."Give me children, or else I die."

Galatians 2:9b - ...they gave to me...the right hand of fellowship:

Chapter Twenty-Six

Galatians 3:26 – For ye are all the children of God by faith in Christ Jesus,

Ephesians 4:15 – But speaking the truth in love, may grow up into him in all things, which is the head, even Christ;

I Corinthians 3:1 – And I, brethren, could not speak unto you as unto spiritual, but as unto carnal, even as unto babes in Christ.

Matthew 10:33 – But whosoever shall deny me before men, him I also deny before my Father which is in heaven.

Job 1:10 – Hast not thou made an hedge about him...?

Matthew 10:28 – *And fear not them which kill the body, but are not able to kill the soul: but rather fear him which is able to destroy both soul and body in hell.*

Jeremiah 32:42 – *Yea, I will rejoice over them to do them good...*

Zephaniah 3:17 – *The Lord thy God in the midst of thee is mighty; he will save, he will rejoice over thee with joy; he will rest in love, he will joy over thee with singing.*

Ephesians 1:6 – *To the praise of the glory of his grace wherein he hath made us accepted in the beloved.*

Acts 14:22 – *Confirming the souls of the disciples, and exhorting them to continue in the faith, and that we must through much tribulation enter into the kingdom of God.*

I Peter 1:6-7 – *Wherein ye greatly rejoice, though now for a season, if need be, ye are in heaviness through manifold temptations: That the trial of your faith, being much more precious than of gold that perisheth, though it be tried with fire, might be found unto praise and honour and glory at the appearing of Jesus Christ.*

Chapter Twenty-Seven

Philippians 3:21 – *Who shall change our vile body, that it may be fashioned like unto his glorious body, according to the working whereby he is able to subdue all things unto himself.*

James 5:11b - *...that the Lord is very pitiful, and of tender mercy.*

Psalms 33:18 – *Behold, the eye of the Lord is upon them that fear him, upon them that hope in his mercy;*

Psalms 103:13 – *Like as a father pitieth his children, so the Lord pitieth them that fear him,*

Chapter Twenty-Eight

Psalms 41:1 – *Blessed is he that considereth the poor: the Lord will deliver him in time of trouble.*

Titus 3:9 – *But avoid foolish questions, and genealogies, and contentions, and strivings about the law; for they are unprofitable and vain.*

Luke 4:18-19 – *The spirit of the Lord is upon me, because he hath anointed me to preach the gospel to the poor; he hath sent me to heal the brokenhearted, to preach deliverance to the captives, and recovering of sight to the blind, to set at liberty them that are bruised, To teach the acceptable year of the Lord.*

Chapter Twenty-Nine

Romans 14:11 – *For it is written, As I live, saith the Lord, every knee shall bow to me, and every tongue shall confess to God.*

Job 10:2a – *I will say unto God, Do not contend with me;*

Matthew 13:25, 30 – *But while men slept, his enemy came and sowed tares among the wheat, and went his way. Let both grow together until the harvest: and in the time of harvest I will say to the reapers, Gather ye together first the tares, and bind them in bundles to burn them: but gather the wheat into my barn.*

Job 8:11 – *Can the rush grow up without mire? Can the flag grow without water?*

Proverbs 15 26b - *...But the words of the pure are pleasant words.*

Hosea 14:4 – *I will heal their backsliding, I will love them freely: for mine anger is turned away from him.*

Luke 17:10 – *So likewise ye, when ye shall have done all those things which are commanded you, say, We are unprofitable servants: we have done that which was our duty to do.*

Chapter Thirty

I Colossians 1:9 – *For this cause we also, since the day we heard it, do not cease to pray for you, and to desire that ye might be filled with the knowledge of his will in all wisdom and spiritual understanding;*

Psalms 113:9 – *He maketh the barren woman to keep house, and to be a joyful mother of children. Praise ye the Lord.*

Proverbs 3:26 – *For the lord shall be thy confidence, and shall keep thy foot from being taken.*

Lamentations 3:41 – *let us lift up our heart with our hands unto God in the heavens.*

Acts 9:15-16 – *But the Lord said unto him, Go thy way: for he is a chosen vessel unto me, to bear my name before the Gentiles...*

II Samuel 5:23a – *And when David enquired of the Lord,*

Psalms 32:8 – *I will instruct thee and teach thee in the way which thou shalt go: I will guide thee with mine eye.*

Revelation 5:5 – *And one of the elders saith unto me, Weep not: behold, the Lion of the tribe of Judah, the Root of David, hath prevailed to open the book, and to loose the seven seals thereof.*

Luke 2:49 – *And he said unto them, How is it that ye sought me? Wist ye not that must be about my Father's business?*

Chapter Thirty-One

Psalms 107:33 – *he turneth rivers into a wilderness, and the water-springs into dry ground;*

Proverbs 17:17 – *A friends loveth at all times, and a brother is born for adversity.*

Daniel 10:19 – *And said, O man greatly beloved, fear not: peace be unto thee, be strong, yea, be strong. And when he had spoken unto me, I was strengthened, and said, Let my lord speak; for thou hast strengthened me.*

1 Peter 5:7 – *Casting all your cares upon him; for he careth for you.*

Chapter Thirty-Two

Isaiah 40:29 – *he giveth power to the faint, and to them that have no might he increaseth strength.*

John 21:12 – *Jesus saith unto them, Come and dine.*

Numbers 4:47b - *…every one who came to do the service of the ministry,*

Genesis 50:20a – *but as for you, ye thought evil against me: but God meant it unto good,*

1 Samuel 7:12c - *…Hitherto hath the Lord helped us.*

John 16:33 – *These things I have spoken unto you, that in me ye might have peace. In the world ye shall have tribulation: but be of good cheer; I have overcome the world.*

Epilogue

Ecclesiastes 3:1-2a – *To every thing there is a season, and a time to every purpose under heaven; a time to be born, and a time to die;*

Luke 12:48b - *…For unto whomsoever much is given, of him shall be much required:*

Luke 20:35 – *But they which shall be accounted worthy to obtain that world and the resurrection from the dead, neither marry, nor are given in marriage:*

I Corinthians 15:55 – *O death, where is thy sting? O grave, where is thy victory?*

Psalms 107:42a – *The righteous shall see it, and rejoice!*

Psalms 116:15 – *Precious in the sight of the Lord is the death of his saints.*

Psalms 86:15 – *But thou, O Lord, art a God full of compassion, and gracious, longsuffering, and plenteous in mercy and truth.*

Job 43:23 – *... he will not lay upon man more than right, that he should enter into judgment with God.*

II Samuel 6:14a – *And David danced before the Lord, with all his might;*

Isaiah 45: 2a-3 – *I will go before thee, and make the crooked places straight: And I will give thee the treasures of darkness, and hidden riches of secret places, that thou mayest know that I, the Lord, which call thee by thy name, am the God of Israel.*

II Corinthians – *Now thanks be unto God, which always causeth us to triumph in Christ, and maketh manifest the savour of his knowledge by us in every place. For we are unto God a sweet savour of Christ, in them that are saved, and in them that perish: To the one we are the savour of death unto death; and to the other the savour of life unto life. And who is sufficient for these things?*

Hebrews 11:4 - *...offered unto God a more excellent sacrifice..., by which he obtained witness that he was righteous, God testifying of his gifts: and by it he being dead yet speaketh.*

Proverbs 10:7a *...The memory of the just is blessed:*

Isaiah 60:1-2 – *Arise, shine; for thy light is come, and the glory of the Lord is risen upon thee. For, behold, the darkness shall cover the earth, and gross darkness the people: but the Lord shall arise upon thee, and his glory shall be seen upon thee.*

II Corinthians 12:9a – And he said unto me, My grace is sufficient for thee: for my strength is made perfect in weakness.

Matthew 16:24 – Then said Jesus to his disciples, If any man will come after me, let him deny himself, and take up his cross, and follow me.

Luke 6:27-28 – But I say unto you which hear, Love your enemies, do good to them which hate you, Bless them that curse you, and pray for them which despitefully use you.

Matthew 5:5 – Blessed are the meek: for they shall inherit the earth.

Ephesians 5:20 – Giving thanks always for all things unto God and the Father in the name of our Lord Jesus Christ;

Isaiah 43:2b - ...when thou walkest through the fire, thou shalt not be burned; neither shall the flame kindle upon thee.

Addendum

Matthew 19:26b – With men this is impossible; but with God all things are possible.

Psalms 30:11-12 – Thou hast turned my mourning into dancing; thou hast put off my sackcloth and girded me with gladness; to the end that my glory may sing praise to thee and not be silent. O Lord my God, I will give thanks unto thee forever.

II Kings 20:1 – In those days was Hezekiah sick unto death. And the prophet came to him, and said unto him, Thus saith the Lord, Set thine house in order; for thou may die, and not live.

<u>Matthew 21: 16b</u> – Yea; have ye never read, Out of the mouth of babes...thou hast perfected praise?

Back of Book

<u>Luke 4:1</u> – And Jesus, being full of the Holy Ghost...was led by the Spirit into the wilderness.

ABOUT THE AUTHOR

Remarried now and in her middle years, Kim resides on the east coast. She enjoys the new family God has brought into her life, as well as loving and serving within her local "church family." Although a self-writer for decades, this is her first published work.

Printed in the United States
34062LVS00001B/39